National Security
and the
Nuclear Dilemma

National Security and the Nuclear Dilemma

An Introduction to the American Experience

Richard Smoke
Wright Institute

ADDISON-WESLEY PUBLISHING COMPANY
Reading, Massachusetts • Menlo Park, California
London • Amsterdam • Don Mills, Ontario • Sydney

Library of Congress Cataloging in Publication Data

Smoke, Richard.
    National security and the nuclear dilemma.

    Bibliography: p.
    Includes index.
    1. United States--National security. 2. United
States--Military policy. 3. United States--Foreign
relations--1945—   . 4. Atomic weapons. 5. Atomic
weapons and disarmament. I. Title.
UA23.S524   1984   355′.033073   83-17916
ISBN 0-201-16420-5

ISBN 0-201-16420-5
ABCDEFGHIJ-PO-89876543

Dedicated to my mother,
Lillian H. Smoke

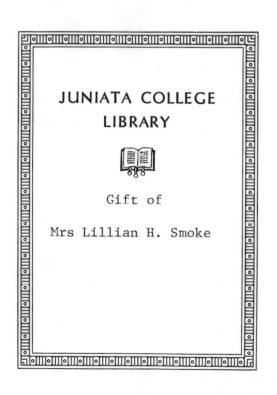

Contents

1   **Introduction**   1

2   **The Political-Technological Background**   5

War in the Modern Age   6
War Becomes Technological   11
The End of the Nineteenth Century World   13
Warfare in the Twentieth Century   15
The Systematization of Technology   18
Summary   21

3 **America Enters the World Military Arena**   **23**
Collective Security   27
A New Conflict Begins to Emerge   31
The East-West Discord Begins   32
The Cold War Begins   36
The Cold War Turns Frigid   38
Summary   41

4 **America Fashions Its National Security**   **45**
Containment   49
Deterrence   52
The Year of Shocks   56
NSC-68   59
Summary   62

5 **The First Era of American Military Superiority**   **65**
The New Look   68
Massive Retaliation   72
The Idea of Limited War   75
Summary   80

6 **Sputnik and the Missile Gap**   **83**
The First Criticism of Massive Retaliation: Credibility   85
Flexible Response   88
The Second Criticism of Massive Retaliation: Vulnerability   92
A Delicate Balance of Terror?   95
Into the Missile Age   96
The Missile Gap Becomes a Public Issue   99
Summary   101

7 **The Second Era of American Military Superiority**   **103**
The American Strategic Buildup   106
Further Conceptual Developments   111
The Cuban Missile Crisis   115
A Defense Against Missiles?   118
The Second Era of U.S. Superiority Passes   121
Summary   124

8   Security Through Arms Control   127

Early History   129
Arms Control Comes of Age   134
The Limited Test Ban Treaty   137
Other Agreements of the 1960s   141
The Nonproliferation Treaty   143
Summary   147

9   SALT   151

SALT I   152
MIRVs   156
A Tragedy of Timing   160
The Vladivostok Accords   162
SALT II   166
Summary   172

10   The Soviet Buildup   175

The Soviet Strategic Buildup   177
The Soviet Buildup of General Purpose Forces   179
The American Reaction to the Soviet Buildup   182
European Nuclear Issues   185
Eurostrategic Missiles   189
Chinese Nuclear Forces   192
Summary   193

11   The American Buildup   197

Flexible Targeting   198
The "Window of Vulnerability"   200
The American Strategic Systems of the 1980s   204
The MX Debate   209
The American Military Buildup   211
Summary   215

12   Strategy and Arms Control in the Early 1980s   219

"Limited Nuclear War"   220
The Peace Movement   223
Controlling Strategic Arms   231
Summary   233

13 **Conclusion: U.S. Security and the Nuclear Dilemma in the Late Twentieth Century** **237**

The Post-World War II Era   241
The Prospects Ahead   243

Epilogue **249**

Appendix: National Security as a Field of Study **251**

Index **263**

Tables

Table 1   American and Soviet strategic forces as of October 1962   109
Table 2   American and Soviet strategic forces at the end of 1969   122
Table 3   The SALT I Agreements   155
Table 4   The Vladivostok Accords   166
Table 5   Most significant provisions of the SALT II Agreements   170
Table 6   American and Soviet strategic forces as of mid-1975   178
Table 7   American and Soviet strategic forces as of mid-1981   211
Table 8   Budget expenditures for defense, in constant
          (Jan. 1982) dollars   213

Acknowledgments

Parts of *National Security and the Nuclear Dilemma* are taken from my monograph entitled "National Security Affairs," published in volume eight of the *Handbook of Political Science*, edited by Fred I. Greenstein and Nelson W. Polsby (Reading, Mass.: Addison-Wesley Publishing Co., 1975). Most of this book is fresh material, but a portion of the monograph, suitably revised and updated, has been included. I am grateful to Addison-Wesley Publishing Company for the opportunity to carry the project to this further stage. I have been fortunate to work with editors Stuart Johnson, Stan Evans, and Debra Hunter, who were most helpful throughout.

The National Strategy Information Center, Frank N. Trager, director, supported in part the preparation of an early draft of the book manuscript. And I am especially grateful to Professors Paul

Gordon Lauren and Michael Boll, of the history departments of the University of Montana and San Jose State University, respectively, for the favor of close critical readings of draft chapters. Other scholars who gave me the benefit of their advice and criticism at the time the original *Handbook* monograph was written are acknowledged therein. The Wright Institute of Berkeley, California, provided office space and other tangible and intangible assistance for which I am also appreciative.

National Security and the Nuclear Dilemma

1
Introduction

How has America tried to preserve its national security in the era of nuclear weapons?

The nuclear era began in August 1945 with the destruction of Hiroshima and Nagasaki. By the early 1950s the Soviet Union had built its own atomic bombs and was able to make a nuclear strike on the United States. In the decades since, the destructive power of the USSR has grown enormously. Today it is enough to wipe out every American city several times over. Together Soviet and American nuclear forces, if fully used, might destroy human civilization.

The dilemma of U.S. national security in the nuclear era is captured by the fact that, in spite of enormous efforts, America is less secure today than it was several decades ago. In the absence of effective, verifiable agreements that would limit Soviet (as well as American) nuclear forces to low levels, each side's ability to threaten the other has grown and keeps on growing.

Any effort to understand America's comparative insecurity raises some basic questions. What in fact has the United States done in the face of the great and growing threat to its security? How have American ideas about security developed in the nuclear era? How have U.S. nuclear forces grown, and how has American strategy come to grips with the evolving technology of nuclear weapons? What efforts have been made to achieve effective, verifiable agreements that would limit and reduce both sides' forces, and hence the threat that each side faces?

This book aims to answer these questions. Presuming limited knowledge of these subjects, it tries to give the reader an understanding of how U.S. national security has developed to the present, and how the nuclear dilemma has grown.

Today's insecure situation is an outgrowth of the developments of past years: technological advances, Soviet decisions, and American choices about strategy and policy. The focus of this book is not on the issues current at the time the book is published, but on the evolution of the nuclear threat as a whole, and American responses to it. Questions current in the early 1980s are given no more attention than the issues of the preceding decades. This book attempts to put the contemporary scene in context by showing how the present developed out of the past. One learns not only something about the current situation, but also a good deal about how the United States came to find itself in that situation. With this knowledge, the reader can approach with some understanding almost any nuclear question that may arise, including those that have emerged since this book was written.

The evolution of U.S. national security in the nuclear era is a subject that could be presented in a very technical way, but will not be here. Over the years the two superpowers have deployed ever larger and more complex weapons systems. Today American "strategic" forces intended for use against the Soviet Union include three kinds of land-based ballistic missiles; two sea-launched ballistic missiles (with a third on the way); several existing and proposed bomber aircraft (each able to carry several kinds of bombs and missiles); and another type of weapon called the cruise missile. Soviet forces are somewhat different and even more complicated. Both sides also deploy other nuclear forces, intended for targets other than each other's homelands, such as Soviet missiles aimed at Europe, and American tactical aircraft on bases abroad and on aircraft carriers. Both sides' forces are supported by reconnaissance satellites that can pinpoint objects as small as a single person anywhere in the world, and by an enormous array of communications, radar, computers, and other technology and systems.

Such large and diverse nuclear forces make U.S. national security seem a forbidding subject. It is made still more forbidding because it is filled with jargon, technical questions, and abstract strategic reasoning. The jargon provides a convenient shorthand for specialists, but it also makes the subject mysterious to anyone encountering it for the first time. Scientists often disagree about technical issues, leaving lay people uncertain. Abstract strategizing is unfamiliar and sometimes discomforting—for instance, what decisions a president should make after hundreds of nuclear warheads have exploded on the United States.

This book tries to introduce its topic in such a way that it does not seem forbidding or mysterious. Technical complexities are held to an absolute minimum. Jargon terms and unfamiliar ideas are introduced gradually. Successive chapters develop more difficult material slowly. Only later in the book does the substance and terminology resemble what is found in most writing about national security. The index gives a page number for the definition and first use of jargon, so the reader may quickly look up a forgotten phrase.

After two chapters that present political background, the book focuses primarily on the evolution of American policy. Weapons developments, world events, Soviet behavior, and other factors are introduced only where they are necessary for a basic understanding of U.S. nuclear policies. Each chapter is followed by a short list of suggested books and articles for those who would like to delve more deeply into that chapter's material.

Any book—like this one—that addresses only the nuclear dimension of U.S. national security necessarily leaves out other dimensions. Although most specialists would agree that the nuclear questions compose its core, national security involves much more. The reader should be aware of important aspects of U.S. national security that have been excluded from this introduction to nuclear affairs:

- *Conventional* (i.e., non-nuclear) forces are not discussed in any comprehensive way.
- Some nuclear issues involving NATO are discussed, but the evolution of that and other American *alliances* is not.
- The *internal processes* and *politics* of U.S. national security policies,

including the roles of Congress, of public opinion, of executive branch decision-making methods, and of the economics of military spending, are not discussed.

- Also excluded is the history of U.S.-Soviet and other *crises* of the cold war period and since. One exception is the single crisis that had a major nuclear component, the Cuban Missile Crisis of 1962, discussed in chapter 7.

All of these are important topics in the American experience of national security, but are not directly part of the nuclear dilemma. Not part of American experience, but an important part of any overall treatment of the nuclear dilemma, is the Soviet perspective. This book discusses Soviet nuclear policies as they affected the United States, but not much about their origins in the Soviet experience since 1945. The Soviet experience of the threat posed by American nuclear forces would deserve major attention in, for example, an analysis of the overall danger of world holocaust.

The nuclear dimension of U.S. national security definitely does include efforts to limit or reduce nuclear weapons — called "arms control" since about 1960. The evolution of arms control is the subject of chapters 8 and 9, and parts of later chapters.

The two chapters immediately following this one set the stage for the remainder of the book. The discussion opens by placing the whole postwar period in its larger context, and suggesting how a variety of trends, most of them relatively recent, combined to give national security a new meaning in the postwar world. The third chapter sketches the American experience of security prior to World War II, then indicates how and why the United States adopted thereafter a role so different from its accustomed one. A summary of the origins of the cold war in the late 1940s is included because that period determined so many of the premises of U.S. policy, even to the present.

2
The
Political-
Technological
Background

Most of the U.S. experience of national security that is significant to Americans today has occurred in the years since World War II. It is helpful nonetheless to begin an account of that experience with a brief glance at some earlier history. The contemporary period possesses qualities that are more easily recognized by drawing comparisons with the past than by taking them entirely on their own terms. Also, if our range of vision is so narrow that it embraces only what is immediately in view, slowly changing features of the background may appear constant, unchanging. In fact, much of what we have experienced in the current era represents a complete reversal of what war and national security used to be about. To see our era in perspective, then, we should step back from it and begin with the long view.

WAR IN THE MODERN AGE

During the Dark Ages and most of the Middle Ages, war could not cover much area at any one time, nor be sustained for very long. There were not enough resources, nor was society organized for it. Armed conflict was frequent, but it was not terribly destructive, and usually did not last very long. In the Arab world, in India, and elsewhere in the Far East, resources and organization were more conducive to war on a large scale. But in Europe, only the Crusades and a few charismatic leaders like Charlemagne could mobilize large numbers of men for sustained military action. Nation-states in the modern sense did not yet exist. Most of the time fighting took place on a small scale. A feudal lord might strip the local countryside of its men to press some quarrel with a neighboring lord, but most of the men would return within a few months. A small army might march through a district and lay it to waste, but that district might then experience many years of relative calm before there was another attack. Fighting went on constantly in one place or another in medieval Europe, but mainly over local grievances and ambitions, and it wreaked mainly local destruction.

As the Middle Ages drew to a close the nature of war gradually changed. Many of the modern European nations began to take shape, allowing them to form larger and more organized armies. Resources increased, as did the means to mobilize them. Armies could be systematically supplied, and kept fighting, or making preparations for fighting, over longer periods of time. As a result the physical damage that war could cause and the casualties it could inflict increased steadily. At first this trend was not universal. In Renaissance Italy, generals for hire, called *condottieri*, rented small mercenary armies to the various principalities and city-states, while agreeing among themselves on rules for an elegant, formal kind of warfare that caused relatively few casualties and little damage to society. But elsewhere in Europe warfare was becoming more deadly and destructive, and eventually the Italians had to follow suit.

The climax of this trend was the Thirty Years War (1618–1648). Armies from all over the Continent came to fight over whether central Europe would be Catholic or Protestant. Neither side could defeat the other, and in the end the dividing lines were drawn not too far from where they had been at the outset. But the scale and duration of the destruction was like nothing Europeans had ever seen. As the fortunes of war ebbed and flowed over the years, cities and towns would be taken and retaken many times. Each time there would be a slaughter of civilians and unrestrained looting and rape. The marauding armies laid waste to farmlands, killed or drove away the farmers, and disrupted all commerce. Millions who escaped the sword died from starvation or were so weakened by hunger that they fell victim to plagues. The population of central Europe fell drastically. In Bohemia, previously one of the most civilized of lands, three-quarters of the people perished, and four-fifths of the towns and villages were destroyed by troops or deserted by the starving populace. In Austria and Germany many of the beautiful medieval cities were left in ruins. In some districts one could ride for days seeing nothing but gutted towns, burned-out farms, and rotting corpses.

The devastation of the Thirty Years War shocked a Europe that in other ways was becoming more, not less, civilized. Dimly people realized that the ideological nature of the conflict was a principal reason why it had lasted so long and gone to such extremes. Both sides had believed that they were fighting not only for material gains but for the deepest kind of values — the whole order of society, the individual's place in society, and even the salvation of souls. Yet the high-minded ideologies had led in practice to barbaric terrors. A reaction against ideological conflict now set in; people recoiled from the intense passions and bitterness that ideologies could generate. This recoil became part of the Age of Reason in philosophy, the arts, and culture. Ideological differences weakened, and a consensus developed that those remaining should not become the fuel for wars. The first European attempt to codify an "international law" was set forth by Hugo Grotius (1583–1645), a Dutch jurist and statesman. With a handful of partial exceptions, there would not be another ideologically-based war for hundreds of years, until the twentieth century.

The nations of western Europe, especially England and France, had largely escaped damage in the Thirty Years War. They had already begun exploring and colonizing other parts of the world, and they continued to channel most of their surplus energy into this effort. As the rest of Europe recovered, a system of limited warfare developed. During the latter seventeenth century and through most of the eighteenth and nineteenth centuries, armed conflict was kept under restraint. There were many wars during this time, but they were allowed to absorb only a fraction of the available wealth and energy. They were mostly wars of position and maneuver, not of conquest and destruction. The various *governments* jockeyed and fought with each other, but the respective *societies* were not much involved. Indeed, they could not become much involved without changing the nature of the political, social, and economic system. Peoples' attention was mostly directed elsewhere—to the cultural flowering, the pursuit of private and national wealth, colonial expansion, the growth of science, and to the beginning of the Industrial Revolution.

Armies of this period were smaller, and for the first time became highly disciplined and professional. Fighting went on within a framework of generally observed rules and did much less damage to the fabric of civilian life. Questions decided "on the field of honor" were mostly limited to narrow political issues, such as which of the European royal families would succeed to some nation's suddenly empty throne. Conflicts between rival colonial empires sometimes became serious, but they were fought out in the colonies themselves and on the high seas, and did not grow into European wars grave enough to demolish the system of limited warfare. During most of these two and a half centuries even actual battle casualties were low, although as armies gradually grew larger again, casualties also rose.

Many factors encouraged this restrained approach to warfare in the modern age. Materialistic and practical motives replaced ideological ones; people did not want to spoil or destroy what they were trying to gain. Expensive professional armies could not be lightly squandered in action. To some unmeasurable but real degree, ethical and moral standards influenced national policies more than they had earlier (at least so far as war among the European nations themselves, as opposed to colonial actions, was concerned). Governments played less of a role in economic life; with the rise of capitalism it became unnecessary for ambitious individuals and groups to work through governmental and political means to achieve wealth. There seemed to be almost unlimited territory overseas where European societies could establish themselves and expand their influence. Partly because of this imperialism, and partly because of the emerging industrialization, overall wealth increased steadily. Each generation could look forward to its children being better off. Every nation found that it could have a bigger slice of pie without taking someone else's slice because the pie itself was getting bigger. Finally, most political and governmental affairs were run by the nobility, who intermarried freely across national boundaries. The nobility had a bigger stake in maintaining a stable social system than in promoting too great an advantage for any one country; and the system it wished to maintain inherently restricted the social resources that could be mobilized for war. (Notice that most of these factors have ceased to apply in our own time.)

For some 250 years, then, until the coming of the twentieth century, warfare played a subordinate and limited role in the life of Western society. Only a fraction of nations' resources went into war or preparations for war. The lives of individuals and the development of culture were far less affected than in our time by the outcome of any particular war. The distinction between what was military and what was civilian was very sharp — on and off the battlefield — and most of life fell clearly on the civilian side. Even during wartime life changed very little for most people. There was no thought of any general "draft" of young men, and people could travel freely to the countries with whom their governments were at war. During the frequent wars between England and France in the 1700s, for instance, English citizens could readily visit France and vice versa, and even travel around without passports. War was the business of governments and professional military men, not of society at large.

In our own time we have almost forgotten how narrow and how tightly defined was this niche that warfare occupied for such a long time in our civilization. Wars broke out in Europe often, yet nations almost never felt much threat to what today would be called their "national security." War had its own place, significant but secondary, and it stayed there.

There was one important exception to these generalizations, and that was the period of the French Revolution and Napoleon. In the 1790s the revolutionaries invented the *levée en masse*, under which all Frenchmen between certain ages were drafted for military service. It was the first time since the Roman Empire that a sizable society had enforced universal conscription, and it vastly increased France's military power. When Napoleon overthrew the Republic he turned this power to aggression. It was primarily because he had behind him the total human resources of his nation, and only secondarily because of his personal military genius, that he was able to conquer nearly all of

Europe for a while. (The resources of the mass, citizen-conscript army became available only after a political and social revolution had released them; as always in history, military institutions were intimately connected with political and social institutions.)

The Napoleonic Wars were another upheaval for Western civilization, comparable in some ways to the Thirty Years War. Desperate fighting, involving huge armies and thousands of casualties went on almost continually for half of another thirty years. Again Europe was shocked and frightened by the scale of the destruction. Statesmen sought to prevent this from ever happening again by restoring "legitimate" rulers and the traditional social order at home, and by reestablishing the "balance of power" and creating new diplomatic means to maintain stability in Europe.

Over the centuries a system had gradually emerged in Europe for balancing the power of any one nation, or group of nations, against another. Now, in the nineteenth century, this system reached its zenith. The Congress of Vienna, called in 1815 when Napoleon was vanquished, carefully redrew the map of Europe to try to prevent power from concentrating in any one place. The negotiators in Vienna also created the so-called "Concert of Europe," a general agreement among the great powers that their own national interests would be considered in the context of what was good for the system as a whole. In times of crisis they would hold international congresses rather than go to war at once. This would provide a cooling-off period and a forum for negotiating disputes. Other congresses of the powers would be held from time to time to make small adjustments in the balance of power – for instance, compensating some nation for a gain a rival had made by giving it (or allowing it to take) a prize of its own. Thereby tensions would be drained off and would not accumulate.

The system worked so well that there was no large war in Europe for the next ninety-nine years. A handful of small wars were fought, but these were brief, very limited in their geographical scope, and involved smaller armies than did the Napoleonic Wars. The nineteenth century (measured, as historians usually measure it, from 1815 to 1914) was the most peaceful era Europe had ever known. For most people during most of the century, another large and very destructive war was hardly imaginable.

There were reasons why the system worked so well, however, other than the wisdom of the Congress of Vienna statesmen and their successors. Primarily because of industrialization, wealth now increased dramatically. For the first time in history, people could see noticeable improvement in their nation's economy within a single lifetime. The pursuit of this wealth absorbed attention that might otherwise have gone toward warfare; achieving it provided rewards that people might otherwise have sought by means of war. The nineteenth century was also the era of burgeoning capitalism, and, except for a small group of munitions manufacturers, the capitalists found that war was not in their interests. War might destroy their factories, and would certainly disrupt trade arrangements and eat up their profits in high taxes. Finally, during most of this period almost all the European nations directed their aggressive energies outwards, in a fresh and even more vigorous wave of exploration, colonization, and exploitation around the globe. All these things, and not just the balance of power system, contributed to the long period of relative peace in Europe.

WAR BECOMES TECHNOLOGICAL

Until industrialization set in heavily during the nineteenth century, the technology of war had changed very little in the modern era. There were few differences between the weapons used in the Thirty Years War and those used in the Napoleonic Wars almost two centuries later. An army of the earlier war could have fought one of the later war, making up for minor disadvantages with only a slight superiority in numbers. Much the same was true in naval warfare.

These factors began to change, with ever-increasing momentum, during the nineteenth century. Shortly after the middle of the century, navies started to abandon wooden ships for ironclads, and wind power for steam. Ships became independent of the wind, and thus able to move quickly wherever and whenever they might be needed. Within a few decades, coal was abandoned in favor of oil as fuel for the steam engines, permitting longer voyages between refuelings. During the same period, naval guns became far more powerful, throwing much larger shells more accurately over longer ranges.

Land warfare also started to change. In 1866 and again in 1870, the Prussian Army won stunning victories thanks, in substantial degree, to superior technology. In the earlier of these conflicts, the Prussian infantry had breech-loading rifles while their opponents, the army of the Austrian Empire, had only muzzle-loaders. In the second war the Prussians pitted accurate, rifled artillery against their enemies, the French, who possessed much less accurate smoothbore cannon. In both wars the Prussians also had the benefit of a more extensive and efficient railway system. (Indeed, it was railways and their steam engines that made large armies practical: many troops could be transported quickly over long distances and still be able to fight effectively when they arrived.) The outcome of the two wars together was to create a large German empire (the second Reich), covering much of central Europe, where previously there had been many small states and principalities — an empire that was basically Prussian in character and under Prussian control.

The significance of superior military technology now became obvious to everyone, and the pace of its advance quickened thereafter. The Prussian Army of 1870 could have been destroyed by an army of the same size using the technology of 1914, when World War I began, and the latter army destroyed in its turn by one of the same size using the technology of 1918, when World War I ended. A similar advance to a new "generation" of military technology has occurred many times since.

Today the importance of military technology has become so great that in any new war we take it for granted that the side with the superior technology will win, if the two sides are not grossly unequal in numbers of weapons and men; and if there are not other, special, factors at work as there were, for instance, in the U.S. war in Vietnam. Yet this decisive role for technology dates back, even in its early, formative stages, only about a hundred years. In all previous time it was almost unknown. In other civilizations, and in our own civilization through most of its history, technology changed so slowly that generally both sides had similar equipment. Wars were almost always won or lost by the numbers of men brought to bear, and by the strategic and tactical skill of commanders — not technology.

In fact, the decisive role of technology is so recent, historically speaking, that we probably have not yet entirely adapted to it. Many of the traditions of today's armies and navies, such as parade-ground drill and emphasis on individual heroism, date back to earlier eras. So do many of the attitudes and feelings that civilians and society at large hold about their armed forces, such as a continuing respect for the mystique of military uniforms and the military life. To some extent these traditions and attitudes may no longer be appropriate; and newer social attitudes, such as valuing the highly educated officer who can make complex decisions, have only partially emerged. In this as in so many other spheres of life, social and cultural change tends to lag behind technology and the practical changes that technology brings.

THE END OF THE NINETEENTH
CENTURY WORLD

It is one of the tragedies of human history that the rapid rise of technology to decisive importance in warfare came just about the same time that the world ran out of frontier areas — around the turn of the century. The machine gun, large accurate ground and naval artillery, the airplane and air-dropped bombs all arrived at about the same moment, historically speaking, that the last habitable lands on earth were marked "claimed" on the maps of Europe. Thereafter, for any nation to control new territory, it had to move into territory already owned, or claimed, or "under the protection of" some nation that possessed weapons of general slaughter. From that time on, all the relations and disputes among nations proceeded within a "closed" universe whose political, social, and psychological outer bounds had been reached.

By the turn of the century an arms race had begun among the six or seven great powers (which at the time did not include the United States). A long series of disputes was developing over the lines marking the European nations' possessions and "spheres of influence" in the now closed universe. The previously flexible balance of power system in Europe itself and the spirit of common interests were degenerating into a confrontation between two increasingly definite and hostile blocs. Unlike the contemporary arms race, however, the turn-of-the-century arms race was mainly for quantity of weapons and men, not superior technological quality. Technology generally was not yet advancing so fast that governments could hope to achieve victory in any imminent war by means of scientific breakthroughs. The arms race was mainly a competition in the numbers of troops that could be mobilized, numbers of naval capital ships (battleships and heavy cruisers) and later, numbers of airplanes. Also unlike the present era, tension between the two blocs mounted fairly steadily, with only occasional and temporary relief.

World Wars I and II, which together set the contemporary stage, can in many respects be considered a single war, interrupted by what the historian E.H. Carr has called a "twenty years crisis." The lineup of the nations fighting in Europe was much the same in both wars, and many historians believe that both were caused by an underlying imbalance in the power relationships in Europe — a unified Germany held too preponderant a position.

The "victors' peace" of 1919 did not really correct this imbalance, and in some ways it worsened the situation by punishing Germany severely without weakening her permanently. The League of Nations, established at the same time but damaged by the absence of the United States, could do little but serve as a vehicle for the main victors, Britain and France, when they wished it to. The peace could have been maintained only if the British and French had cooperated with each other and had continued through the 1930s—in fact indefinitely—the stern measures enforcing German military inferiority that they had relished taking in 1919. After a passage of time, a depression, and many changes in domestic politics, they could not. Germany emerged even more powerful, relatively, than before.

Although the physical destruction, particularly to the cities of central and eastern Europe, was greater in World War II, and although that conflict included the war against Japan, in more fundamental ways World War I was probably more destructive. To a much greater degree than the second, the first war destroyed an entire generation—the "lost generation" that perished in the long, drawn-out agony of the trenches, or survived benumbed with pain, grief, and cynicism. World War I also began to destroy the distinction, taken for granted earlier, between civilians and combatants, as evidenced by the introduction of a new expression, "the home front."

All the European nations suffered shocking casualties in that war. The French, for instance, lost over 1.33 million men dead, and about an equal number permanently maimed. To appreciate the impact of this loss, one must realize the limited size of the population at the time—these casualties represented about one out of every five adult males in France. (For comparable impact the United States of today would have to suffer over fifteen million dead and crippled, or approximately the entire adult male population of New York, Pennsylvania, and the six New England states.) Even more numerous Russian casualties, and the austerities and disruptions of the war, triggered the overthrow of the czarist regime. For Britain, Germany, and the other European nations involved the losses were almost as serious. In the long battle of Ypres in 1917, for instance, the British lost almost half a million killed and wounded in only twenty weeks. (This is over five times the number of Americans killed or seriously wounded in all of the Vietnam War.) For this hideous price, the British succeeded in pushing forward their trenches some two miles, along a ten-mile sector of the front.

The fantastic absurdity of such battles and of the endless, stalemated trench war as a whole, was deeply destructive in psychological, cultural, emotional, and spiritual ways—all the more so for its total negation of the spirit of optimism and belief in inevitable progress that previously had reigned supreme. It is almost impossible for us now to recall the feeling of confidence that people in the late nineteenth century had in the steady, peaceful progress of mankind. People then took it for granted that wars, if they occurred at all, would be brief; and that the steady expansion of wealth, of beneficent science, of culture, and of the rule of reason would scarcely be interrupted, ever again. Western civilization was triumphant, and peoples' confidence in its continued, orderly perfection was complete. The gigantic absurdity of the First World War dealt this confidence a blow from which it never recovered.

WARFARE IN THE TWENTIETH CENTURY

World War I began what the French sociologist Raymond Aron has called "the century of total war." In wartime, twentieth-century societies have devoted nearly the totality of their energies and resources, and almost the whole attention of their citizens, to the conflict. Even in peacetime they now devote large expenditures to war preparations, and "national security" considerations have first claim upon all social resources, tangible and intangible. And, not infrequently, one or more advanced nations finds itself caught in a preoccupying, often costly state somewhere between peace and full-scale war (for example, Britain and France in the years just before World War II; Europe and the United States during the various Berlin crises of the cold war; the United States during the Korean and Vietnam conflicts; everyone during the Cuban Missile Crisis). The lines between peace and war, civilian life and military matters, have grown fuzzy. In this century war and preparations for war, which once occupied such a narrow niche in the life of Western societies, have enlarged their influence tremendously.

There are several reasons for this. In part it stems from the return of ideological conflict. Since the time of the Thirty Years War, the deeper values of Western society and the basic nature of the social order had rarely been at stake in international politics. In the twentieth century, threats at that deep level have reemerged, stronger than ever. Nazi, Communist, and fascist ideologies have seized power in major European countries, warped them into totalitarian dictatorships, and then used them as a power base from which to threaten their neighbors. The democracies of Europe and North America, which represent the main line of the evolving Western social order, have felt themselves threatened almost continually, for over four decades now, by totalitarians coming from one ideological direction or another.

In part, the seeming omnipresence of war-related activities in our era stems from the closure of the political universe at the beginning of the century, and from the ever-multiplying connections among the nations inside that universe. Previously the technically advanced nations had been largely disconnected from tribal, religious, racial, and other hostilities that have existed for a long time in the Southern Hemisphere and Asia. Where they were connected, by way of colonies or conquests, they were so dominant that they often were able to constrain conflict (as Britain and Russia did, for instance, in the regions northwest of India in the late nineteenth century). In our era the colonial connections have largely dissolved, but new and more complicated connections, involving economics, natural resources, and political alliances, have been formed between the developed and less-developed countries. Meanwhile ancient hostilities are refought with modern weapons. Racial conflicts that, once, would have been of local significance only, pose dangers for the whole world (for instance, the Middle Eastern wars and the conflicts in southern Africa). By now, these intertwining interests form a single, highly complex global web, along which the ramifications of major events reverberate. It is hard to think of any area on the globe where a spark might be struck without igniting a spreading fire of interests, fears, and involvements.

Perhaps the largest reason for the "total" presence of war-related activities in our century is accelerating technology. Nuclear weapons are the most obvious factor. The threat to survival that nuclear warfare poses can motivate the most far-reaching measures to prevent or deter it. But the impact of technology goes far beyond the danger posed by these and other weapons of mass destruction. The increasing flexibility and speed of twentieth-century transportation and communications has meant that nations can expect no time to gather their strength and get ready to fight after a major war begins. In preceding centuries, a war would start and *then* the belligerents would build up their armies; or a race to be first with one's forces mobilized would precede the outbreak by only a few weeks. In recent decades, nations have had to plan on fighting a major war with nothing more than the forces already "in being" the moment it starts. (The only significant exception is "counterinsurgency" wars such as the American war in Vietnam.) Since one must always be ready, all necessary forces must be continuously "in being."

It is primarily *this* technological factor, not nuclear weapons, that makes it necessary for twentieth-century states to maintain large, ever-ready military establishments, with everything this implies for the enlargement of the "national security" sphere in the life of society. If nuclear weapons had never been invented (and were thought, say, to be impossible), the advanced nations' military establishments would be, in most respects, just as large. Possibly they would be larger, since nuclear weapons can substitute partially for such things as very large armies and huge fleets of bomber aircraft. It is the transportation and communications technology that we all take for granted, not nuclear technology, that makes contemporary military forces so large and so permanent.

Advancing technology has also meant a rapid change in peoples' personal experience of what war and security mean. The suddenness with which a nation can be attacked by airplanes or missiles produces a kind of insecurity that never used to exist, but which now seems permanent. This too does not necessarily derive from atomic weapons, although those also create their own pervasive background insecurity. Suddenness alone has its effect. Most people know that a missile attack can occur with little or no warning. In many places, less "ultimate" (and more likely) attacks can also arrive very suddenly. Many cities of Europe, Japan, and the Middle East lie within ten to twenty minutes flight time from bases inside the territory of probable enemies. Hostile warplanes can appear overhead with hardly any warning, and in the Middle East this has happened. The psychological sense that enemies and danger were far away, which civilized humanity used to take for granted, has vanished.

Less recognized, but perhaps more far-reaching in its subtle effects, is the steady advance of the impersonality of warfare. In a few decades, in fact, the whole quality of warfare as a human experience has changed drastically. As recently as 1866 the Austrian army marched into battle to the music of bands, wearing gaily decorated costumes displaying all the colors of the rainbow. True, their enemies, the more technologically inclined Prussians, were already wearing a gray green drab; yet they too had their bands along. There may still be people in Europe who can remember their grandfathers recounting this experience. By now, though, mechanization has created a kind of warfare so drastically different, in the personal experiences it creates, as almost to need a different name.

The significance of this alteration is not limited to the personal feelings of the individuals directly involved. Throughout history prior to this century, war (whatever its costs) was also valued positively for its opportunities for individual heroism, sacrifice of narrow self-interest, and other victories of character. Indeed, the central role that war has played in the literary and artistic life of our culture and most other cultures, prior to the present, derived from peoples' experience that life in wartime was in many ways a microcosm of life as a whole. Opportunities for good and evil, and for moral choice, were distilled and concentrated, and hence magnified. This "romantic" dimension of war, in the higher literary and philosophical sense, lasted through the nineteenth century but, so far as major warfare was concerned, died before the thousands of machine guns and was buried in the muddy trenches of World War I. In peripheral aspects or theaters, though, it persisted through that war — for instance, in the duels between primitive airplanes over France and in the exploits of T.E. Lawrence in Arabia. It even lingered in the geographically limited and technologically somewhat old-fashioned civil war in Spain. But World War II produced no Red Baron or Lawrence of Arabia, only a Kilroy who was distinguished mainly by his anonymity, if he existed at all. We remember no heroes from Korea or Vietnam.

In wars of moderate size, fame and a measure of heroism could be achieved until recently, however, and perhaps still can be, by a dazzling strategic feat — a dramatic and well-publicized concept, perfectly executed by a top commander. We do remember the brilliance of MacArthur's Inchon landing of 1951 or Moshe Dayan's air-tank blitz in the Six Day War in 1967. But this too is departing, and so far as large-scale war is concerned, has already departed. In the U.S. war in Vietnam, strategic decisions were made mostly by anonymous groups and committees, not by vivid individuals; sometimes they were made by staff officers interacting with computers. Computers now are taking over more and more aspects of decision making in war. The advanced nations are preparing for what is called "the automated battlefield," over which most of the fighting will be done by automatic and remote-controlled devices. Robot flying machines, for instance, might be shot down by a computerized air defense system. In this kind of war men will take their instructions from machines at least as often as machines from men; and the battle may be so complex and so fast-moving that no one individual can grasp it completely. In not much more than a century, the depersonalization of war has gone about as far as it can go.

THE SYSTEMATIZATION OF TECHNOLOGY

The rapid and relentless pace of technological development, which has had so profound an impact upon warfare in our time, ironically has also fed itself on war and the threat of war. The extreme motivation that war provides has fueled technical research and engineering to an extent that no economic motive can match under any social system. In fact, with the exceptions of the automobile and the radio, most of the technology we take for granted today had its source and/or much of its development in the pursuit of national security.

Airplanes, submarines, and the tank were all either invented during World War I or were developed then from an experimental to a practical stage. Radar, essential for air travel independent of daylight and weather, was a laboratory curiosity at the outset of World War II, but was highly developed and used routinely at its end. Approximately the same was true of rockets. All the basic research and development for television, jets, and atomic energy took place during World War II. The first civilian jetliner, the Boeing 707, was largely derived from a U.S. Air Force bomber of the early 1950s, the B-47. Subsequent commercial airplanes, as well as the air traffic control systems that make high-volume air travel possible, have also drawn heavily from aeronautical and electronic technology first developed for military uses. Much, although not all, of the development of computers has been at the behest of the Defense Department, as has much of the research on lasers. Home computers and the hand-held calculator derive in part from microminiaturization and from an electronics development called "large scale integration," both originally created for U.S. military purposes, chiefly aircraft and missile guidance and control systems. The manned space program began in the early 1960s with rockets and other hardware that had been developed for military reasons, and since then has constantly benefited from (and contributed to) military missile and space developments. Many other technological aspects of contemporary life, too numerous to mention, derive directly or indirectly from national security research and development. Most of the technology we now accept as a normal part of our existence, in fact, is in one way or another a product of two world wars, a cold war, and the never-ending arms race.

The First World War contributed least to this onrush of technology. The development of military technology then was still unorganized, haphazard, and not much emphasized. The tank, for instance, took over two years to make the short step from demonstration of feasibility to battlefield use on any scale, because the British possessed almost no organized system for developing, testing, procuring, and deploying a new technical item. Putting these things on a systematic basis came with the next war. By the end of the Second World War, the complete sequence, from preliminary research to placing quantities of a new weapon into the hands of combat troops, had been organized for maximum speed and efficiency. The research and development process had been systematized and the "R and D" approach could be applied to any hardware problem. It was mainly *this* development, not the size of the expenditures or the number of people working on technical devices, that launched the true technological revolution of our times. In effect, the process of advancing any technology, and technology as a whole, was itself put on a systematic, scientific basis for the first time. A *technology of technology* had been created.

This byproduct of World War II was a major social innovation, one with profound consequences. Previously there had been only an occasional, ad hoc connection between the advancement of technology on the one hand, and scientific research and the systematic use of scientific methods on the other. With a few exceptions (mainly among the large chemical companies like I.G. Farben and DuPont) new technological developments prior to World War II had not come from an organized research effort. They had come from independent engineers and inventors who exploited ideas as they had them—the Wright brothers, for example. Among other consequences, this greatly limited the pace at which technology could advance. The development of the R and D system yoked scientific research and technological advance together, and enormously increased the need for (and the influence of) scientists and engineers. Following the war, the speed of technological change increased enormously in every field to which the new system was applied. It spread through private industry and before long being an "inventor" was almost a forgotten profession. Almost all innovation, at least in things tangible, came to be organized in the new way.

After the war, too, the scientists, engineers and experienced technology managers were on hand, among the military services and the military equipment manufacturers, to carry the R and D system on into the cold war. Comprehensively applied to military affairs first in the United States and, on a lesser scale, in Britain, the system was copied with differences in detail and style by the Soviet Union and subsequently by the European nations, Japan, and others. By midcentury, all the more advanced nations had learned, or were rapidly learning, how to develop ever more sophisticated technology in a speedy and highly systematic fashion. In this way, all the necessary conditions were established for a continual and expanding technological arms race, which decades later nobody knows how to halt, and which appears to have no intrinsic end.

SUMMARY

National security in its contemporary sense emerged as a fundamental and continuing challenge in the years following World War II. It emerged as the culmination of an interwoven series of trends that had shaped themselves during the previous five or six decades, and that represented complete transformations and reversals of the circumstances within which the nations of the West had always sought security. During those five or six decades, humanity reached the outer limits of its possible political space and was thrown back upon itself in a newly "closed" universe. After centuries in which supranational, ideological motivations had been largely absent from conflict, new ones appeared to threaten our deepest values in a "total" fashion. Yet paradoxically, the romantic element drained out of war and conflict became steadily more impersonal. For the first time, technologies appeared that could sow mass destruction, and on an ever-growing scale. Airplanes and their bombs grew steadily larger, and with the appearance of the atomic bomb destruction could be truly wholesale. High-speed transportation and communications forced nations to maintain large standing military forces at all times. A technology emerged for further developing all military technologies at a rapid pace.

The combination of these things set the contemporary stage. By the middle of our century, threats to national security could appear across a wide and growing spectrum of violence; could appear very suddenly in a military strike; could evolve into new technical forms quickly; and could be coupled with thoroughly intolerable political demands.

FOR FURTHER READING

Aron, Raymond. *The Century of Total War.* Garden City, New York: Doubleday and Co., 1954. A broad sociological and philosophical assessment of the change in character that war has undergone in our time.

Brodie, Bernard, and Fawn Brodie. *From Crossbow to H-Bomb: The Evolution of Weapons and Tactics of Warfare.* Paperback edition: Bloomington, Ind.: Indiana University Press, 1973. A general history of the evolution of warfare, written from a contemporary perspective and in a semipopular style.

Carr, Edward H. *The Twenty Years' Crisis: 1919-1939.* Second edition, London: MacMillan Company, 1956. Perhaps the leading historical analysis in English of the international politics of the period between the world wars.

Clausewitz, Karl von. *On War.* Edited and translated by Michael Howard and Peter Paret. Princeton: Princeton University Press, 1976. The most famous analysis of warfare of all time. Essential reading for any serious student of the subject.

Fuller, J.F.C. *The Conduct of War, 1789–1961.* New York: Funk and Wagnalls Co., 1961. A classic introductory history of warfare in the last two centuries, by a major military historian.

Nef, John U. *War and Human Progress.* Paperback edition: New York: W.W. Norton Co., 1963. An exploration of the thesis that war has had a stimulative effect on technological and other progress, particularly in the West.

Preston, Richard, Sydney Wise, and Herman Werner. *Men in Arms: A History of Warfare and Its Interrelationships with Western Society.* New York: Praeger, 1956. A nontechnical and very readable presentation of how the arts and technology of war have evolved since ancient times.

3

America Enters the World Military Arena

For a very long time the United States of America enjoyed an extraordinarily favored, indeed almost unique, status in the history of nations: it was almost totally secure, and this security was achieved at very little cost to itself. Most societies have had to pay considerable attention to security and then have found it incomplete. Even the European countries, during the limited warfare of the seventeenth and eighteenth centuries and the relative peace of the nineteenth, devoted significant resources to military affairs; and while the European social order might not have been threatened, regimes and territorial possessions certainly were.But until remarkably recently, the security of the American people was granted, nearly free of charge, by "nature." Uniquely situated far from any powerful state, easily supreme on their own continent, and protected by oceans on two sides, Americans for a long time had no reason to be concerned with their security.

This absence of threats was unprecedented in its duration and completeness. At the beginning it took one war, the Revolutionary, for the country to break free from the old world, and another not long after, the War of 1812, to seal the victory against a mother country that had not given up hope of reestablishing her rule. Thereafter the United States was able to evolve for a full century and a quarter while devoting minuscule energy—economic, political, social, or psychological—to foreign relations or to military precautions. At no time in recorded history has any major nation been able to prosper and develop so long, while devoting so few resources to security. Not even ancient Rome or imperial China so completely escaped military concerns for such a long time.

The only possible threat to the United States was itself—the Civil War was a costly experience in every way. But shielded from Europe by an ocean that took many days to cross, the nation found that nothing external presented any real hazard. After the War of 1812 Canada was no threat. Mexico, and later the Spanish Empire, were defeated very quickly, using only fractions of the potentially available power. Even smaller forces dealt with the indigenous tribes. Communities in frontier areas might be vulnerable to Indian attack, but behind the advancing frontier the country as a whole was profoundly secure.

It is hard for us today to imagine how confident and at ease our forebears were in this respect. In 1837 Abraham Lincoln, then a young man, said in a speech:

> *All the armies of Europe, Asia, and Africa combined, with all the treasure of the earth (our own excepted) in their military chest, with a Bonaparte for a commander, could not by force take a drink from the Ohio or make a track on the Blue Ridge in a trial of a thousand years.*

Except for their eloquence, these sentiments drew no particular notice. They simply expressed what everyone felt, and continued to feel until well into our own century.

Actually there was some element of naïveté in this sense of security, and at the time they were spoken Lincoln's words were probably not literally true. Nineteenth-century Americans tended to overlook the significance of the Royal Navy, whose complete mastery of the seas kept others far from our shores; and of the European balance of power, which kept any one state or combination of states (including the state that commanded the Royal Navy) from becoming too preponderant. A Napoleonic Empire, for example, that had become permanently established over all of Europe might have mounted a serious threat. That one must reach to such a farfetched example, however, shows the approximate truth in Lincoln's words.

The power position of the United States, relative to the rest of the world, grew as time passed, and was at its height in the first half of the present century. At the dawn of the century the United States won an easy victory in the Spanish-American War. The country entered an imperialist phase when it decided to keep some spoils of the war—colonial possessions in the Caribbean and Pacific. These never played the important political and economic role in American life that the imperial possessions of the European countries did in theirs. America did not go on to win greater possessions, although the navy and marines did intervene in Latin America from time to time in both the nineteenth and twentieth centuries to further U.S. interests.

In 1917 the United States awoke further to its potential as an emerging world power. An "American Expeditionary Force" of modest size was sent to France. Arriving fresh when the European nations were exhausted, it helped settle the outcome of World War I and returned home in eighteen months. Its cost, both in dollars and in casualties, was extremely low compared to the size and resources of the society that supported it. Its very name indicated that that society viewed it as an exception, a one-time venture. After the brief flurry of postwar diplomatic activity, the nation subsided into "normalcy" and, as it was soon to be called, "isolationism." That this term was first coined in the 1930s is significant. Before then Americans had been so inattentive to the external world that it had not even occurred to them to call their position isolated, or to feel any need to express that as a preference.

The United States, then, was able to progress for about 125 years, almost to 1940, with scarcely any anxiety concerning threats from beyond its borders. Such felicity has its social effects. Contemporary Americans have forgotten not only the security of their forebears and their freedom from military concerns, but also their distaste for things military. Through most of their history Americans have thought of themselves as a very peaceable people, with no use or wish for a military presence in their society. Except for the Civil War years, American military officers during this long period were few in number, and most of the time completely lacking in influence. Decade after decade the military budget was minuscule. Military affairs and military life proceeded in their own niche at the edge of American society.

Something similar applied to foreign affairs as a whole. Americans were just not much interested. Diplomatic relations were maintained with the major countries of Europe and later, of Latin America and Asia, but until the approach of the twentieth century there was very little business to conduct. At that time it began to increase, but it was still mostly ignored by the public – almost totally ignored outside the few largest cities. Until after the First World War, intellectuals gave little attention to foreign relations or to questions of war and security; even in the twenties and thirties their attention was limited mainly to international law and international organizations. Until well into this century, "intelligence" consisted mostly of a few army and navy officers copying statistics out of foreign publications, and of U.S. embassy personnel abroad keeping their ears open at parties. The American people generally were a bit suspicious of professional military officers, and of the well-to-do "men in striped pants" who manned the small State Department.

But mostly Americans paid no attention at all to these people or their activities. Until about 1940 (and excluding the Civil War years) what we would now call national security was simply not a significant part of Americans' awareness. They were absorbed with building the country, settling the West, expanding business and the economy. Preferring, in any case, a small government acting within a limited sphere, they certainly had no interest in a sizable standing military establishment or, except for the imperialist phase, in active foreign involvements.

If some unavoidable threat did appear, the traditional American attitude was to dispose of it quickly, efficiently, and thoroughly, and then return at once to normal life. If the *Maine* were blown up in Havana harbor (1898) or if German U-boats sank American shipping only a few miles outside the port of New York (1916), Americans got excited and took prompt action to deal with the aggressor. As soon as this was accomplished, their attention turned back almost entirely to ordinary things.

This attitude persisted long after the United States had ample power to play an active role on the world stage, and to adopt policies aimed at helping to prevent the emergence of new threats. However *feasible* it might have been in the early twentieth century, an active foreign policy in this preventive spirit was inconsistent with the traditional attitude. In the 1920s and 1930s the country remained largely aloof from European concerns and problems, and did not believe that the rise of fascist and Nazi dictatorships in Europe and Asia was its business. As late as 1938 the annual military budget of the United States was only about *one* billion dollars. Even by 1940, when World War II was already under way in Europe, the United States Army consisted of only six divisions, badly equipped, with a skeleton cadre of a few thousand officers. The navy was substantial but somewhat antiquated, and short of both officers and men. A fledgling "Army Air Corps" had only some 2,000 combat planes, many of them obsolete.

The reversal that followed was profound. In the next five years the United States created an armed force of over twelve million men to vanquish the world-empire dreams of Hitler, Mussolini, and the Japanese warlords. It deployed more than a hundred divisions all over the globe, and two complete, mostly new navies, each stronger than any rival's. It built over ten thousand new aircraft; at one point aircraft production was about thirty planes a day. It expended more than a third of a trillion dollars, and the lives of well over a quarter million young Americans. It orchestrated the efforts of a dozen allies. It seized and used every conceivable source of national power, and ultimately tapped one of the basic physical energies of the universe.

In a single bound the country leaped onto the world stage and became, unchallengeably, the mightiest nation on the planet. Even so, at the war's end the traditional American attitude was to reassert itself strongly.

COLLECTIVE SECURITY

Hiroshima was destroyed on August 6, 1945, and Nagasaki on August 9. On the 10th the Japanese sued for peace, and on the 14th the American terms of surrender were accepted in Tokyo. The enthusiastic celebration of V-J Day in the United States was followed by a public outcry to "bring the boys home." During the succeeding days and weeks the White House, Congress, and the Pentagon were flooded with calls and letters demanding that the troops, so long separated from their families, be brought back at once. The armed services, not expecting the war to end so suddenly, had not completed their preparations for demobilization; the resulting delays only exacerbated the impatience of the public and of the millions of men in uniform. Mounting political pressure on Washington finally led to a crash demobilization in which everything was sacrificed to the goal of getting the troops back to the United States and discharging them from service as speedily as possible. Never has a giant war machine been dismantled so completely and so quickly as the one that had just won the greatest war in history.

Even so, most Americans did not intend the United States to withdraw from the rest of the world's affairs as totally this time as it had after the First World War. The inescapable preponderance of the United States in a world in which virtually every other advanced country had had its cities and industries bombed did not permit a complete withdrawal. The memory of what had followed from America's refusal to participate in the League of Nations warned against any repetition. And the moral leadership that the nation had assumed during the war could not suddenly be dropped. In 1945 the rest of the world looked primarily to the United States as the shaper of things to come. Many Americans recognized, too, that aircraft had now made the world much smaller. And even though the secret of the atomic bomb was known only to the United States, the bomb cast a chill over the future.

Rather than let the rest of the world look after itself, American policy this time was to join with other nations to maintain "collective security" on behalf of all. An international organization, which the United States would sponsor and support, and which would include most (eventually all) of the world's nations, could carry out the kind of preventive policy that America had not undertaken in the 1930s. Such an organization, presumably dominated by the Western democracies, would also help to assure world markets and a free-enterprise economic order favorable to American commercial interests. From the security viewpoint, however, the primary purpose and justification for the organization would be its ability to prevent new threats to the peace. Should new tyrannies arise and be tempted to aggression, they could be stopped by economic—and if necessary, stronger—sanctions by the rest of the world, already banded together.

This idealistic goal of collective security, which for a period seemed achievable, had for some time been the stated objective of the United States as it planned its policies and actions for the postwar era. As early as 1943 the United States had persuaded its most important allies, Britain and the Soviet Union, to include this in the Allied statement of their main purposes in fighting the war. The three heads of state, Franklin Roosevelt, Winston Churchill, and Joseph Stalin, committed their signatures to this declaration at the Tehran Conference in November of that year. Thereafter, Allied propaganda referred frequently to a "United Nations Organization" as the embodiment of the Allies' moral ideas for a better world after the war.

Nor did Washington intend to allow good intentions to dissipate following the victory, as they had in 1919 when the democracies, after emerging victorious, had squabbled among themselves over the terms for the League of Nations. This time the organization would be created while the alliance was still united in military action. At American initiative, the international conference to draft the United Nations Charter and create the organization was held in the spring of 1945, when it was expected that the war in the Pacific would continue another one to two years.

At home, too, Roosevelt and his advisers were determined to prevent any recurrence of the situation following World War I when, after bitter controversy, the Senate had rejected Woodrow Wilson's demand that the country join the League. Long before the war's end the Roosevelt administration began an elaborate political effort to win strong congressional support for active American involvement in the United Nations. To make it hard for Congress to keep the country out, it was decided that the United States should be the host for the 1945 conference, convened in San Francisco. To make it still harder, and to make it difficult for the United States ever to ignore the United Nations in the future, it was planned that the organization would be headquartered in New York rather than in Switzerland. These efforts paid off: when the United Nations treaty came before the Senate for approval it passed almost unanimously.

In one sense, this drive to create the United Nations, and the senatorial approval of the treaty, represented a complete reversal of the traditional American stance toward the world. Rather than withdrawing from international politics, henceforward the country would be involved in them heavily and permanently. In another and deeper sense, though, it represented much the same traditional stance in a new guise. The shift from prewar minimal attention to national security, to the postwar standing policy of collective security, was actually intended to bring back the previous state of affairs as nearly as mid-twentieth century conditions allowed.

It was hoped that the potential weight of the world's nations united would so discourage potential aggressors that resort to military threats would hardly ever be required. In any case the United States would not have to take sole responsibility for guarding against aggression. By shifting the burden of vigilance to an international organization, the United States would be merely one of many nations that might be called upon to carry out, collectively, some form of preventive diplomacy if necessary. The need for the United States to cope in any sustained way with security threats could be avoided, as could the usual accompaniment, a large standing military establishment. The United Nations, acting on the basis of international law, would see to the security of all, and if once in a while it requested some temporary American military assistance, this too would be entirely in the U.S. tradition of occasional, strictly temporary resorts to force.

The American planners of the new organization were quite explicit that the UN was intended to make it unnecessary for the United States to concern itself further with problems of force and security. They sold the concept to the Senate substantially on that basis. Late in 1944, President Roosevelt told a joint session of Congress that the plan "ought to spell the end of the system of unilateral action, the exclusive alliances, the spheres of influence, the balances of power . . . we propose to substitute for all these a universal organization. . ." The president was being literal in saying that the United Nations was to *substitute* for national security involvements. American planners intended to continue only small military forces in existence after the war, similar to those that had existed before it. The United States had no military "strategy," indeed scarcely any military plans of any kind, for the postwar world. It intended to make no military alliances.

Only the victorious wartime alliance of America, Britain, and Russia, now joined by France, was to be continued, or rather institutionalized, in the form of the UN Security Council. (Washington insisted that the Republic of China be given a fifth permanent seat on the Council; three other seats would be held on a rotating basis by other nations.) As its name implied, the Security Council would be the true instrument and decision maker for the collective security of the world. If a new threat to the peace emerged, the Security Council would decide upon, and oversee the implementation of, any actions (up to and including military actions) necessary to prevent a new war.

In this fashion, Americans tried to re-create in a new form that *uninvolvement* with international politics that had always been their desire and their habit. At the end of World War II they believed that they could return to a life with only small expenditures and little attention devoted to security. This could be achieved, they thought, not by removing America from the world — that was no longer possible — but by involving it in the world in a special way. By acting with other nations collectively to forestall aggression, the United States would not have to arm itself heavily again.

A NEW CONFLICT BEGINS TO EMERGE

The weakest point in this bright dream was that everything depended upon maintaining unified purpose among the victorious wartime Allies. Each of the great powers seated on the Security Council held a veto over its decisions. Without this provision the whole concept would never have been accepted by Congress, nor by the other powers. Any permanent member could prevent the world organization from taking action that it regarded as detrimental to its own interests by wielding its veto in the Security Council. The system of collective security, therefore, would continue to work only so long as the great powers on the Council considered their interests to be in harmony and could continue to work in unison.

It took less than a year for this system to begin to break down. A rift opened and steadily widened between the USSR and the Western democracies, for many reasons. Since the democracies dominated the Council (and in those days, the UN as a whole) the Soviets feared that the international organization would take sides against them in the growing discord. To prevent it they found themselves saying "nyet" more and more often in Security Council meetings. Soon it became clear to all that the collective security concept, as conceived by the United States, was breaking on the wall of Russian vetoes. By the beginning of 1947, the United States government was looking for another approach to security.

To be sure, some conflict had begun among the Allies even before the war had ended. Churchill, who had always been staunchly anticommunist, had been suspicious of long-range Soviet motives all along. In private conversations with Roosevelt he had argued that the main American-British assault on Hitler's Europe should move up through the Balkans, rather than on the shorter path from Normandy across France, to prevent the Red Army from seizing all of Eastern Europe on its way toward Germany. Roosevelt, the final arbiter by right of commanding the larger forces, had overruled him, partly to avoid jeopardizing Allied unity.

Even so, before the end of the war Russia and the Western Allies had sharp disagreements over a number of issues, including the postwar government of Poland. Early in 1945 the Soviets established a provisional government there, a government quite different from the Polish government-in-exile that in 1939 had fled the Nazis to London, and, with Western support, claimed still to be the legitimate government of Poland. After the European war was over the Soviet-installed provisional government was made permanent despite Western objections. More and more disagreements regarding eastern Europe, Germany, and other matters began developing between the USSR and the democracies.

This is not the place to discuss in detail the many events, motives and perceptions, stretching over years, that led to a hostile and fearful state of cold war between the Soviets and the Western nations led by the United States. The story is a complicated one, with many interpretations, and even in its standard Western version demands a lengthy treatment to be presented adequately. The story is also somewhat controversial—or it has been. Two decades later an entire literature was to flower in the West, offering a "revisionist" interpretation of these events that argued that Soviet intentions were unaggressive and that the cold war was caused partly (or in some versions, entirely) by unnecessary belligerence on the part of the United States. More recent and balanced scholarship suggests that the onset of the cold war is best seen as a tragedy of misperceptions on both sides. Soviet actions probably had primarily—not exclusively—a defensive and self-protective motive. Yet these actions were such that they would inevitably be seen as dangerously aggressive by Americans and most Europeans, who were sincere in looking to their own defense. Let us sketch briefly, in the remainder of this chapter, only the bare outlines of how these misperceptions occurred and the rift between the Soviets and the Western allies developed.

THE EAST-WEST DISCORD BEGINS

When World War II ended, the Soviet Union, unlike the United States, did not demobilize its army. Instead, most of the Red Army remained in place in those portions of Europe which it had occupied. The United States enjoyed a monopoly on atomic weapons, and the United States and Britain withdrew nearly all their forces from France, Belgium, and other countries liberated from the Nazis, and kept units only in occupied Germany. The Russians continued to occupy not only their portion of Germany but also all the countries of eastern Europe, with the exception of Czechoslovakia, from which they shortly withdrew. These countries were not permitted to choose their own governments. Instead, governments controlled by local Communist parties were installed and maintained by the power of the Red Army in Hungary, Romania, Bulgaria, and Albania as well as Poland.

As the events of late 1945 and 1946 showed ever more clearly what was happening in Europe, the United States and Britain protested, to the UN and through diplomatic channels, but to no avail. The war-time Allies had worked out few definite arrangements for postwar Europe, partly because no one had known when Nazi Germany would surrender or what the European situation would be at that point. Also, no one had wanted to divert much attention from the consuming, immediate problems of winning the war to difficult and potentially divisive questions.

At the Tehran Conference and elsewhere the Allied leaders had agreed in general terms, and publicly declared, that all European countries liberated from the Nazis would be granted freedom and self-determination. Presumably this applied to eastern Europe as well. However, Roosevelt and Churchill had also informally agreed with Stalin that, by reason of geography, the Soviet Union would need regimes in eastern Europe that were friendly to the USSR. The Western leaders *hoped* that this consideration and the declarations about freedom and self-determination would not prove to be inconsistent. To Stalin, though, this informal understanding meant more than the propagandistic statements of idealistic principles, and in any case he was not about to give up, after the war, the control over eastern Europe that the Red Army's victory over the Wehrmacht had given him.

In retrospect it seems fairly clear that Stalin was mainly after a protective layer of small nations that could serve as a buffer between the USSR and the West. This essentially defensive motive was not well understood in Western countries at the time, nor for some time afterward. Russia had always been in a painfully insecure, even precarious, position. As Louis Halle points out in his insightful book *The Cold War As History*, the experience of the Russian people over the centuries had been the exact opposite of the American experience. Americans had always been unusually *secure*, whereas the Russians had always been unusually *insecure*. During the Middle Ages they had been overrun repeatedly by hordes of barbarian invaders who came out of central Asia to put the torch to Russian cities and towns, and who exacted tribute for long periods. In its formative era the Russian nation had almost been snuffed out several times.

More recently the attacks had come, time after time, from the west. Nature provided no natural defenses there; an unbroken plain stretches from France all the way across Europe and deep into Russia beyond Moscow. In the seventeenth century Poland had conquered and ruled much of Russia and burned down Moscow. When after much sacrifice the Poles were ejected and subdued, new threats had emerged— from Prussia, Sweden, the Austrian Empire, and from further west. Early in the 19th century Napoleon had invaded, and destroyed much of the capital, St. Petersburg. In World War I Russia had endured terrible casualties, worse than those of any other nation, and in 1917 had been compelled to surrender to the enemy. Only three years later the new Soviet regime found itself at war on several fronts with "armies of intervention" that were sponsored, paid for, equipped, and to some extent manned by Western countries. Ultimately these "white" armies failed to unseat the "reds" and reestablish a counterrevolutionary regime, but at several moments it was touch and go. In less than a generation Germany attacked again, more terribly than ever. Most of the industrialized part of the country was overrun and destroyed and some *twenty million* Russian soldiers and civilians lost their lives. This was a scale of death and destruction almost unimaginable for Westerners, and especially for Americans, whose homeland had scarcely ever been touched by any enemy.

In light of this history it is not surprising that after the war Stalin was determined that this should *never* happen again. By retaining a layer of nations on his border whose governments he could control, he established a barrier against new onslaughts from the west. His Communist ideology told him that the capitalist countries were bent on the destruction of the homeland of communism. The lessons of centuries of Russian insecurity and ideology together drove him to keep potential enemies as far away as possible and his neighbors under control.

Even so, had circumstances been a little different Stalin might not have insisted that the eastern European governments be entirely Communist. He did not do so in the case of Finland, which the Soviets also wished to use as a buffer state. Finland in the 1940s had a canny diplomat, and subsequently prime minister, in Juho Paasikivi. He skillfully negotiated agreements with the Soviets by which Finland was freed of Soviet occupation and permitted substantial (although not complete) freedom in its internal affairs, in return for Soviet control over its foreign policy. Stalin might have liked to find statesmen who could carry off a similar tightrope act in the other eastern European countries. He remarked at one point, discussing the problem of Poland, that what was needed was a Polish version of Paasikivi.

But the east Europeans were more thoroughly inundated with Red Army troops than were the Finns. They were also less patient and experienced with appeasement of their huge neighbor. With the exception of the Bulgarians, who are closely related to the Russians ethnically, they hated and feared the prospect of Russian hegemony. History had already given them as much taste of it as they wished: the czars had partitioned and continuously occupied Poland with troops, had ruthlessly put down the popular Hungarian revolution of 1848, and in many other ways had threatened and oppressed eastern Europe. There was no reason to expect more kindness from the new Soviet masters of a Russia grown even more preponderant in power.

A "Finnish solution" to the problem of eastern Europe was not possible. As the populations began to resist, the local Communists had to take strong-arm measures to ensure a pro-Soviet government, such as using force to limit the role of non-Communist political groups in the governmental process. These measures generated more popular resistance, hence stronger measures of control, and so on, until there was no alternative left for the Communists but totalitarian regimes, equipped with secret police and backed by the Russian army, which took up permanent residence.

This, in turn, was very different indeed from what the Americans and the other Western allies had intended. Insofar as they had thought about eastern Europe at all, they had expected it to turn out after the war somewhat as Finland did: subservient to Moscow in foreign affairs but largely free in internal affairs. Certainly they had not intended (though some pessimists had feared) totalitarian police states and a permanent Soviet occupation.

From the Western point of view this clearly was aggression. The perception was reinforced when the Soviets tried to make permanent their occupation of the northern part of Iran, begun during the war as a defensive measure with Western agreement. Again the Soviets wanted a buffer zone. In this case, strong Western protest compelled a withdrawal.

People in the West were suspicious of any events that reminded them of the history of Nazi Germany. The image of totalitarian aggression was vivid in everyone's mind, and it was easy to suppose that another totalitarian regime was behaving similarly. People began to fear that the USSR, like Nazi Germany, would never set any limit to its ambitions and would have to be stopped. The possibility of a defensive motive for Soviet behavior was overlooked. Where it was recognized, it often met the rejoinder that Hitler too had asserted defensive justifications for German aggression.

During an American tour in 1946, Churchill gave a speech in Missouri in which he declared that

> *From Stettin in the Baltic to Trieste in the Adriatic an iron curtain has descended across the continent . . . I do not believe that Soviet Russia desires war. What they desire is the fruits of war and the indefinite expansion of their power and doctrines . . .*

The U.S. government was still hoping at that time to make the United Nations work, and did not accept Churchill's suggestion of a Western military alliance against Russia, but his "iron curtain" phrase passed into the language.

THE COLD WAR BEGINS

Concern in the United States mounted when it became clear how weak the European allies were. In the earlier great conflicts of this century, Americans had counted on Britain, at least, to resist the tide of aggression while they made up their minds that a U.S. response might be required. But the British economy had been badly damaged in the war, and in the period following it failed to recover as hoped. Indeed, in some ways it worsened. In February 1947 the British officially informed Washington that they would be unable to go on protecting against Communist encroachments in Greece and Turkey. And a Soviet veto prevented the United Nations from acting.

Greece was immediately threatened by a civil war in which one side was pro-Communist. In March Truman made a strong speech before Congress declaring that henceforth the United States would "support free peoples who are resisting attempted subjugation by armed minorities or outside pressure." American aid started flowing into Greece and Turkey. How far this "Truman Doctrine" could reach was hardly envisioned at the time. In future years it was invoked many times as a justification for U.S. actions around the world.

Later that spring Bernard Baruch, an American elder statesman, gave a speech in South Carolina. "Let us not be deceived," said Baruch, summing up his assessment of Soviet-American relations, "today we are in the midst of a cold war." Picked up and spread by Walter Lippmann, the famous newspaper columnist, the phrase "cold war" quickly caught on. By summertime Americans were using the phrase routinely to describe the situation they felt they were being forced into by the Soviets.

Meanwhile Secretary of State George Marshall had proposed a plan by which the United States would send many billions of dollars worth of aid to Europe. The Marshall Plan was not actually approved by Congress for nearly a year. Almost at once, though, an expectation sprang up that it would be, and this gave a great psychological boost to the Europeans, whose devastated economies had been strained by unusually severe weather the previous winter. Marshall carefully held open the door for Soviet participation in the plan and for aid to Eastern as well as Western Europe, though with conditions. Because of the conditions and for other reasons, the Soviets refused and commanded the governments under their control to refuse also. This act, and the American and West European implementation of the plan in spite of it, created two economic blocs on the Continent and went far toward completing the division of Europe into East and West.

Americans have not always understood, at the time or since, how aggressive and how threatening the Soviets felt this American economic intervention in Europe to be. It was not just that the Soviet economy was also weak and damaged, and might be left permanently inferior to a rapidly rebuilt Western European economy (which in fact is just what happened). More than this, the Marxist ideologues in the USSR believed deeply that economic arrangements are always the supreme and ruling expression of political, social, and moral purposes. To them economic arrangements are not, as they are to most Westerners, a somewhat separate part of life, secondary to moral and political fundamentals such as liberty and democracy. Most Americans felt the Marshall Plan to be primarily altruistic and humanitarian, a one-time gift to cousins who had experienced misfortune. The Soviets saw it as something vast, political, and sinister: an intervention by capitalist America into the profoundest wellsprings of the European social order. (It is also true that many American officials hoped that the Marshall Plan would help forestall the election of Communists to public office in Italy and France.)

After the war, Marxist theoreticians in the USSR had been unanimous in predicting that the capitalist order in Western Europe could not survive the shock of the war's devastation, and that the historically "inevitable" proletarian revolution would come quickly. Now Washington and Wall Street were intervening on the grandest scale to forestall the revolution that was so inevitable, necessary, and right, and to turn back the clock of history. Short of outright war, a blacker deed could scarcely be imagined, or a more dangerous one to the Soviet Union. Little wonder, then, that the Soviets not only rejected the Marshall Plan absolutely within their own sphere, but from mid-1947 on adopted more cautious and defensive policies in all their dealings with the West.

By this time, too, the attention of the American people was returning to the problem of security, which had been gladly forgotten at the close of World War II. In late 1945 and through 1946, the possibility that the USSR might become some kind of threat had concerned a growing, but as yet small, segment of society. In 1947 this changed. The security question intruded again.

Some Americans believed that more effort should be made to find an accommodation with the USSR and to work through the United Nations. But the majority found themselves concluding that just as the UN had been unable to intervene in Greece and Turkey, it would be unable to intervene in similar situations in the future. The Soviet veto made it impossible.

This meant that the American concept of "collective security" had failed, at least so far as any conflict involved in the cold war was concerned. If collective security would not work, then another approach would have to be found to ensure the nation's security.

It was in 1947 that the term "national security" came into general use in America, for the first time in its history. It was also in 1947 that the United States government accepted a new doctrine for "containing" Soviet power, and began to create specific institutions and programs to protect national security, which will be detailed in the next chapter.

THE COLD WAR TURNS FRIGID

Even so, nothing that occurred in 1947 necessitated the deep and intense cold war that was to follow. The Communist threat was successfully turned back in both Greece and Turkey. The actual size of the Marshall Plan had not yet been determined because it had not yet passed Congress. If the East-West conflict could have been frozen at this point — that is, if neither side had taken any more initiatives that the other would have to see as hostile—the cold war might have become little more than a cold peace: a continuing *political* competition, perhaps not too different from many that have occurred in modern history.

But this could not be. In a world in which American economic power was intervening massively in Europe, and in which only America possessed the atom bomb, the Soviets felt threatened. Especially, they felt themselves in danger in Czechoslovakia and in Germany.

Czechoslovakia after the war possessed the largest and most genuinely popular Communist party in eastern Europe, and one that had a role in the coalition democratic regime that was formed. But Czechoslovakia was also the only eastern European country bordering on the USSR that the Soviets did not control. As Europe increasingly became divided into Western and Eastern blocs and as talk of cold war grew in the West, the Soviets evidently grew worried about the gap in their layer of buffer states. In February 1948 the Kremlin engineered a coup which brought the Czech Communists to full power and converted the country into another police state subservient to Moscow.

This coup stunned the West. It reinforced the belief that the Soviets would stop at nothing to expand their power and produced a general hardening of attitudes toward the USSR throughout Western Europe and America. It led almost directly to prompt congressional passage of the Marshall Plan and to the signing of a military alliance among Britain, France, and the Benelux countries.*

Meanwhile disagreements were becoming increasingly serious between the Soviets, who occupied the eastern part of defeated Germany, and the French, British, and Americans who occupied the western part. In 1948 the crucial issue was currency reform. After long negotiations had broken down completely, the Western allies introduced their own currency plan in their zones. Continuing economic chaos was too reminiscent of the conditions that had aided Hitler's rise to power. But to Soviet eyes this meant that once again the West was intervening unilaterally in the all-important economic sphere. The Soviets complained bitterly (and with some accuracy) that the Western action meant dividing Germany on a lasting basis.

Since 1945 the Western allies had also occupied part of Berlin, though the city lay far within the Soviet sector. Concluding that they

---

*Belgium, the Netherlands, and Luxembourg have usually acted together in their foreign affairs since World War II and are designated with this abbreviation.

could use the leverage of geography to make the West back down, in June the Soviets announced a blockade until the Western allies renegotiated the currency issue along Soviet lines — or alternatively, agreed to give up their share of Berlin. All ground access from the West was blocked and all food, coal, and electricity from Soviet-occupied Germany was cut off.

The Soviets did not try to blockade air traffic from the West to Berlin, because there was no way to do so without shooting down the airplanes (which would put on the USSR the burden of firing the first shots) and because supplying the city by air seemed impossible. The West decided to try it.

An immense drama now unfolded, a drama that gripped the whole world and further locked East and West into the deep and bitter antagonisms of the cold war. Food could be airlifted easily enough. The challenge was to bring in enough coal to keep the West Berliners from freezing to death in the winter. More and more planes were flung into the effort, until an airplane was landing in Berlin every few minutes, twenty-four hours a day. Week after week this grueling pace was maintained. When spring came the Soviets tacitly admitted failure and, in May, lifted the blockade.

To the USSR this was an immense blow. So soon after the tremendous sacrifices of the war, the Soviets had lost control over the larger and richer portion of divided Germany. It would join the West politically as well as economically; before long it might even be allowed to rearm. And the Soviets had not even been able to consolidate their own portion of Germany. A Western bastion deep within it would be a source of endless trouble for them in the future (as it was).

Meanwhile, Westerners were shocked that the USSR had held an entire city hostage so cold-bloodedly. The Berlin Blockade had a much greater personal impact on the average American and West European than anything else that had happened. The emotional, political, and moral effect in the United States was so great that for many years thereafter it was almost impossible for any American political leader to see the USSR as anything but a cynical aggressor.

The Soviets have not always understood how aggressive and how threatening Westerners felt this act of coercion (and to a lesser degree, the Czech coup) to be. Westerners felt deeply that this use of force against unwilling people was profoundly immoral. Where the Soviets saw it as a logical move in a competition between rival and ultimately irreconcilable social systems, Westerners saw it as an action that invited comparison with the Nazis — a deliberate, cynical threat of death by freezing to two million human beings. Short of outright war, a blacker deed could scarcely be imagined, or a more dangerous one to the West. The Red Army, hitherto passive, was immensely more powerful than all the Western armies in Europe combined, because the latter had been all but totally demobilized. Now that the Soviets had shown that they were ready to use that power aggressively, what might they do next?

It was in the wake of the Berlin Blockade that the United States and most of the Western European countries created the North Atlantic Treaty Organization — NATO. The treaty was signed in Brussels in July 1949, and approved by the Senate with the knowledge that it implied sending American troops back to Europe. Four divisions were committed there in 1951, partly in response to the outbreak of the Korean War.

These troops, plus the modest forces the European allies were able to muster, were still enormously outnumbered by the Red Army forces deployed in Europe. To help partially redress the balance, West Germany was admitted to NATO in 1955 as the fifteenth member country, and with American assistance began an ambitious rearmament program. In response, the Soviet Union and its East European satellites created the Warsaw Pact, and the USSR began beefing up (while retaining effective control over) the satellites' military forces. The two military alliances have faced each other, across the frozen division of Germany, ever since.

SUMMARY

America's colossal effort in World War II, and her leadership of the worldwide antifascist alliance in that conflict, represented a radical reversal of her previous stance in the world. For 125 years Americans, uniquely secure on their own continent, had built their country with negligible interest or involvement in military matters. Except for a relatively brief flirtation with imperialism at the turn of the century, Americans had resorted only rarely to military might, and had soon returned to a life unconcerned with security. They hoped to continue this tradition, in a new form, when they withdrew and demobilized their forces almost completely after winning humanity's greatest war, and tried to turn all questions of future security over to a "collective security" system, the United Nations.

But the UN Security Council could not work without unanimity among its permanent members, the great powers. The Soviet Union wielded its veto repeatedly to prevent UN "interference" in its pursuit of its own policies after the war. Deeply insecure through the centuries, invaded and ravaged time after time, the Russians were determined to create a layer of buffer states around their border to increase their security against the danger of attack.

Both historical circumstance, and misperceptions that arose between two very different social systems, generated out of this situation an ever-growing conflict between East and West. It was historical circumstance that only in Finland did popular attitudes and skillful leaders emerge to permit a mixture of Soviet hegemony and internal democracy. It was historical circumstance that a power vacuum developed after the war in central and western Europe, where victor and defeated nations alike retained tiny armies and tottering economies. It was historical circumstance that these Europeans, watching American power ebb away over the seas, felt deeply insecure in the shadow of the huge Red Army; yet the Soviets too felt insecure and overshadowed, by the atom bomb that only archcapitalist America possessed. And it was historical circumstance that the victorious Allies' arrangements for occupying Germany would exacerbate conflicts once they split, and that the most urgent issues there were economic ones that East and West viewed in profoundly different ways.

But it was a Soviet misperception that the Marshall Plan was a sinister intervention by capitalist America to return Europe, now teetering on the brink of inevitable revolution, to a reactionary social system. It was a western misperception that the conversion of occupied eastern Europe into totalitarian dictatorships, the Czech coup, and the Berlin Blockade, were highly aggressive deeds comparable to the early career of Nazi Germany. And there was an element of misperception on both sides about the geopolitics and timing of events: The West did not understand that the Soviet hegemony looked to the Soviets like a defensive barrier only, or that their steps to complete that hegemony were triggered by Western actions. In their turn the Soviets did not understand that, from the outside, all their actions looked like a steady and relentless forward march, or that outsiders would have to be alarmed when each step was more violent than the last.

By 1947 the West, led by the United States, was turning away from collective security as its principal means for ensuring the peace, at least so far as conflict involved in the cold war was concerned. Thereafter "collective security" remained a phrase often used to describe American intentions, but with a new and different meaning—security for *one* collection of nations united against another. And the United States, as leader of its group, arrived finally at a problem which it, alone among the world's nations, had never before had to face—coping with a serious, continuing menace to its security.

FOR FURTHER READING

Ambrose, Stephen E. *Rise to Globalism*: *American Foreign Policy 1938-1980*. Second edition, revised. New York: Penguin Books, 1980. A quite readable overview of the development of U.S. foreign policy, including a balanced presentation of postwar events.

Churchill, Winston S. *Triumph and Tragedy*. Boston: Houghton Mifflin, 1953. Churchill's own account, colored by his personal attitudes but beautifully written, of the closing months of World War II and the period immediately following.

Gaddis, John L. *The United States and the Origins of the Cold War, 1941-1947*. New York: Columbia University Press, 1972. A leading historical assessment of the cold war "origins" question, widely respected for its balance.

Goldman, Eric F. *The Crucial Decade*: *America 1945-1955*. New York: Alfred Knopf, 1956. This history of the period is particularly effective in evoking the feeling and tone of the experiences that Americans lived through.

Halle, Louis. *The Cold War As History*. New York: Harper and Row, 1967. Perhaps the premier "grand" history of the cold war, in which events unfold in a lofty perspective.

Truman, Harry S. *Memories. Volume II: Years of Trial and Hope, 1946-1952*. New York: Doubleday, 1956. This defense of the Truman administration's policies illuminates how the administration perceived and coped with the national security problems of the postwar years.

Ulam, Adam. *Expansion and Coexistence*: *Soviet Foreign Policy 1917-1973*. Second edition. New York: Praeger, 1974. This general account of the USSR's foreign policy includes a well-balanced assessment of the Soviet role in the origins of the cold war.

4
America Fashions Its National Security

As it became increasingly clear, in the period after the Second World War, that the United Nations would not be able to guarantee peace and security for the United States, attention began to turn to how the United States could do so for itself. For a while both possibilities were pursued. As late as 1948 the United States was proposing to destroy all of its atomic bombs and turn over the secret of their construction to the United Nations. (The Soviet Union rejected the idea for reasons that will be discussed later.) But meanwhile the Truman administration had prepared a bill for Congress that would create permanent institutions within the U.S. government for guarding the nation. The National Security Act, passed in July 1947, created a governmental structure for national security affairs that, with only minor changes, has continued to the present.

Throughout previous American history, the navy and the army (including since World War I an Army Air Corps) had been separate departments. In peacetime the army had been responsible to a civilian secretary of war and the navy to a secretary of the navy, and these cabinet-level officials only to the president. In wartime the services had reported directly to the president through their highest-ranking officers, the chief of staff of the army and the chief of naval operations. The most controversial feature of the new National Security Act was the "unification" of the services, though this really was quite limited. The services continued to have their separate identities, but were made responsible to a single, civilian secretary of defense. (Separate service secretaries remained also, but at a subcabinet level.) The act also split the air corps from the army and renamed it the United States Air Force, a co-equal military service within the new Department of Defense (DOD, pronounced dee-oh-dee). The Office of the Secretary of Defense (OSD, pronounced oh-es-dee), created fairly weak in 1947, was strengthened several times in later years and given research and other agencies of its own, in amendments to the act passed by Congress and in executive orders from the White House.

Partly to compensate the military services for having inserted a new civilian layer between them and the president, the National Security Act put on a permanent, legal basis the institution of the Joint Chiefs of Staff (JCS). Worked out less formally during World War II, the JCS had originally been little more than a committee of the service chiefs. Now it was given permanence, more support (the Joint Staff), and the standing right of direct access to the president on request.

The National Security Act did not confine itself to military organization, but also addressed national security more broadly. During the war, the American effort to gather general intelligence and conduct espionage and secret operations had been conducted by a clandestine agency, the Office of Strategic Services. Now the Act took the OSS, rechristened it the Central Intelligence Agency (CIA), and gave it the same responsibilities on a permanent basis. However, the three military services also retained the intelligence organizations they had long possessed for gathering military intelligence about other nations' air, naval, and ground forces. In the 1960s these military intelligence services were partially unified to form the Defense Intelligence Agency (DIA), which is responsible to the secretary of defense.

Finally, the Act created the National Security Council to advise the president. Essentially a cabinet for national security, the NSC includes, under the terms of the Act, the vice president and the secretaries of state and defense. Statutory advisors to the NSC are the director of the CIA and the Chairman of the Joint Chiefs of Staff. Over the years others have often been invited to join the NSC temporarily, and the NSC has been given a staff. When the presidents, beginning with Eisenhower, decided to appoint a "special assistant for national security," these senior White House officials have also joined the NSC. They have often chaired its meetings and they direct the NSC staff. The position of national security assistant, though, is a creature of presidential authority and has not been written into law by Congress. This means, among other things, that Congress cannot require the national security assistant to appear before congressional committees to testify, as it can all the other members of the National Security Council.

About the same time, Congress passed a second measure, the Atomic Energy Act of 1947. The main purpose of the Act was to place the atomic bomb program under firmer civilian control. During the war this program had been run by the army, under the deliberately misleading name of "the Manhattan Project." The Act created an Atomic Energy Commission, headed by five civilians, with responsibility for research and development of new atomic weapons, all aspects of their manufacture, and their delivery to the military services. Storing, deploying, and guarding the weapons remained military functions. Civilian applications of atomic energy—for instance, the development of reactors for generating electricity—also were given to the AEC. In the 1970s the AEC was merged with some other governmental bodies to create a Federal Energy Agency, which shortly became the nucleus of the Department of Energy.

All the steps Congress took in 1947 represented less of a change than they seemed at the time. Often the same people continued working in the same offices, and merely used paper with a different letterhead. Congress had a justifiable confidence in the organizations and arrangements that had been so dramatically successful in winning World War II, and since the United States had been involved so little with military matters for more than a century, there was little experience with other ways of doing things. The tendency was to make few and modest changes. Those that were made, were made partly for reasons of efficiency, but perhaps mainly to ensure civilian control of what would be, for the first time in America, a large, standing military establishment.

Also for the first time there would be large military expenditures, year after year, in time of peace. Drafting military budgets to take to Congress was the responsibility of the Office of the Secretary of Defense. At once OSD found this to be no easy task. Previously the army and navy had lived with whatever small budgets their secretaries could secure for them at the cabinet level of executive policy making. But now they were faced with the prospect of a single defense budget, which would have to be divided *within* the department among the separate services. Not only the size of each slice, but also the method of cutting the pie would set precedents for future years, so disputes among the services erupted almost at once. These became all the worse when it was discovered that President Truman insisted that the first DOD budget come to only about half the total that the services separately requested. Particularly vehement was a USAF/navy argument whether primary emphasis should go to a "70-group air force" or to "supercarriers" (that is, the Forrestal-class aircraft carrier which is now the standard size, but which was much larger than the World War II aircraft carriers). The army's needs were secondary because they could be partially met by mobilization after a war began. But aircraft and ships were "long lead-time items" that would have to be bought in advance, and each service felt that its own needs should get priority.

Disputes like this were to become common as the years passed. Despite the public pledge of every president to "spend whatever is necessary for the defense of America," in fact each administration has given DOD a budget ceiling that may not be exceeded. Naturally, what the services believe they need comes to more than this, so there is a continual need to make hard choices. The same thing can occur within a single service, as when the "brown shoe navy" (naval air and aircraft carrier officers) compete with the "black shoe navy" (combat ship and submarine officers) for the same pot of money. Although it can be argued that a certain amount of competition among and within the services is a good thing, great efforts have been made to reduce its intensity, and also to minimize duplication of tasks between one service and another. In the late 1940s and early 1950s, disputes and duplication were limited somewhat by negotiated agreements among the services, defining "roles and missions." In the 1960s, mathematical techniques were introduced into military planning that sometimes helped. But the competition is never entirely resolved, only coped with, and it can always arise anew. During the Vietnam War, for instance, the USAF complained that the army had deployed so many types of helicopters and small aircraft that it was creating practically another little air force, and intruding onto air force roles and missions.

These are conflicts *within* the established system, though. The consensus that the system itself is sound is so complete that proposals for making basic changes (such as the one Canada made, to put all its military into a single uniform) are rarely heard. There are, of course, endless small modifications. Organizations and agencies have been added from time to time, such as the Directorate of Defense Research and Engineering within OSD.

One major organization, confusingly called the National Security Agency, was also added outside the military services. It is responsible for supplying the United States with unbreakable codes, for trying to break foreign codes, for intercepting foreign communications and other electronic intelligence, and for making U.S. communications and electronic systems secure from similar interceptions by others. Such additions do not alter the fact that the basic structure of national security institutions created by Congress in 1947 has stood for over thirty-five years without major change. (The identities and missions of these organizations are not discussed further in this book.)

When the United States turned to fashioning its own national security in the years following World War II, creating institutions was only half the challenge. There was also the deeper and more complicated question of what needed to be *done* (and not done) with those institutions, and with American power generally. To this we now turn.

CONTAINMENT

The bare beginning of U.S. national security policy was provided some six months after the end of World War II. In the American embassy in Moscow worked a staff officer named George Kennan, who sent Washington a secret cable, sixteen pages long, in February 1946. In his message Kennan analyzed the history and nature of the Soviet regime, and concluded that unless prevented, it would probably expand into the power vacuum in central and western Europe that the war's devastation had left. He reminded the U.S. government that America had fought two wars in this century to prevent all of Europe from coming under the control of a single militaristic regime. He suggested that this danger could arise again, and he recommended that Soviet expansionism be "contained" by American policies while there was yet time to do so without having to fight again.

Kennan's analysis, and his recommendation of the "containment"

concept, was not immediately accepted in Washington. It was still
U.S. policy to work with the Soviets and to try to make the United Nations succeed. But his articulate and obviously thoughtful essay was
circulated, first around the State Department, then more widely
through the government. Kennan himself was recalled to Washington
to explain his ideas further. As the months passed and Soviet actions
in Europe disappointed and frustrated American hopes more and
more, Kennan's view gained ground. His analysis provided a way of
understanding what was occurring, and why the ideal of organizing
world politics in the framework of the UN system was failing. As the
course that the United States was trying to take in the world proved
more and more impossible, Kennan's approach gained favor as an alternative. By the winter of 1947 it was largely accepted by policy makers,
and incorporated into a formal document establishing it as a fundamental U.S. goal. As the cold war mounted thereafter, containment of
the Soviet Union became the very bedrock of U.S. foreign policy.

So that the American public could better understand the premises
of U.S. actions, Kennan published an edited version of his long cable,
with secret information about the USSR removed. Entitled "The
Sources of Soviet Conduct," it appeared in the July 1947 issue of
Foreign Affairs, at the time the only important American journal
devoted to international relations and foreign policy. The article's
author was given as "Mr. X," since the U.S. government and its high-ranking officials rarely publish official policy in private journals, but it
became widely known that the article presented what was now the
American government's view. As the main justification for containment to appear publicly, the Mr. X article became probably the most
famous essay on foreign relations written in the English language in
this century.

In retrospect it is easier than it was at the time to see exactly what
containment was and was not. Kennan argued the need to imprison
Soviet influence within approximately its existing boundaries, and he
justified this with a careful analysis of Soviet practice, Communist doctrine, and the threat that an expansion of Soviet power in Europe could
pose. But containment was offered as a *policy* only in a loose sense of
the term. It was really a concept, and a policy *goal*. Which among many
possible foreign policies and/or military policies would *accomplish* the
goal of containment was not discussed in the cable or the Mr. X article.

Still less did containment represent a full-scale national security
doctrine or theory. Although the concept seemed to have military implications, no serious attempt was made at first to study what military

resources might be needed to sustain containment, or how different approaches to military strategy related to that foreign policy goal. In fact, the Mr. X article did not even discuss what overt, immediate military threat might be posed by the USSR, or how it might be met.

Shortly thereafter the Truman Doctrine and the Marshall Plan were developed as policies in support of containment. Kennan, who worked on the latter but not the former, was skeptical of extending containment outside democratic, industrialized Europe. He helped design the Marshall Plan as a way of rebuilding that region, so it could defend itself in the future without continuing American subsidy. It was hoped that once the Western European democracies enjoyed economies that functioned productively again, their current political instability would fade and they would be able to choose their own destinies without undue influence from the East.

The containment line *was* extended, though, to the Far East after the Korean War broke out, and then to the Middle East in the so-called Eisenhower Doctrine of the mid-1950s. Kennan himself was more aware of the concept's limitations than many who flocked to the containment banner. He opposed these extensions, and also the somewhat harsher, more militant cast that containment developed as the cold war deepened. In a simplified form the concept took on a life of its own, however, and as late as the 1970s was still being appealed to as a justification for the Vietnam War even though that conflict was far removed in place, time, and circumstances from the Europe of the late 1940s, and involved a different opponent.

Part of the reason why the concept became simplified in the period following its introduction may have been that people believed it would apply for only a few years. At this time there was no expectation of a "long haul" competition with the USSR. It was thought that after the tyrant Stalin died, the Moscow regime would become less aggressive. Material progress and better education would gradually make the Soviet Union a "have" rather than a "have-not" nation, and give the regime a stake in peace and stability. Containment, in Kennan's sophisticated sense of the term, was not merely a negative goal—prevention of Soviet expansionism—but also a positive one. It supposed that Soviet as well as West European economies would be rebuilt, and that the Soviets would gradually find themselves having more to gain from continued peace than from making trouble. Hence containment would not be required forever; as the Soviet system mellowed the need for it would gradually fade. The common view in the West in the late 1940s was that this process might take, at most, ten or fifteen years. The cold war was expected to be over in less time than that. This may be one of the reasons, often forgotten now, why Americans allowed their feelings and behavior in the cold war to become so harsh and militant; they thought it would be quite temporary.

We know now that these assumptions, which lay behind the containment concept in ways not wholly articulated, were both right and wrong. After about fifteen years the Soviets did indeed start acting less aggressively. The cold war lasted longer, in its intense phase, than expected—into the mid-1960s—but thereafter modified its form. The East-West competition continued, but without the intense crises or sense of major war being an imminent possibility that had existed earlier.

However the Soviet system has changed far less than Kennan and his fellow planners expected. They did not foresee a "mature tyranny," in which the worst excesses of the Stalin era have been left behind but dissent continues to be repressed systematically. They did not foresee how the regime would use modern technology (much of it imported or copied from the West) to build an awkward but workable economy that can supply both a giant military machine and enough consumer goods to secure a mixture of approval and acquiescence from the people. Thus they did not foresee how a threatening competition between East and West, though less acute, would come in time to seem a permanent fixture in the world. This permanence, along with other things, has brought an element of pessimism into the American people's sense of the long-term evolution of world politics, which was not present in the early years of the cold war even though fears about immediate dangers were much stronger then.

DETERRENCE

At the time that containment of the Soviets was becoming the central goal of U.S. foreign policy, the West had astonishingly little military power available to deploy along the containment line. American, British, and French occupation forces in Germany had been reduced to a very low level. The Western European nations, straining to recover from the war economically, were supporting only token armed forces in their home territories. Facing them across the iron curtain were over one hundred Red Army divisions. The U.S. Army, now almost completely demobilized, had approximately *two* divisions, and these were stationed in the United States. It was obvious that if the Soviets ever decided to conquer Western Europe, they would hardly have to fight. People said, in a phrase that became famous, that "all the Russians would need would be shoes" to march all the way to the Atlantic Ocean.

The United States, though, was the only nation that had atomic bombs. By 1948 it also had a new bomber, the B-36, a large, propeller-driven, long-range airplane, as well as many bombers built during World War II. On the drawing boards was a jet bomber, the B-47. In the event that war broke out, Russian cities and industrial areas would be vulnerable to atomic bombing by the Strategic Air Command (SAC, pronounced "sack"), the bombing division of the U.S. Air Force. This was stated by high-level American officials with increasing explicitness as the cold war deepened.

American strategy at this point was to deter the outbreak of a new war by making a drastic threat. Although the Soviets could not be physically stopped from seizing Europe, their own homeland would be destroyed behind them if they did. The Soviets could not risk this, hence — according to the strategy — they would never attack in Europe. And since they would never attack, the drastic threat would never have to be carried out.

In this way *deterrence* of a third world war became the principal function of American military power. As a strategy, deterrence seemed straightforward and basically simple. At this point it had not taken on the complications that it would in a few years. The strategy played to America's strength, its atomic monopoly, and it seemed to offer a way to maintain peace and the freedom of Western Europe without having to pay the political and economic costs of maintaining a large standing army there.

There were two possible alternatives to the deterrence strategy. One was to launch a preventive war. In theory, the United States could have taken advantage of its atomic monopoly to attack the source of the threat, the Soviet Union, remove the Communist regime and replace it with a democratic government that, presumably, would cooperate thereafter with the United Nations and a collective security system. This possibility was never given serious consideration at any time within the U.S. government, although it was recommended by no less a figure than Bertrand Russell (who feared atomic wars in the future when many nations had such weapons).

It is worth recalling the option of preventive war, because more recently people have forgotten the moral significance of the fact that the United States never considered it. America is the one nation in all of recorded history that for a few years probably had—to put it bluntly—the chance to rule the world. The atomic monopoly would almost certainly have carried the United States to victory in a war against the USSR, something that undoubtedly the Soviet leaders were keenly aware of at the time. Thereafter the United States might have enforced a *pax Americana* on the world indefinitely, either directly, or through a UN that America controlled. This possibility was never seriously entertained in Washington, and that fact has a permanent moral meaning. However uncomfortable Americans may have felt, and still feel, about Hiroshima and Nagasaki, and more recently about the war in Vietnam, it will always be to their nation's credit that the United States of America possessed the one opportunity in history to be master of the globe, and was not even seriously tempted.

Besides preventive war and deterrence, the other option available to an America worried about the Red Army looming over Europe was to send a big American army there. A large conventional force (that is, one without atomic weapons) stationed there indefinitely could defend the Europeans directly against a Soviet attack, should it come. This *defense* strategy would be a more visible expression of containment than the *deterrence* strategy, and perhaps a resort to the atomic bombing of Russian cities might not be necessary in a war. But in the late 1940s, this option was thought to be politically and economically out of the question. The American people had never been willing to station a large army far from home indefinitely, and had insisted on almost complete demobilization at the end of World War II. A controversial proposal for universal military training of America's young men was defeated in Congress in 1948, in favor of "selective" service by some of them instead. It was believed, too, that the economy could never sustain the large military expenditures that would be required, year after year.

Throughout the late 1940s the defense budget was held almost constant, and fairly low—around $40 billion a year in 1983 dollars. (This was $10 to $12 billion a year in the dollars of those years.) The Strategic Air Command was well supported with this budget, and so was the atomic weapons program, which received almost the entire AEC budget of about $2 billion a year. But other military forces received only modest support, and not remotely enough to station in Europe an army big enough to have a chance of defeating a Red Army attack. The budget could support a strategy of deterrence, but not one of European defense.

This left the United States in the awkward position of having to tell its allies that it could not protect them from being overrun by the Soviets. American war plans during these years assumed that "the next war," if and when it occurred, would begin with a Soviet assault on Europe that would succeed immediately. The weak ground forces available to the West would try, though, to hold the Channel against any amphibious assault on Britain. Meanwhile, according to the plans, SAC would carry out atomic strikes on cities and industrial districts inside Russia.

One of the most closely guarded secrets of this era was the fact that the United States actually had very few bombs with which to do this. The American public, U.S. allies, and foreign powers, including the Soviet Union, all assumed that the United States was stockpiling hundreds, if not thousands, of atomic bombs. American defense officials carefully allowed this impression to stand, because the deterrence strategy depended on everyone, especially the Soviets, believing that the USSR would be almost wiped out if SAC attacked. In fact, the technology of the day produced bombs very slowly. After Hiroshima and Nagasaki, the United States could not have had another bomb ready to drop on Japan for months, and even as late as 1949 there were only about a hundred bombs in the arsenal. Since some of the bombers carrying them would be shot down on the way to their targets, every bomb that could be built was important.

When the nuclear stockpile was used up, the war plans called for continued bombing of Soviet and East European factories, railroad yards, and other war-making resources, with conventional bombs. Meanwhile the United States would mount another grand mobilization of its military potential, as it had in 1942 after Pearl Harbor. All of Europe would be liberated by American armies just as Western Europe had been in 1944–45.

In short, American plans visualized a replay of the European part of World War II, with a nuclear prelude. This scenario and variations on it were the only ones seriously planned for. The image of the great war so recently experienced was vivid in everyone's mind, and this image completely dominated peoples' thinking about "the next war." Other and more complicated possibilities were little considered. Although actual crises involving military force were occurring in Greece, Czechoslovakia, Berlin, and elsewhere, these events were scarcely connected to American military planning, and hardly any forces were developed that might be useful in such situations. U.S. planners had almost no concept at this time of small-scale or "limited" warfare and made almost no preparations for such a possibility. On the assumption that the next war would be a third world war, they believed that the military forces America needed were those required to deter an all-out attack, and if necessary, to strike rapidly and devastatingly at the enemy's homeland should deterrence fail and the attack actually came.

Furthermore, deterrence in this sense was thought to be supplied almost automatically by SAC and the nuclear monopoly. Probably it would succeed and no war would occur; if it failed this would be for some reason outside American control. Either way deterrence seemed almost effortless, more a fact than a problem or a policy goal. In this respect it differed greatly from containment, which might prove hard or relatively easy to achieve (and differed also from the way deterrence too would seem in a few years). Though containment might be pursued in many ways that required study, deterrence at this time seemed to require little analysis.

Such was the American approach to national security in the first years of the atomic age. Containment and deterrence reigned supreme, each in its own sphere. Containment was pursued by various political, diplomatic, and economic means; deterrence was provided by SAC. The United States not only had its atomic monopoly, but also was the only major power whose industries and economy had survived the war intact. Vastly richer than any conceivable combination of foes, America was a colossus bestriding the globe, and limited only by its own values and form of government from ruling it. The national security of the United States, though challenged in a way previously unfamiliar to Americans, could be reliably preserved by deterrence. The challenge would gradually lessen as containment did its work and Europe regained its strength. Security was no longer free of charge, and a world of collective security could not be achieved yet, but national security could be gained and kept, at a not too burdensome cost, by American strength.

THE YEAR OF SHOCKS

In the second half of 1949 occurred two events that severely shook Americans' sense of relative security. One was the final victory of the Communists in the Chinese civil war. For a dozen years starting in the 1920s, Mao Zedong and his Peoples' Liberation Army had fought the Nationalist government headed by Chiang Kai-shek. After the Japanese attacked in the 1930s, the two Chinese parties had made an alliance to fight the invader, each in the part of the country it controlled. But with the defeat of Japan in World War II, the civil war had erupted again more violently than ever, and the Communists began making rapid progress. By 1949 the Nationalists were evacuating their forces to the island of Taiwan, leaving Mao in possession of the mainland and its huge population.

Mao had briefly been interested in American assistance when the civil war had resumed; after being rebuffed he turned to the USSR. In exchange for increasingly close ties he received some aid, and after he formed a government the relationship was formalized in a treaty of friendship. The American people, who traditionally had felt a special, somewhat sentimental, attachment for China, were shocked when it was taken over by Communists and allies of the USSR. At one blow this doubled the territory and quadrupled the population controlled by Communism.

Even more stunning was the first atomic test explosion by the Soviet Union. American specialists had expected that this would not occur for several more years at the soonest; optimists had thought longer. Now, on September 23, the White House announced that it had already happened. Trying to forestall panic, it coupled the announcement with reassurances. Government spokesmen pointed out, for instance, that this explosion (like the first American test) was of a "device" too big to carry in an airplane, and that real bombs, even when designed, could not be manufactured rapidly. But people knew that they would be built as soon as they could be, and that before long America might become vulnerable to atomic attack. In the following years thousands of Americans would sign up for "Operation Skywatch," in which volunteers would scan the heavens with binoculars, looking for incoming Soviet bombers.

The "fall" of China and the Soviet atomic test, occurring back to back, shocked and worried Americans more than anything that had happened yet. Although the danger might not be immediate, the implications for the future were very ominous. The USSR and China together ruled over a quarter of the world's people, and controlled most of the world's greatest landmass, from the middle of Europe all the way around half the globe to the South China Sea. If the Communists had atomic bombs also, what might they try to take over next?

In response to this new and graver challenge, President Truman took two initiatives. One was to order a complete review and reanalysis of the world situation, with recommendations for new U.S. national security policies. (The results are discussed below.) The other was to proceed with a more terrible weapon that had now become possible.

Atomic bombs worked by the sudden fission of heavy uranium or plutonium atoms into smaller fragments. American scientists now knew that it would also be possible to set off even mightier explosions by the sudden fusion of lightweight hydrogen atoms into heavier elements. In a less explosive way this was the power that was keeping the sun bright and hot for untold ages. Plans had been drafted for developing a fusion bomb, initially called Super, and now the president ordered that Super be built.

There was little choice, Truman believed, because the Soviets would be working on a fusion bomb as well. He ordered that work on Super proceed as rapidly as possible, and the United States was the first to explode a hydrogen device, on a Pacific island in 1952. Even so it was the Soviet Union, not the United States, that was first to test a bomb, working partly on fusion, that was small enough to drop from an airplane. (This fact was not revealed to the American public for many years; and indeed it was not as significant as it would have seemed to the public at the time because the United States tested a fusion bomb soon after, and a better one.)

The U.S. and Soviet decisions to develop hydrogen bombs were of deep importance, because fusion weapons can be enormously more destructive than fission bombs. There is an inherent upper limit to the explosive power, called "yield," that a fission weapon can have, but there is none for fusion bombs. While the force of a fission bomb is awe-inspiring, that of a fusion bomb is almost incomprehensible. The yield of a fission weapon is measured by how many thousands of tons of the strongest chemical explosive, TNT, would be required to create a blast of equal size. The Hiroshima bomb, for instance, was the equivalent of about fifteen thousand tons of TNT, or fifteen "kilotons." But hydrogen weapons are measured in *millions* of tons of TNT, or "megatons."

The difference is more important than the average man on the street is likely to think offhand. A fission bomb of fifteen kilotons dropped on the Statue of Liberty in New York harbor would do little more than break windowpanes at the distance of Times Square (some seven miles away). But a ten-megaton hydrogen bomb dropped at the same place would utterly devastate all of Manhattan and, indeed, the entire New York City and harbor area. Although the public did not fully realize it when news of the hydrogen bomb was released, the step from fission to fusion bombs was at least as significant as the earlier step from the largest conventional bombs to fission. The wholesale death of most of a nation's people and the destruction of civilization—most peoples' image of "the end of the world" in atomic war— would actually be fairly difficult to accomplish with fission weapons only. With hydrogen weapons it becomes all too feasible.

Truman's other initiative, the reanalysis of the overall national security challenge, was carried out by a special task force drawn from several departments of government. The study it produced was to become a landmark in U.S. national security affairs.

NSC-68

The study was submitted to the National Security Council in the spring of 1950, and became known as NSC-68 (that is, the 68th policy document prepared for the council). The task force had taken seriously Truman's request for a complete and general reassessment of the United States' overall position in the world. Drawing on all available intelligence, NSC-68 analyzed the American national security situation broadly and traced through the logic of existing and anticipated problems. In doing so it created something the United States had never had before: a comprehensive national security policy and strategy.

NSC-68 began with a review of the overall world situation. Stating that the USSR "seeks to impose its absolute authority over the rest of the world," and that Soviet political values are incompatible with those of a free society, the report identified the Soviet Union as a grave threat to American security. It reviewed the political and economic strengths and weaknesses of the two societies, and pointed out that the USSR devoted a "far greater proportion" of its total resources to military purposes than did the United States. It also concluded that international control over atomic weapons would remain impossible until such time as Soviet aggressive designs were so thoroughly frustrated that a drastic change in Soviet policy might follow.*

NSC-68 then distinguished and analyzed four courses of possible American action: to continue present policies, to retreat into isolation and seek to defend only the Western Hemisphere, to launch a "preventive war," or to build up American power. It argued against the first

---

*A citation to the published text of NSC-68 appears at the end of this chapter.

three and strongly for the last. A substantial military buildup would be needed "to deter, if possible, Soviet expansion, and to defeat, if necessary, aggressive Soviet or Soviet-directed actions of a limited or total character."

The Soviet threat was now more urgent because the USSR possessed atomic bombs and could be presumed to be working on hydrogen bombs. NSC-68 estimated that by 1954 the Soviets could have 200 fission bombs and cautioned that its estimate might be low. Without an American buildup, the Soviets could then destroy enough of Western Europe to make any defense against the Red Army impossible, destroy Britain sufficiently to preclude its use in any subsequent effort to liberate Europe, and make devastating attacks on the United States.

Several things would have to be done. Clearly one was "to provide an adequate defense against air attack on the United States." Up to this time, the United States had never made any serious effort to protect its airspace. Now it must. This was one concrete recommendation of NSC-68 that was carried out. In the following years several lines of radar stations were erected across Canada, and extended out to sea on ships, to spot attacking Soviet bombers while they were still some distance away. A substantial force of fighter aircraft and of surface-to-air missiles (SAMs) was also deployed. Inevitably some Soviet bombers would get through, however.

NSC-68 also concluded that the United States must provide "an adequate defense against air and surface attack on the United Kingdom, Western Europe . . . and on the long lines of communication to these areas." This meant a large increase in U.S. *conventional* forces. Although the report did not point it out explicitly, defense against the enormous Red Army formations in Eastern Europe would mean a large commitment of American ground troops to Europe. An effort to defend Europe against the Soviet Air Force would also mean a significant USAF commitment. The NATO allies would not be able to carry this burden by 1954. In turn, American ground and air forces in Europe would have to have their supply line across the Atlantic protected by adequate U.S. naval forces. Furthermore the United States should have conventional forces "in being and readily available to defeat local Soviet moves with local action," so that a limited attack did not become "the occasion for [all-out] war."

The conclusion that Europe would have to be defended represented a major departure in American thinking. Up to this time it had been assumed that the Red Army was deterred by SAC from marching into Western Europe. A Soviet invasion would mean all-out war, and all-out war would mean American atomic strikes on the USSR. Implicit in NSC-68 was a new logic. Soon the Soviets would also have the ability to make atomic strikes on an enemy's homeland. An American strike on the Soviet Union would presumably be answered in kind, by Soviet atomic attacks on America and Western Europe.

A new situation was developing in which each nuclear power would know that striking the other side's cities would invite a counterstrike on one's own. In effect the two nuclear forces would balance and *mutually deter each other*. A nuclear stalemate would develop, in which neither side would dare launch an atomic attack on the other.

This meant, although NSC-68 did not develop the argument explicitly, that another way would have to be found to protect the European allies. SAC might *not* be unleashed if the Red Army invaded, or at any rate the Soviets might not think it would be. If they didn't think so they might not be deterred from invading. In a strategy of deterrence, what the enemy *thinks* is all important. If he does not believe your threat, he may attack and deterrence will have failed. It does not help then that you really did mean it.

So the United States would have to station conventional forces in Europe after all, and since they would hardly be sufficient by themselves, the NATO allies would have to contribute forces also, as their postwar recovery enabled them to. A combined force of American and West European armies, though probably not large enough to match the Red Army man for man, might be large enough to make an invasion too costly for the Soviets. Rather than a quick and predictable victory they would face a real European war, the results of which could not be foreseen. The risks to the Soviet empire in Eastern Europe, and even to the USSR itself, would be high in such a war. Hence the Soviets would be deterred from attacking. They would be deterred on the "level" of violence of a European war, just as they would be deterred at the level of war by long-range bombers by the mutual deterrence that would exist at that level.

By now deterrence was far from simple and far from effortless. The assumption of the first postwar years, that deterrence was almost automatic, had been blown up in the first Soviet nuclear test. Deterrence had now become an analytic problem and a vital policy objective—one that might be achieved only at considerable cost and trouble.

From an analytic point of view the first Soviet atomic explosion was more significant, in a sense, than the first American one. One nation that possessed nuclear weapons in quantity was, quite simply, supreme on the planet. What raised complicated and novel problems was the existence of *two* or more nuclear-weapon states. Implicit in NSC-68 was a grim logic of deterrence and counterdeterrence on multiple levels, a logic that was to become characteristic of national security problems in our era.

The report did not include estimates of how much it would cost to carry out its recommendations. State Department representatives on the team that wrote it guessed it might be $35 to $40 billion or more, in 1950 dollars. (This is roughly $130–$150 billion in 1983 dollars.) This amount was approximately triple what the defense budget had been over the immediately preceding years.

Through the spring of 1950, the paper was studied and debated in the upper circles of the government. Before a consensus could be reached or President Truman make a final decision, however, the Korean War broke upon the world. NSC-68 and the problems it raised were put aside while this newest emergency seized everyone's attention. The defense budget did go up to about $40 billion, but to meet the attack in Asia, not the demands of doctrine or a possible future attack in Europe. The approach to national security taken by NSC-68 was never finally approved by the president, and by the time the Korean War was over a new administration in Washington had decided on a different approach. Almost another decade would pass before the philosophy of NSC-68, under a different name, would finally triumph in American national security policy.

SUMMARY

The impossibility of creating a workable collective security system in the period just following World War II led the United States to fashion its own national security. Not surprisingly, organizational arrangements and a foreign policy goal, containment, came first. Next developed policies in support of containment, the Truman Doctrine and the Marshall Plan. Finally came a full-fledged national security analysis, NSC-68. In this sense, the step-by-step fashioning of American security followed a path of development that, in retrospect, seems almost predictable.

It did not seem so at the time, however. With the possible exception of Kennan's original cable, the direct cause of each of these steps was not any desire to sculpt a new American stance in the world, or to carry the development of American security to a new stage, but a pressing need to solve a specific, immediate problem. Until this operational need arose, the development did not occur. For example the full-fledged analysis was not operationally needed, and did not appear, until the American atomic monopoly was broken and the existence of two nuclear powers created novel analytical challenges.

The cumulative effect of these developments, though, was enormous, and from a security viewpoint the United States of early 1950 was very different from the United States of 1946. National security goals, concepts, institutions, policies, and programs were now in place that would have been almost inconceivable just after the war's end. Most of them would last a long time and prove successful. The central objectives of U.S. policy makers in that era, after all, were to forestall a third world war and to halt what they saw as a westward tide of Soviet power in Europe. Both of these objectives were accomplished fully.

At the same time the United States was becoming less secure than before. The surprisingly early Soviet atomic test created a new situation in which all of America would be vulnerable within a short time to direct and devastating attack. No comparable threat had appeared before in American history, and absolutely nothing could be done to prevent its emergence. At best it could be hoped that a combination of offensive nuclear striking power and air defense could deter any actual attack, and limit the destruction if deterrence failed.*

The fundamental danger lay in the vast destructive power of nuclear weapons and the impossibility of maintaining the American monopoly for long. No complete defense was possible, because no air defense system could stop all incoming bombers and only a few atomic bombs dropped on American cities could wreak terrible destruction. By the time of NSC-68 it was becoming ever clearer that even increased defense expenditure could purchase only the uncertain kind of national security promised by deterrence. Future years would show that as nuclear weapons multiplied in numbers and variety, this approach to security would involve never-ending expenditures and hazards.

---

*Here and throughout the remainder of this book, the term "nuclear" will be used as a generic name to cover both fission and fusion weapons. This is consistent with common practice, although technically fusion processes (explosive or otherwise) are termed "thermonuclear." Most weapons now in the U.S. and Soviet arsenals are fusion weapons, but some are not, and yields of almost any size from very great down to quite small are available. Normally in wartime a military commander or civilian policy maker would want to know the approximate yield of weapons being used but would have little reason to be interested in whether they were fission or fusion.

FOR FURTHER READING

Campbell, John C. *The United States in World Affairs, 1948–49*. New York: Harper, 1949. This assessment of the period when the cold war was beginning is particularly interesting today because it was written when the events of the period were quite fresh, and their full consequences as yet unknown.

Gaddis, John L. *Strategies of Containment: a Critical Appraisal of Postwar American National Security Policy*. New York: Oxford University Press, 1982. This work is opposite from the previous one, in the sense that it represents an analysis in depth written more than thirty years later, and uses information publicly unavailable at the time.

Hammond, Paul Y. *Organizing for Defense: the American Military Establishment in the Twentieth Century*. Princeton: Princeton University Press, 1961. Perhaps the best general analysis, from a political science perspective, of the evolution of the U.S. military from its original small size to its very large, cold war form.

Huntington, Samuel P. *The Common Defense*. New York: Columbia University Press, 1961. A detailed analytic history of the evolution of U.S. national security policy from the postwar years through the end of the Eisenhower administration.

Kennan, George F. *The Nuclear Delusion: Soviet-American Relations in the Atomic Age*. New York: Pantheon, 1982. This collection includes essays decrying Washington's misinterpretation of the roots and rationale of containment and the resulting militarization of U.S. foreign policy.

NSC-68: A Report to the National Security Council. In the *Naval War College Review* 27: 51–108. Reading this classic policy document is interesting not only for its conclusions but also for the moral and political assumptions it states regarding the goals of U.S. and Soviet policy.

Spanier, John W. *American Foreign Policy Since World War II*. Eighth edition. New York: Holt, Rinehart & Winston, 1980. A standard text on the history of American foreign policy, including much information about the broader factual and policy context within which national security policy evolved.

"X", "The Sources of Soviet Conduct." *Foreign Affairs* 25: 566–582. The classic essay by George Kennan, advocating the containment policy, appeared in July 1947.

Wells, Samuel F., Jr. "Sounding the Tocsin: NSC-68 and the Soviet Threat." *International Security* 4:116–158. A detailed historical account of the drafting of NSC-68, and assessment of its political and military context.

5

The First Era
of American
Military Superiority

The Korean War broke out about dawn on June 25, 1950, when the army of Communist North Korea suddenly attacked South Korea across the 38th Parallel. The United States, with backing from the UN and some modest forces from other UN members, intervened on the South Korean side. In about six months the U.S.-UN forces were on the point of defeating the North Koreans, and perhaps unifying the peninsula under a pro-Western government. The mainland Chinese then intervened, sending large numbers of troops across the Yalu River, the

Chinese-Korean border, to fight for the North Korean regime. The U.S.-UN troops were forced into a long retreat, then spent two more years slowly winning back territory to about the 38th Parallel. Finally an armistice was reached on July 27, 1953. The outcome was the restoration of approximately the same situation that had existed before the war began. There has never been a final peace treaty.

Over three years of fighting, and the costs and casualties incurred, for so little gained were a frustrating experience for Americans. Just as a generation later in the Vietnam War, initial enthusiasm and confidence in victory gradually turned to bitterness and confusion. Even in the army a group of high-ranking officers grew weary of the war and formed a "Never Again Club" — never again should the United States fight a ground war in Asia.

In the 1952 presidential campaign Dwight Eisenhower said that, if elected, "I will go to Korea." In World War II "Ike" had been the supreme commander of the allied forces of the West that had assaulted Nazi-held Europe, and in the American popular imagination he was the man who had put down Hitler. In November he was swept into office by a landslide, and in fact the war ended within six months of his taking office. Thereafter the new administration set as one of its main goals avoiding any more wars like Korea.

The new Republican administration was also determined to balance the federal budget while keeping taxes moderate. This policy was necessary, the administration believed, to maintain prosperity without much inflation, a goal that would be important for national security as well as for domestic reasons. The Eisenhower administration, unlike its predecessor, believed the United States faced a "long haul" competition with the Soviet Union that might stretch over decades, and in that kind of competition continuing American economic strength would be as important as the military balance. Eisenhower himself was concerned that excessive military spending could damage the American economy. High taxes or a deficit budget could not be permitted. But a balanced budget with moderate taxes would make it impossible to maintain the defense budget at its Korean level, and hence impossible to maintain a large, standing conventional army.

At the same time Washington still perceived a serious Soviet threat to Europe, and now the Soviet bloc had demonstrated that it might attack the free world at other points as well. How could the United States keep the Soviets from being tempted to new aggression, while still keeping defense expenditures down? How could the administration keep its promise that there would be no more Koreas, if it could not deploy enough troops to stand up to a Soviet, or Soviet-inspired attack?

The Eisenhower administration's solution to this problem came in two parts. One was diplomatic. The new secretary of state, John Foster Dulles, was convinced that both world wars and many other conflicts could have been avoided if the aggressors had not made a certain miscalculation. Hitler, Kaiser Wilhelm, and others would never have launched their wars, Dulles believed, if they had foreseen how many nations would band together as allies against them. The secretary intended to prevent the Soviets from making a similar miscalculation by creating the great alliances in advance. Then the Kremlin would know the array of forces it faced and would not be tempted.

NATO alone would not be enough. Dulles proceeded to create an organization designed along similar lines for the Middle East, first called the Baghdad Pact and subsequently CENTO, for Central Treaty Organization. Another in the Far East was called SEATO, for Southeast Asia Treaty Organization. These, plus the North Atlantic Treaty Organization and mutual defense treaties with Japan, South Korea, and the Nationalist Chinese on Taiwan, were intended to encircle the "Sino-Soviet bloc" with an unbroken defensive ring of allied countries, all backed by the United States.*

When Secretary Dulles was finished the United States was linked to over fifty countries in alliances that could invoke military action. The Eisenhower administration regarded this network as a foreign policy success—a strengthening of the American position and a powerful caution to the Soviets. (It was around this time, incidentally, that the term "collective security" came to mean, nearly always, this effort of *some* nations to find security in alliance; and the original meaning of collective security in which *all* nations unite in a single world peace-keeping organization, was largely lost.)

In later years, though, much of Dulles's immense network proved to have little meaning in practice. CENTO became little more than a formality even in the 1950s; the Middle Eastern nations were far more concerned with regional hostilities than with a hypothetical threat from the Soviets. SEATO also proved mostly empty and played little role in any of the wars that have occured in Southeast Asia since. The mutual

---

*In addition the United States had helped create the Rio Pact in 1947, in which all the nations of the Americas agreed to consult on joint action in the event of aggression in the Western Hemisphere; and had signed the ANZUS mutual defense treaty in 1951 with Australia and New Zealand.

defense treaty with the Nationalist Chinese on Taiwan was canceled by
the United States in 1979, as part of the American rapprochement
with mainland China.

By the time Eisenhower left office the strategy of building large
alliance networks was being discredited, though in later years several
treaties were signed with individual nations, for instance Thailand.
Even so the treaties with Japan and South Korea, and of course
NATO, remain strong and meaningful commitments to this day. It is
no accident that the defense relationships that have lasted are the ones
where the United States has close ties anyway—intimate historical and
cultural attachments (NATO, ANZUS) or deep involvements created
by recent history (Japan, South Korea.)

THE NEW LOOK

The second part of the Eisenhower administration's strategy, and the
part more directly military, involved the exploitation of U.S. technological prowess, in a way new in American policy. To understand this,
one must comprehend the technological situation of the early and
mid-1950s.

By the time Eisenhower entered office some of the specific recommendations of NSC-68 were being carried out, even though the document as a whole had never been approved. A substantial air defense
system was under construction, including radar stations across
Canada. Jet intercepters, more radar, and a ground-launched antiaircraft missile called Nike were on the way. Equally great improvements
were coming in offense. The Strategic Air Command was now receiving a jet bomber, the B-47, that could carry an atomic bomb to the
Soviet Union much faster than the propeller-driven B-36s, and was
much less vulnerable to Soviet air defenses. A larger and more advanced
jet bomber, the B-52, was on the drawing boards. One B-52 aircraft
would be able to carry six nuclear bombs.

Most important of all, the United States now had an ample
atomic stockpile. Ways had been found to speed up production, and
by the early 1950s there were so many bombs available that planners
no longer had to worry about husbanding them carefully in the event
of war, or having to fall back on conventional bombs before the important targets had all been struck. Hydrogen bombs would be coming into the arsenal before long.

Meanwhile the USSR seemed to be lagging behind. U.S. intelligence agencies believed that the Soviets had, as yet, manufactured only a few atomic bombs, compared to America's many hundreds. The Soviets also had only propeller-driven aircraft with which to deliver them. Their air defense system could be penetrated by U.S. jet bombers, and their propeller bombers would soon be faced by jet intercepters in the U.S. air defenses.

The Eisenhower administration entered office, then, to find the United States coming to enjoy a greater degree of strategic superiority than most people outside the government realized. Conventional warfare on the ground would be, of course, another story. Here the Red Army still loomed hugely over anything NATO could put into the field in Europe, although contributions from the European allies were making the imbalance less extreme than it had been. At the level of strategic warfare, though, the new administration found itself with a great and growing superiority. This happy position had resulted partly from the decisions of the previous administration to pursue strong strategic programs. More basically, it resulted from the overall primacy of American technology and industry in a world where nearly every other advanced nation was still recovering from World War II.

Eisenhower and his colleagues decided to press the advantage. The "New Look," as they called their policy for the Pentagon, would stress technology over manpower. This would play to America's strength, while saving money. It would be less expensive to develop fully the jet bombers, the air defenses, and the armory of bombs, than to keep lots of men in uniform; this kind of defense posture could be afforded even assuming a balanced federal budget and moderate taxes. The New Look in America's defenses would be a lean and tech nological look. And such a stance, being more economical, would also be suitable for a "long haul" competition with the Soviet Union.

With minor modifications the New Look philosophy was to guide American defense decisions throughout the two Eisenhower administrations until 1961. Throughout these years the defense budget was held nearly constant, at around $140 billion a year in 1983 dollars. (This was approximately $45 billion a year in the dollars of those years.) This was considerably more than any defense budget of the years preceding Korea, but less than that implied by NSC-68.

In this period the army, contrary to its own wishes, was held to a small number of divisions. Its role in air defense, though, was well funded, and the original Nike antiaircraft missile, soon dubbed the

Nike-Ajax, was followed by a more powerful version called the Nike-Hercules. The navy was fairly well supported, particularly its fleet of aircraft carriers, which was regarded as one of America's main contributions to the network of alliances.

Best supported of all were SAC and the Air Defense Command of the air force, and the nuclear weapons program. Their supremacy was a top priority. In the mid-1950s, for instance, it seemed that the Soviets were building more long-range bombers than U.S. intelligence had previously estimated. Fears of a possible "bomber gap" were laid to rest when the administration ordered an expansion in the fleet of B-52s. By the end of the decade the United States had more than 600 of these large jet bombers, each capable of delivering six hydrogen bombs over thousands of miles, with in-flight refueling from tanker aircraft.

The "forward basing" of many SAC bombers, in England and other points abroad, also reached its zenith during the New Look years. From some of these forward bases a U.S. atomic strike by B-47s and B-52s could reach the Soviet Union in less than two hours, while the Soviets had no comparable bases near the United States and would take considerably longer to strike.

During the 1950s all three services also started receiving nuclear weapons for delivery over medium to short ranges. These included bombs for USAF and navy aircraft, and atomic artillery shells for the army's biggest, longest-range cannons. All these came to be called "tactical nuclear weapons," partly because the air force and navy aircraft that could deliver them had always been known as tactical aircraft.

The term "tactical nuclear weapons" was a misnomer, although it continues to be used for all manner of nuclear weapons designed to be delivered over short or medium ranges. There is a clear and real difference between the strategic *use or* tactical *use* of weapons, nuclear or otherwise—that is, whether they are employed against homelands or in a local theater. Most of the weapons can be used either way. For example, through all the years since the mid-1950s the United States could have struck the Soviet Union or China with nuclear bombs delivered by tactical USAF planes based in Europe and the Far East, and by navy planes from aircraft carriers in the Mediterranean and western Pacific. Indeed the USSR could be seriously damaged, and China almost wiped out as an industrial nation, by the so-called tactical forces that the United States has maintained at all times—without any need to dip into what is usually called the American strategic arsenal. Conversely, weapons generally regarded as strategic can be used in a tactical mode. The United States used the B-52 this way in Vietnam, employing conventional bombs with devastating results, although the airplane was designed and justified to Congress for nuclear bombing of the Soviet Union. What is strategic or tactical is also a matter of geographical perspective: what may seem tactical to faraway Americans may be strategic to the Vietnamese, or to Germans, or Israelis, in a European or Mideast war.

However mislabeled, nuclear weapons for short- to medium-range delivery began to enter the American arsenal in quantity as the 1950s wore on. Here too the Soviets lagged behind, and there was a period in the second half of the decade, and perhaps into the early 1960s, when the United States was far superior in this category. This was already anticipated as the New Look was becoming policy, and became one of its rationales.

The growing American superiority in so many categories—jet bombers, quantities of nuclear bombs, air defenses, and nuclear weapons for tactical uses—created a spirit early in the Eisenhower years of something approaching optimism, especially within the administration. The immediate postwar confidence in U.S. global supremacy had turned into alarm when the Soviets had begun testing atomic bombs in 1949; now the psychology reversed again, as the basic American technological and industrial superiority of the midcentury era reasserted itself. Although everyone conceded that some U.S. cities would be lost and many Americans killed in the event of a nuclear third world war, the USSR and its allies would be completely wiped out by the forces that America now had in its arsenal. No one wanted to speak, at least publicly or casually, of "victory" in such a terrible war, but administration spokesmen did say (in a phrase that became famous for a while) that should such a war come, "we would prevail."

American war plans of the 1950s supposed that in an intense crisis, American air defenses and strategic strike forces could be brought rapidly to a high pitch of readiness. If war then broke out, the bombers on the forward bases could strike very fast; under some circumstances they might destroy some of the Soviet bombers before they had taken off. Indeed, if the United States began the war by striking *first* (a possibility to be discussed further in a moment), the SAC jets might catch a large number of those bombers on the ground. The Soviets would then have to send their remaining bombers against the Nike missiles and jet intercepters in the U.S. air defenses; although some would get through many might be shot down. True, the war plans had to acknowledge as the decade wore on that the number of Soviet bombers (and bombs) was growing; but so were the SAC strike forces and the U.S. air defenses. Through most of the decade, at least, the administration continued to argue that in a nuclear war, the United States would prevail.

MASSIVE RETALIATION

The strategic superiority that the Eisenhower administration inherited on entering office, and attempted to perpetuate and enhance at moderate cost by its New Look military policy, became the main basis for a new departure in its broader national security policy. The network of alliances that Secretary Dulles created was only half of the administration's strategy for deterring new Soviet military adventures and forestalling another Korea. The other half was an attempt to deter Soviet aggression by explicitly threatening to *use* superior American strategic power against the USSR itself in the event of a new attack.

In a speech delivered about six months after the Korean War ended, Secretary Dulles announced that henceforward the United States would not feel itself obliged to fight "on the enemy's terms." Instead, should there be a new Communist encroachment on the free world, the United States would "by means and at places of our own choosing" retaliate "instantly" and "massively" against the centers of Communist power. The secretary was apparently threatening that in the event of another attack like Korea America would retaliate by immediately launching atomic strikes against the heartland of the Soviet Union and/or China!

This speech was made in the depths of the cold war years, at a time when the costly war in Korea had only recently ended, and when the United States was enormously superior to a Soviet Union that had, as yet, relatively little atomic striking power. Under these circumstances Dulles's threat was received with little objection and considerable approval from Congress and the American people. Though in subsequent years it was to attract sharp criticism, the policy of "Massive Retaliation" (as it was quickly dubbed) remained, at least officially, U.S. strategy until 1961.

The Eisenhower administration did not believe that Massive Retaliation would ever have to be carried out, and of course it never was.

Rather, Massive Retaliation was intended as a doctrine and a policy of *deterrence*. It was an attempt to keep the defense budget relatively modest and prevent new wars like Korea, while protecting the security of the free world, by extracting the greatest possible deterrent effect out of U.S. military power. Under this policy, America would not merely enjoy strategic superiority over Soviet nuclear forces; the potential value thereof would be exploited to the full. The superiority was so great, it was believed, that SAC could deter not only its inferior Soviet counterpart, but also deter conventional attacks on U.S. allies. As proponents of Massive Retaliation put it, "the dog we keep to lick the cat can lick the kittens too."

This was a novel concept of deterrence, at least in American policy. It was also the third concept of deterrence that the U.S. government had entertained in six or seven years. The first concept, in the immediate postwar period, had been that the deterrence of a new *big* war was an automatic by-product of America's nuclear monopoly—a fact, rather than a problem or a policy goal. The second concept, embodied in NSC-68 but not yet carried out in policy, was that deterrence was a complex problem that had to be solved differently on different levels of possible threats. Now Dulles was introducing a third idea of deterrence—that it was neither automatic, nor a difficult challenge, but a tool to be used vigorously. Deterring the USSR, in Dulles's view, was a task requiring a lot of attention and energy. The Massive Retaliation doctrine was reiterated many times over the following years, and the nuclear striking power that backed it up was carefully nurtured by the Eisenhower administration. But it was also something, Dulles felt, that could be done so successfully that the invocation of SAC could prevent not only a new big war but new *small* ones as well. The deterrent effect flowing from American superiority was powerful enough to be "stretched" to cover the prevention both of World War III and of new Koreas.

The limitations and dangers of this idea will be discussed in the next chapter. But it is worth noting, especially in the light of the severe criticism that Massive Retaliation received before long, that the doctrine was not quite as unsubtle or "Neanderthal" as some of its critics were to suggest. The administration was always careful not to specify too exactly what kind of attack would trigger the massive nuclear strike. Very small, "brushfire" conflicts, it was said, would be the responsibility of U.S. allies, with American technical and material assistance to be sure. Administration spokesmen never stated how large a conflict would have to grow before it was no longer in the brushfire category and became a candidate for Massive Retaliation. Hence the Massive Retaliation policy involved a strategy of *calculated ambiguity*. The administration deliberately kept the Kremlin uncertain about what kinds of conflicts would receive what kinds of American response. The administration reasoned that the Soviets would probably err on the side of caution and would avoid beginning anything that might pose any risk at all of nuclear war. Thus the deterrent effect of the strategy would be increased further. The ambiguity would be useful in another way as well: if a war of medium size did break out, the United States could always decide against a nuclear strike and say that, after all, it had not committed itself definitely.

In fact there were no cold war military conflicts of any size during the Eisenhower years. Whether or not this meant that the Massive Retaliation strategy "succeeded" is impossible to say. In international relations as in everything else, one can never prove why something has *not* occurred. This applies to all deterrence policies. Deterrence can never be proved successful because one never knows whether the opponent did not attack because he was deterred, or for some other reason.

One thing that can be said of the Eisenhower period is that the administration not only assigned brushfire conflicts to the allies, but also retained significant U.S. conventional forces, to provide some options other than a nuclear strike. In one crisis during these years, a small fraction of these forces was actually used. In 1958 the president sent a sizable contingent of troops to Lebanon at the request of the legal Lebanese government, then faced with severe internal strife. This was not a cold war challenge, however, or not clearly so, and other crises that clearly were received responses that were less military. When the mainland Chinese bombarded the offshore islands of Quemoy and Matsu, held by the Nationalist Chinese Army, in 1954–55 and again in 1958, the United States provided some assistance to its Nationalist allies and deployed some U.S. forces to the area, but did not take military action. An intense crisis in Berlin in 1958–59 was fielded by diplomatic means.

There were, however, three instances when the Eisenhower administration did actually deliver a threat of Massive Retaliation in coping with cold war challenges. Almost immediately upon entering office early in 1953, Eisenhower sent a private message to the Communist Chinese that unless the stalled negotiations to end the Korean War bore fruit soon, the United States might resort to nuclear strikes on China. Not long thereafter, the Chinese accepted the UN proposals for an armistice, in only slightly modified form. The administration concluded that its nuclear threat had succeeded in ending the war (although Joseph Stalin had died in the meantime, and this may have been another reason for the change in Chinese policy).

The second threat was communicated between the lines of a formal armistice day statement by Washington, warning the Chinese not to resume the war. The third came a few months later, implicitly threatening nuclear retaliation if the Chinese intervened in the civil war then raging in Vietnam. Although it was unclear, then and later, that Beijing intended either of these actions, the administration wished to deter the possibility.

All three were threats against China, not the USSR, and China was not yet a nuclear power. At the time even the Soviet Union had only a few nuclear weapons. Its capacity to make atomic strikes on the United States was limited, and any attempt would invite a crushing counterblow from the greatly superior U.S. forces. Obviously these were circumstances under which making an atomic threat held little risk. As the Soviet atomic arsenal grew during the 1950s, Washington made no more specific threats of the Massive Retaliation type.

However, Massive Retaliation was never officially abandoned as a policy doctrine during Eisenhower's presidency. Twice in 1958 the Joint Chiefs received secret directives to prepare to use nuclear weapons, if necessary, in the Mideast and Quemoy crises of that year. More recent administrations have also made implicit and even explicit nuclear threats. During the latter part of the Vietnam War, Henry Kissinger suggested to the North Vietnamese leaders that Richard Nixon might consider using nuclear weapons in Southeast Asia; and at the time of the battle of Khe Sanh in 1968 there was public as well as private discussion of it in Washington. More recently still, the Carter Doctrine asserting U.S. interests in the Persian Gulf included the statement that the United States would defend its interests "by any means necessary." On assuming the presidency Ronald Reagan reaffirmed the commitment, saying he trusted the Soviets would not take on "a confrontation which could become World War III." As will be discussed later, the United States has never pledged itself to a "no first use" of nuclear weapons. Nuclear threats remain possible, and are made.

THE IDEA OF LIMITED WAR

The Massive Retaliation doctrine was a direct product of the Korean War. Although the enormous U.S. superiority of the early and mid-1950s would have materialized even if there had been no war in the Far East, the Korean experience led the United States to exploit that superiority to the full. Massive Retaliation was an attempt to avoid any more such experiences—while still holding Soviet-inspired aggression firmly at bay—by stretching to the utmost the deterrent value of U.S. superiority. The impact of Korea did not stop here, though. It also led to a new departure in strategic thinking in the United States: the development of the idea of "limited war."

The old-fashioned European idea of limited war, discussed in an earlier chapter, had not been part of the American experience of warfare. The American experience had always been either grand conflict with other major powers for grand objectives (the two world wars), or else minor actions to get rid of nuisances (e.g., the Mexican rebels in 1916). The Korean War, though, was nothing like these. Korea had turned out to be surprisingly costly, painful, and long-lasting; yet for all the effort expended its goals were not terribly important, and even those had to be scaled down, from what some Americans had wanted, to little more than reestablishing the situation that had existed before the conflict.

Now there were at least two possible ways of looking at this frustrating experience. One, which was the Eisenhower administration's viewpoint, was that it was too intolerable to be contemplated, and that something—the Massive Retaliation policy—must be done to ensure that the United States never got into any similar kind of war again. The other viewpoint, gradually developed during the 1950s by specialists outside the administration, was that Korea might be the prototype of a new kind of conflict that ought to be completely understood and might, under some circumstances, have to be accepted.

What was so interesting about Korea to these specialists was the fact that the war had remained so very limited compared to what it might have become. The two sides had fought for years inside a narrow area, with large forces and huge potential for destruction poised and ready for use—but never used. The U.S-UN side had not only refrained from using nuclear weapons; it had also prohibited its aircraft from flying north of the Yalu River, even though Chinese air bases, army staging bases, and supply routes on the other side, crucial to the Chinese war effort, could have been bombed easily. The Chinese had observed a similar hands off policy regarding Japan, which the West had used as its main staging and supply area for the war. Thus each side had respected the other's "sanctuary" and had confined its operations to the arena of the Korean peninsula itself, although neither was constrained by military or technical reasons. This had happened, furthermore, in spite of the fact that both sides found the war, limited in this way, very costly, and the outcome unsatisfactory.

Here was a phenomenon that was not understood. Why hadn't the warring powers attacked each other's bases? Would the same thing happen the next time a war like Korea broke out? Or was there something about this kind of conflict that kept it "controlled"? How large can a "little" war get and still be controlled? How does one know if such a war is about to get out of control? Would some kinds of restraints be "stronger"—more successful in keeping the war limited—than others? A whole package of questions had been opened up that transcended ordinary military considerations. Answers to these questions seemed to have something to do with each side's political attitudes in the conflict, and with the perceptions held by each side's decision makers of what the other side's objectives were and of what the other side might do. Dissecting these things went well beyond military analysis in the traditional sense. Yet these problems concerned decisions in war and the uses and manipulation of force and violence, and hence were not the same thing as diplomacy or international affairs in the usual senses either.

Slowly a new field of study began to take shape. From the mid-1950s until the early 1960s a number of specialists investigated this area, and as they became increasingly convinced of its importance a whole body of literature on limited war emerged. This became one of the important early developments in the dawning field of national security affairs. One of the earliest contributors to this literature was Bernard Brodie, who argued that the universal fear of nuclear warfare was crucial. It would always guarantee, as it had in Korea, strong pressure on governments to keep any new wars non-nuclear. Therefore, Brodie argued, among nations possessing atomic arsenals, or allied with those that did, limiting war deliberately in this way would become a general pattern. (Brodie's argument, and others to be mentioned momentarily, was presented in writings listed at the end of this chapter.)

As the nuclear forces on both sides of the iron curtain grew during the 1950s, more and more analysts came to agree, and to carry the argument further. The growing nuclear arsenals of the superpowers were stalemating each other. This would make possible—even likely—new wars "under their umbrella," and these wars might remain relatively stable. Neither side would dare resort to atomic weapons, at least so long as the other side's objectives remained reasonably limited, because atomic war would be too awful to contemplate. In this way, Korea came more and more to seem a likely prototype of things to come.

From today's perspective it seems obvious that the fear of atomic war could have this result, but in America in the 1950s it certainly was not obvious. The American military tradition had always been to fight all out if one fought at all. This tradition was strongly reaffirmed in conservative, and some military, circles during the Korean War. The American commander in Korea, General Douglas MacArthur, so publicly and so often demanded a freer hand to escalate the war that eventually he had to be relieved of his command. He returned to the United States to give speeches in which he told cheering audiences that "in war there is no substitute for victory."

The fact that the Soviet Union could now destroy American cities meant that the United States would have to rethink its attitudes about the use of force. Many specialists now stressed that future wars might have to be deliberately limited, even though this would mean that, at best, only limited objectives could be achieved. Henry Kissinger, for example, argued this in his first book on contemporary strategy, *Nuclear Weapons and Foreign Policy.*

Even as a consensus was forming among analysts, some were wondering how hard it might be to put limits on wars. Perhaps we had been lucky in Korea. Finding "ground rules" that could remain stable was not automatic and might prove difficult in a future war, because both sides might find it difficult to know what the other side's intentions were. Even if both sides wanted to avoid a much larger war, it might be hard to keep a limited conflict from escalating out of control. The example that haunted everyone's mind was World War I, which had grown out of relatively minor events into a cataclysmic conflict. And there were plenty of other examples of wars that had grown larger than the nations involved had really wanted.

How limited wars could be kept limited thus became one of the main items on the intellectual agenda, and a few conclusions were reached. Avoiding the use of atomic weapons altogether, in spite of temptations that might present themselves to use "just a few," was one obvious one. Once atomic bombs started going off, it would be hard to prevent more and more from being used. Analysts also suggested that having a clear "arena" with outside "sanctuaries" (as in Korea) would be helpful, as would maintaining firm civilian control of the basic wartime decisions. Strictly military considerations should not be permitted to determine the scope of a war. For instance, deciding what geographical limits might be respected by the enemy, and be feasible for oneself, required diplomatic and political judgments that transcended military factors.

Some further conditions that would help were contributed by William Kaufmann: restricting oneself to limited objectives; keeping ample forces in reserve to deter the enemy from escalation; maintaining channels of communication with him even during the fighting; and finally, developing in advance and carrying out flexible and multiple strategies, so that one did not become locked into a single course of action.

As the study of limited war developed, these and related ideas were explored more and more, both in the abstract and in the context of various "scenarios" for hypothetical future wars that analysts constructed. An important theoretical advance came in the late 1950s in a series of articles by Thomas Schelling, which were gathered together into a widely hailed book in 1960. Schelling suggested that limited war should be seen as a kind of "bargaining" process, in which the bargaining was tacit. That is, each side bargained with the other about what the ground rules should be, by deliberately escalating the conflict a certain amount but not more, or by ostentatiously holding itself to some particularly obvious self-limitation. American aircraft bombing targets in Korea right up to the Yalu River, but not a yard beyond it, was an obvious example of the latter. How the wartime situation might offer "saliencies" of this sort, and how these could be signaled, reinforced, deliberately violated, or manipulated in other ways, were explored by Schelling and others as the years passed.

Limited war was getting to be like deterrence: as technology evolved and the military possibilities grew more numerous, the ideas became more complicated. The debate got hotter, too, when high-ranking army officers, who disliked having their forces curtailed by Eisenhower's cost cutting, embraced the limited war concept. Recently retired General Maxwell Taylor, for instance, wrote a book arguing that to avoid defeat in a limited war, without having to resort to nuclear weapons, the United States would have to maintain sizable conventional forces at all times. Otherwise the United States and its allies might not be able to contain another Korea-sized attack, and would be faced with the agonizing choice of accepting defeat or beginning an atomic war. Maintaining a sizable conventional army at all times, of course, was exactly what the Eisenhower administration had decided not to do, in order to keep the Pentagon budget down.

In the late 1950s the administration tried to meet the rising tide of interest in limited war as an alternative to all-out nuclear war, and growing pressures in favor of Taylor's point of view, by coming up with a new idea of its own. American superiority in "tactical nuclear weapons" could be brought to bear, it said. The United States and its allies would be able to defeat another Korea-sized attack by using a relatively few nuclear weapons against enemy troops in the local war zone, without having to expand the war geographically. In this fashion, the United States would still not have to bear the cost of a large standing army, and might also avoid having to make a Massive Retaliation attack on the Soviet Union and China. This idea was called "Graduated Deterrence," and for a while it was supported by some nonadministration specialists in national security as well, including Henry Kissinger.

But many other specialists could not accept that it was prudent or wise for the United States to adopt a posture in which America would *have* to be the one to convert a conventional war into an atomic war. In any case, these analysts argued, the Graduated Deterrence idea would be good for a short time only, because it depended on the United States being highly superior in nuclear weapons for tactical use. Within a few years the USSR would also possess large numbers of these weapons, at which point the United States would be deterred from such a strategy. Any American resort to tactical use of nuclear weapons in a new war would invite the same kind of attack on U.S. forces.

At a more fundamental level, these analysts believed that the "firebreak" between nuclear and conventional weapons should never be crossed. If it ever was, they feared, there would be no way to guarantee that one could halt the process of escalation. A few atomic blasts would be followed by more, and there would be no place to stop, short of all-out nuclear war. The debate around Graduated Deterrence and the questions it raised was still raging when Eisenhower left office in 1961 and was followed by a president who wanted to put his own ideas into policy.

SUMMARY

The first era of American military superiority lasted through most of the decade of the 1950s. During this period the United States possessed long-range jet bombers — the B-47, later joined by the B-52 — while the USSR had only propeller-driven bombers; and possessed a rapidly improving air defense system while the USSR had an inferior one. Most importantly, early in the decade the United States already had quantities of nuclear bombs for strategic delivery, while the Soviet arsenal grew to this size only somewhat later.

The Eisenhower administration inherited some of this advantage when it came to office in January 1953 and decided, in its New Look policy, to enhance and continue it as long as possible. The New Look amounted to a policy to press the American technological advantage, while simultaneously cutting back U.S. forces for fighting conventional war, especially army divisions. The administration pushed, for example, the development of nuclear weapons for short- and medium-range delivery (misnamed "tactical nuclear weapons") and for a significant period in the middle and late 1950s, and perhaps into the early 1960s, the United States led the USSR by a substantial margin in this area as well.

Meanwhile the Korean War was having a far-reaching impact on the evolution of American national security doctrine. Indeed, the policy consequences and intellectual consequences of Korea were probably greater than those of the Vietnam War a generation later, even though Vietnam had a greater emotional impact on the national consciousness. The Soviets proved in Korea that they might sponsor sizable, but non-nuclear, attacks on nearby nations, and the United States now had to come to grips with both the policy and analytic implications of that kind of attack.

The Eisenhower administration produced two kinds of policy responses, both intended to *deter* Moscow and Beijing from launching that kind of aggression (or larger-scale aggression) again. One was to construct an extensive network of military alliances, intended to convince the Communist capitals that any future large-scale attack would be countered by many countries acting together. The other was the policy of Massive Retaliation, intended to convince them that future attacks of significant (but not exactly specified) size would call down U.S. atomic strikes on the Soviet Union and China themselves. The Massive Retaliation policy depended heavily on the assumption of great strategic superiority, and as that gradually waned the administration abandoned the specific nuclear threats that it had made several times during its first year in office. As a general policy of deterrence, though, Massive Retaliation remained in effect until 1961.

Meanwhile specialists in national security outside the administration, joined later by elements within the army, were developing the idea that "limited wars" like Korea might become a pattern for the future, as the two superpowers' nuclear arsenals stalemated each other. Or at least, such wars would be preferable to atomic warfare, *if* ways could be worked out to keep them stable. Analysis of the intellectual implications of the first limited war of the nuclear age was pursued strongly as the 1950s proceeded, the Korean experience sank in, and the Soviet atomic stockpile grew.

FOR FURTHER READING

Brodie, Bernard. "Unlimited Weapons and Limited War." *The Reporter* 11: 16–21. Probably the earliest (1954) influential essay arguing the emergence of limited war as a novel problem.

Dulles, John Foster. "The Evolution of Foreign Policy." Address to the Council on Foreign Relations, 12 January 1954; reprinted in the *Department of State Bulletin*, 25 January 1954. This is the secretary of state's speech introducing and justifying the Massive Retaliation policy.

Kaufmann, William W. "Limited Warfare." In W.W. Kaufmann (ed.), *Military Policy and National Security*. Princeton: Princeton University Press, 1956. A leading statement of the requirements that must be met if a limited war is to remain limited.

Kissinger, Henry A. *Nuclear Weapons and Foreign Policy*. New York: Harper & Bros., 1957. The first major attempt to rethink American foreign policy on the premise that the Soviet Union had attained the capacity to destroy American cities.

Osgood, Robert E. *Limited War*. Chicago: University of Chicago Press, 1957. The principal book written in the 1950s on the problem of limited warfare. It includes a lengthy history of how war was limited in earlier eras.

Schelling, Thomas C. *The Strategy of Conflict*. Cambridge, Mass.: Harvard University Press, 1960. By general consensus the leading theoretical contribution to date on the logic of limited war and escalation, and one of the premier works on strategic theory generally in the contemporary period.

Taylor, General Maxwell. *The Uncertain Trumpet*. New York: Harper & Bros., 1959. A widely read statement of the army's position, in the 1950s, that larger conventional forces were needed if America was not to find itself choosing between nuclear war and defeat.

Wells, Samuel F. Jr. "The Origins of Massive Retaliation." In the *Political Science Quarterly*, Vol. 96, pp. 31–52. A recent historical treatment, assessing Massive Retaliation in long hindsight, and emphasizing its roots in policies and programs originated by the Truman administration.

6
Sputnik and the Missile Gap

On the western side of downtown Santa Monica, California, is a five-story pinkish building. From the rooftop one can throw a stone almost to the beach of the Pacific Ocean. Here, as far from Washington D.C. as it is possible to get within the continental forty-eight states, is the RAND Corporation—the first, and for many years the most influential, of the nonprofit research corporations serving government policy making.

The RAND Corporation was established in the late 1940s by General H. H. ("Hap") Arnold of the U.S. Air Force, who was among the first men, in or out of uniform, to realize that the nuclear age would create military problems that would go beyond the usual confines of military science. Arnold understood that traditional military analysis, as taught, for example, by West Point and the other military academies and war colleges, would not meet all of the novel challenges that would appear in the coming years. He convinced the air force that a new kind of analysis would be needed and that it would be best performed by specialists, not necessarily uniformed military officers, who could pursue their studies in a quiet atmosphere far removed from the hurly-burly of the Pentagon. Its name stood originally for Research ANd Development—though no actual development of military hardware takes place there. RAND was staffed mainly by scientists, principally "hard" scientists and engineers at first, and later by many social scientists as well.

Though created and permanently sustained by the air force, RAND took an increasingly broad perspective on the overall national security problems of the United States as the 1950s progressed. No other institution—no university, no branch or office within the military, no other organization—was doing this at the time, and people from a variety of backgrounds and disciplines who wanted to take this kind of perspective gravitated to RAND in this period. A "critical mass" of thinkers appeared at one place: dozens of individuals attacking related problems in a new topic area, coming from different but mutually intersecting academic and scientific backgrounds, stimulating each other through their interactions. This coming together of diverse specialists to focus on one policy area was an innovation. The idea of a nonprofit "think tank" that does research, not production, and works partly or entirely on problems of public affairs has grown familiar to us since. But in the 1950s it was not. The RAND Corporation was a new invention, and in many respects the model for the hundreds of similar nonprofit research corporations, working on many kinds of policy and social problems, that were to follow.

The mid-1950s through the early 1960s also proved to be the time when the most interesting intellectual challenges appeared in the area of national security. This was simply an accident of technology. Progress in the development of weapons took a course that, as it happened, created at this time problems of strategy and policy that were both important and solvable. (This latter aspect was a necessary condition: insoluble problems, such as the mythical "absolute defense," do not attract talented thinkers for long.) Neither before the mid-1950s nor since the early 1960s has this combination existed, at least not to anything like the same degree.

The development of the limited war concept and the analysis of how such wars could be kept limited, a topic discussed in the previous chapter, was an example of the kind of question that arose in this period. Many of the specialists who concerned themselves with this problem did their work at RAND. But limited war proved to be only one topic within what came more and more to seem an entire field of study—the field that came to be called "national security affairs." The national security specialists, or "defense intellectuals" as they were sometimes dubbed, came increasingly during the middle and late 1950s to see themselves as working in *this* field, whatever other disciplines—mathematics, economics, political science, etc.—they may have come from. By the early 1960s this sense of national security as a field of study was well developed in the American intellectual world. It was increasingly recognized by, for instance, major universities, many of which set up their own national security study programs, either in separate centers or within a traditional academic department (usually political science).

What national security involves when it is approached academically, as a field of study, will not be pursued here. The appendix to this book explores that further. It is enough to note that it was in the late 1950s and the early 1960s that this field emerged as a distinct specialty, attracted a substantial group of specialists, and enjoyed its greatest successes (at least to date) attacking important problems. Limited war was only one of these, and not the most important. The central problem that emerged for national security analysts in this period was the *strategic policy* of the United States, and the immediate reason was the Massive Retaliation policy of the Eisenhower administration.

THE FIRST CRITICISM OF MASSIVE RETALIATION: CREDIBILITY

Massive Retaliation disturbed many of those who were starting to think of themselves as national security specialists. They were distressed that some of the Eisenhower administration's rhetoric—which was deliberately ambiguous—sometimes seemed to suggest that America might begin an atomic World War III over a relatively minor intrusion upon a rather ill-defined line demarcating the "free world." They saw such a policy as dangerous if it were a bluff—if called, it might leave the United States embarrassed and helpless. It was even more dangerous if it were not a bluff—for then it might trigger a nuclear war. These specialists began to subject the administration's policy to an intense critical analysis, and as a body and method of thought began to take shape they published with increasing confidence and sophistication the objections they uncovered to Massive Retaliation. In the process they created the foundations of what came to be called "strategic studies," which in turn has been regarded ever since as the heart of national security affairs.

Hence it was the creation of a sustained, well-analyzed criticism and rebuttal of Massive Retaliation, together with work on how to limit wars, that first generated the new field of national security. Later the field was to expand greatly, but its genesis lay in a widespread and deep concern, among a significant number of intellectuals in the mid-1950s, with the limitation of warfare in the nuclear age, and especially with a danger that American power might be misused to begin an atomic war. It is worth recalling these origins because national security as a field came under fire, especially on American university campuses, a dozen years later during the Vietnam period, when it was often seen as a handmaiden to an unpopular war. But the intellectual roots of the field lay not in an attempt to make American policy more violent, but in a *criticism* of what was seen as excessive (potential) violence and an attempt to find a less dangerous way of life.

The critics of Massive Retaliation in the mid- to late 1950s developed two main objections to the Eisenhower administration's policy. The first was that the Massive Retaliation threat was not *credible* in the face of growing Soviet strategic power. As the Soviet arsenal of atomic bombs, and of long-range bombers to deliver them, grew during these years, it became less believable that the United States would actually launch an atomic war over some invasion in Asia or elsewhere. This might have been plausible, the critics conceded, when the Soviets had such a small strategic force that little or none of it could have penetrated to American cities, but by 1956 that time had passed. From then on, a Soviet or Chinese attack on most places around the world simply would not be important enough to place American cities in jeopardy. (This argument, and others to follow, was not made prominently by one person at one time, but was developed by many hands over a period of years. Several of the most important writings are mentioned at the end of this chapter, but here the discussion will simply refer to the "critics" collectively.)

The criticism just summarized involved an important analytic argument, not merely a statement of opinion. The critics were not merely saying that *they* did not believe that American cities should be or could be placed in jeopardy this way, or that they thought the Eisenhower administration was bluffing. The point was that even if the administration spokesmen really meant it when they implied that this was the policy, people in other capitals would not believe it. America's allies in Asia or the Middle East would not believe that the United States would hazard its cities this way. More importantly, the Soviets and Chinese themselves would not believe it. As the Soviets gained more and more power to devastate the United States, Moscow and Beijing simply would stop believing that Washington would begin World War III over an attack like the one that had taken place in Korea. *This* disbelief was what really counted, for if America's enemies did not believe the threat, they would not be deterred from attacking.

The criticism was a fundamental one. Deterrence, as the administration acknowledged, was the whole point of the Massive Retaliation policy. If the threat was losing its credibility to the very people whom it was supposed to deter, then the policy had lost its point.

It is worth noting that a similar argument has been made, ever since the late 1950s, by some circles of European opinion concerning the standing American security guarantee to Europe. The American commitment to NATO has always implied that the United States will accept nuclear war to defend Europe, but over the years some Europeans (especially the late President DeGaulle and a number of French military officers) have doubted the commitment. Essentially the same argument is made: would the United States really place its cities in jeopardy by accepting nuclear war if the Soviets attacked in Europe?

American national security specialists—including most of those who were critics of Massive Retaliation in the 1950s—have responded that Americans value the cities and lands of Western Europe as much as their own, and that New York would indeed be jeopardized for the sake of London or Paris. Most American (and some European) analysts have felt that this commitment is plausible enough that the Soviets probably find the threat credible. Even so, the NATO allies have always insisted that the United States station in Europe such a large number of troops that any conflict of significant size in Europe would automatically involve those troops in the fighting. In this way the United States would be drawn into the conflict automatically, and any last-minute doubts about the American commitment to Europe would be irrelevant.

This coupling of the United States to NATO is called the "tripwire" or "plate glass" function of the American forces in Europe. They are not powerful enough themselves to defend Europe against a full-scale Soviet assault, but such an assault would "trip the wire" or "break the plate glass." The United States could not stay out once divisions of its own troops were fighting the enemy. In effect, the troops stationed in Europe make the American commitment to NATO inescapable, and hence highly credible. That, and not their fighting value per se, is perhaps their main function.

Western Europe, however, is a special case. Many other places around the world, which the Eisenhower administration seemed to be trying to protect in the 1950s with the deterrent threat of massive retaliation, did not carry the same intrinsic value to the United States (and also did not enjoy the presence of "trip-wire" American forces). Hence, the critics argued, that deterrent threat was not credible in the face of mounting Soviet power. If deterrence was not credible, the Soviets might actually launch some kind of attack, or sponsor one by a "proxy" as they had in Korea.

The Eisenhower administration tried to come part way toward meeting this "credibility" argument against Massive Retaliation when it put forth its concept of Graduated Deterrence in the late 1950s. As mentioned earlier, this was a way of reinforcing the threat, by stating that a moderate number of nuclear weapons might be used against military targets in a local theater. In this way the administration implicitly conceded that it was not credible to threaten *strategic* war as a response to many kinds of *local* attacks. In effect it raised the threshold at which a massive retaliation might be first considered, and filled the gap with the threat of "tactical nuclear war." But the critics responded that within a very few years the Soviets would also have nuclear weapons in quantity for tactical use, whereupon the United States could not resort to them easily. This new threat would be just about as non-credible as unadulterated Massive Retaliation. The basic problem would emerge again: how would America make the deterrent threat credible?

FLEXIBLE RESPONSE

As their own answer to this problem, the critics developed and put forward a new concept, which came to be known as "Flexible Response." This never became a highly explicit theory nor was it written in a single authoritative source, and there has been some variation in its interpretation among its advocates. Nevertheless Flexible Response in all its versions includes certain core ideas. Nuclear weapons, and means for delivering them, must be available at all times both for strategic war should that ever arise, and for tactical use in local theaters. But the main function of these nuclear forces is simply to deter the opponent from using his own nuclear forces of the same kinds. The American strategic arsenal deters the Soviet (and later, Chinese) strategic arsenal, and American capabilities for using nuclear weapons in a tactical theater deter the Soviet (and Chinese) capabilities of the same kind. *And vice versa*, since the Communist powers' forces deter their American counterparts. In addition, some advocates of Flexible Response believed the United States might threaten under some circumstances to escalate to the tactical use of nuclear weapons in the event of a very large-scale invasion by conventional forces. Other advocates of Flexible Response disagreed.

In essence, the Flexible Response theorists argued that a *stable deterrent balance* was emerging between East and West, with respect to nuclear weapons for both strategic and tactical use. They advocated that this stability be accepted and even promoted, for the sake of a stable international situation, and to help keep the lid on crises when they appeared.

At the level *below* nuclear weapons, the same idea should be pursued. Flexible Response called for the United States to maintain sizable conventional forces "in being" at all times. These should be large enough that, added to the forces of America's allies, the total would deter the opponents from using their own conventional forces; and this should be their primary function. Ideally, then, these conventional forces serve the same kind of stable deterrent function that the two kinds of nuclear forces serve. At the conventional level as well as the nuclear level the forces of East and West deter each other. However, if necessary America could also use its conventional forces to fight limited wars. Should deterrence fail and a conventional attack come, forces would exist to meet it; and Washington would not be faced with an agonizing choice between accepting defeat and resorting to nuclear weapons.

The reader will have noticed a strong similarity between this point of view and the arguments that had been made in 1950 in NSC-68. That document too had implied that deterring the Soviets would have to be accomplished in different ways at different levels of violence. It had suggested that the two superpowers' nuclear forces would come to deter each other, and that the United States and its allies would have to develop sizable conventional forces to deter the Red Army. This logic of deterrence operating at multiple levels had been obscured by the Eisenhower administration's attempt to exploit the strategic superiority of the United States in the 1950s. That superiority had been thought so great that it could cover, as it were, all the levels (or later, that it could do so if supplemented by nuclear weapons used tactically). The Flexible Response doctrine argued that this obscuring of the complexity of deterrence was only temporary. As soon as the Soviets caught up, the real problems of deterrence at multiple levels would reappear. It is not much of an exaggeration to say that Flexible Response represented the same philosophy as NSC-68, brought up to date.

The Eisenhower administration's objection to large standing conventional forces was that they would cost too much, but the advocates of Flexible Response developed an answer to this as well. In the first place, the European allies had largely recovered from the destruction of World War II by now, and were economically able to support substantial armies. Their contribution, added to American forces, could make a sizable NATO conventional army. And secondly, an argument was put forward that the real potency of the Red Army in Europe had been exaggerated all along. The tendency, for example, had been to count divisions, and to discover that the USSR had over a hundred available for deployment in Europe, while the West could mount, at best, only a few dozen. But the Soviet Union had structured its army differently from Western armies; a Soviet division is a smaller unit than a Western division. On top of this, there was real doubt whether Moscow's satellites in Eastern Europe would fight in a European war, and some Soviet troops might have to be diverted to keep the satellites under control. For all these reasons, Flexible Response advocates believed that it would be quite possible for the West to maintain conventional forces large enough, if not to match the Red Army man for man, at least to come so close that the Soviets would be deterred from undertaking the risks and costs of a large conventional war.

A final element in the Flexible Response doctrine emphasized, as the name implied, flexibility. Technological improvements were now making it possible to transport more units and larger equipment by air, and to improve and accelerate sea transport as well. This meant that major army units could be kept stationed inside the United States (to save money) and still be brought quickly to bear should a war erupt. Advances were also being made in the technology of communications, so that military forces could be centrally commanded and controlled down to smaller units. (This was to be displayed, for instance, in the Cuban Missile Crisis of 1962, when the movements of each U.S. Navy vessel were minutely controlled directly from Washington.) Overall, these technological improvements in transportation and communications meant that U.S. forces could be deployed and used more flexibly than before, and the advocates of Flexible Response believed that this should be reflected in doctrine and planning. They stressed the value of having "multiple options" available in crises, rather than a few preset war plans. Giving the president multiple options would allow him to apply just the degree of force needed to control a crisis or attack, without either losing, or having to escalate for lack of alternatives.

Having multiple options, especially conventional ones, would also add to the credibility of American strategy, since there might be many circumstances in which the United States might actually be willing to use lower-level options. The doctrine of Flexible Response was designed above all to be highly credible. Maintaining adequate forces and multiple options at every level of violence—strategic nuclear, tactical nuclear, and conventional—would make it improbable that America would want or need to resort to nuclear weapons should a major conventional war break out, and certainly not quickly or in desperation. No deterrent threat would need to be made, therefore, that would be unlikely to be believed. Being believable, deterrence would be effective; being effective, it would preserve the peace.

When John F. Kennedy decided to campaign for the presidency, he chose advisers who were associated with the Flexible Response school. The argument for multiple options to control crises appealed to Kennedy, as did the whole Flexible Response philosophy. After Kennedy was elected, some of its important advocates, from the RAND Corporation and elsewhere, became high-level officials or advisers in Washington, and Flexible Response became official U.S. government policy. Its essentials have remained so ever since. Although there are always differences from administration to administration, and even from year to year, over *what* options should be available and what flexibilities should be emphasized, Flexible Response as a general philosophy has continued down to the present. (It is roomy and imprecise enough to permit many arguments and many differences over specifics without sacrificing the basic point of view.) No other doctrine of the same generality has risen to challenge it, and none seems likely to. Under some American pressure, the NATO allies also accepted Flexible Response as general NATO doctrine in 1967. Again the interpretation of it, and especially of what contributions the various

NATO nations should make in conventional forces, has remained a matter of debate within the alliance (as will be discussed further, below).

THE SECOND CRITICISM OF MASSIVE RETALIATION: VULNERABILITY

The second of the two main arguments against Massive Retaliation that its critics produced also hearkened back to the era of NSC-68. At that time the Truman administration had become concerned about the way SAC's bombers were concentrated on a small number of bases, all of which might be struck by a well-timed surprise Soviet attack. During the years following this hazard was alleviated by dispersing the bombers to more bases, by basing some of them in England and elsewhere overseas, and by creating a much better air defense system. But as the 1950s advanced and the Soviet bomber force grew in numbers, the danger seemed to emerge again. The B-47s and B-52s flown by SAC were still based at well under fifty locations, counting both overseas and domestic bases. The USSR was thought to possess or to be building hundreds of bomber aircraft, which meant that a number of bombers might be sent against each SAC base. Even with good air defense it seemed likely that at least one might get through, and with nuclear bombs on board one bomber alone could completely destroy the largest base. Although there were uncertainties about timing, about how much notice of attack might be available, and other questions, it seemed likely that the American strategic striking force was gradually becoming more and more vulnerable to a surprise, Pearl Harbor type attack.

The first identification of this danger to have major impact came in late 1957 in a top secret report to the National Security Council from an advisory group. The Gaither Report, as it was called after the group's chairman, made various recommendations for improving U.S. strategic capabilities, and especially for making SAC more secure from attack. Ultimately many of these recommendations were accepted by the administration, though in some cases only under pressure from Congress and from administration critics in the national security community (pressure made possible because the main contents of the Gaither Report had been leaked to the press).

To the specialists most inclined to be critical of the administration, its tendency to base so much of America's overall position on SAC's striking power seemed foolish indeed when SAC was becoming more vulnerable. If a new war broke out somewhere, Soviet leaders would be fearful that Washington might be tempted to use the strategic power it seemed to rely on. If at that point they thought that a massive retaliation strike might arrive soon from the United States, they would have the strongest incentive to try to destroy the SAC bases from which that strike would come. At such a moment they might be more willing than usual to start a nuclear war, if they thought that most of SAC's bombers could be destroyed on the ground. In this way, the growing vulnerability of American bases to surprise attack might be turning the Massive Retaliation policy into something that could make a nuclear war *more* likely, not less.

As the decade advanced, national security specialists focused on the question of the vulnerability of strategic forces with increasing urgency, and extended this theme well beyond the criticism of a particular administration's policies. Deterring any kind of Soviet nuclear strike, they pointed out, would always depend upon the USSR never acquiring the ability to *disarm* the United States by striking first. This hypothetical ability was called a "first-strike capability," a term that remains important today. In the strategic lexicon, a first-strike capability does not mean the ability to strike first—anyone can do that—nor does it mean the ability to make a first strike of some general kind. It means the ability to make a *disarming* strike: by striking first and well, to destroy the enemy's ability to strike back with any effectiveness. In the late 1950s many analysts feared that the USSR might be developing a first-strike capability against the United States; or at any rate the leaders in the Kremlin might think so, which would be equally dangerous.

Putting it the other way around, these analysts urged that the United States make sure that it was maintaining a "second-strike capability." This is also a term that remains important today. A second-strike capability does not quite mean the ability to strike back after the other side has struck first. It means the ability to absorb the other side's strike and retain enough operating forces to strike back *effectively*. It means, to introduce another term from the strategic lexicon, that one has the ability to "ride out" the enemy's attack and still have plenty of punch left afterwards. Any nation that has this ride-out ability is said to have a secure, second-strike capability. Clearly, having this means that the enemy does *not* have a first-strike capability, and in this way the terms are opposite.

How secure the U.S. second-strike capability really might be was called into question in the late 1950s. Since warning that Soviet bombers were approaching might be unreliable, or come too late to do much good, many SAC bases might be destroyed with their bombers still on the ground. How many bombers would be airborne in time, or remain at bases still intact? These surviving bombers would have to fly to the Soviet Union, and then hundreds of miles within the Soviet Union to their targets, through a Soviet air defense system that would be at its highest pitch of readiness. How many bombers would actually reach their targets? In other words, how many Soviet cities or other targets would the U.S. second strike actually destroy? Yet the threat of *that* destruction—not what SAC could do on a clear day when it had the initiative and could move first—was what deterrence depended upon.

In short, said a growing consensus of national security theorists, successful deterrence, and hence the prevention of World War III, always rests on having a secure, second-strike force. What counts is not the total size of one's strategic capabilities before a war begins, but how much of it is "survivable" and can "penetrate" to the enemy. Only that part that does survive and does reach its targets is a real threat to an enemy who may strike first (and who will certainly strike at one's strategic forces).

How vulnerable American forces were actually becoming was a matter of dispute between the Eisenhower administration and its critics. But the principle of securing one's forces was generally acknowledged. It is a principle that remains of central importance to this day and as far into the future as anyone can see. It is a key to the perennial question of "how much military power is enough?" in a way that is not always understood clearly. Many people who criticized the U.S. defense establishment in the 1950s and 1960s for having too many strategic forces, for example, did not take this principle properly into account. They pointed out that the U.S. forces were much larger than would be necessary to destroy every important target in the USSR—which was true if one assumed that the American forces remained intact and that all of them were used. But what really counts is only that fraction of the forces that can survive a full-scale Soviet attack, and then penetrate Soviet defenses and destroy their targets. Strategic deterrence of the USSR rests only on this second-strike force. This has been true ever since the Soviet Union developed, in the 1950s, significant forces for attacking the United States, and will remain true as long as that threat exists. (This does not mean there is no legitimate argument over how large the second-strike force needs to be; there certainly is.)

A DELICATE BALANCE OF TERROR?

The national security specialists who developed this reasoning also pointed out that it applied equally well in reverse. If the *Soviet* air bases were becoming vulnerable to a strike by SAC, then the United States might soon have a first-strike capability against the USSR. Superficially this might appear desirable, but in fact (argued many analysts) it was not. Such a state of affairs could lead to great anxiety among the leaders in the Kremlin, and this would be dangerous for world peace. In an intense crisis, or if a war broke out somewhere, they might become extremely anxious to launch the Soviet Air Force bombers before their bases could be attacked by SAC. In the strategic jargon, the Soviets might *preempt*. Fearing that an American attack was likely, they might get their strike in first.

The situation that seemed to be arising, in fact, was one in which *both* sides might have a first-strike capability against each other. Or to put it the other way, it was a situation in which neither side enjoyed a secure second-strike capability. A novel state of affairs seemed to be developing in which the United States and the USSR could each destroy a large part of the other's strategic forces, depending on which one struck first. Or at least, the growing vulnerability of each side's bases to surprise attack suggested that this state of affairs might come into existence before long.

If it did, this would be the greatest danger to peace that the nuclear era had yet seen, because it would mean that in a severe crisis both sides would feel great pressure to preempt. If a war broke out in the Far East, say, or some intense crisis erupted in Europe, leaders in each capital would wonder if a third world war might be imminent. They had wondered this before, in other crises, but in the past there had not been much urgency about striking first. But under conditions of mutual vulnerability there would be. Each side would know that it risked having its forces destroyed—and losing the war—if it held back, and that it had an excellent chance of winning if it struck first.

Indeed it would be even worse than this, because each side would also know that the other was in the same situation. Each would know the other was also strongly tempted to preempt. Hence each would be all the more anxious, perhaps desperate, to strike quickly.

The vulnerability of each side's bases was not extreme yet, but the more vulnerable they became the more real this danger would become. The strategic balance of power, which had been stable, would become increasingly unstable. Ever since the nuclear era had begun, deterrence had seemed to be the key to maintaining the peace. But deterrence in a time of growing mutual vulnerability would become an ever more "delicate balance of terror."

This was the title of a famous essay, published in 1959, that made powerfully the argument that has been summarized here. Written by Albert Wohlstetter, one of the senior national security analysts working at the RAND Corporation, "The Delicate Balance of Terror" was the culmination of specialists' mounting concern about the vulnerability of strategic forces—American and Soviet. Peace would be most surely preserved, Wohlstetter argued, when the strategic deterrent balance between the United States and the USSR was and remained stable. And that stability would be greatest, not when either side possessed a great advantage over the other, but when both sides enjoyed relatively secure second-strike forces.

Complete invulnerability to attack (the ideal case) was probably not to be hoped for. But a number of things could be done to make American forces more secure from a Soviet strategic strike; and American national security analysts did not always shy away (at least in private) from hoping that the Soviet leaders might do similar things to make their forces less vulnerable to American attack. Even as Wohlstetter's article was appearing in print, SAC bombers were being dispersed to more bases, so the Soviet forces would have more targets to try to hit. Plans were also drawn up for transferring some SAC bombers to civilian airports in times of crisis, to add further to the Soviet targeting problem. (This was actually done, for example, at the time of the Cuban Missile Crisis. For some days in October 1962, Strategic Air Command B-52 bombers were stationed at many of the airports attached to major American cities.)

As an additional measure, SAC also came up with a new system for keeping a portion of the bomber fleet on "ground alert" at all times. A rotating fraction of the bombers were kept fueled and armed with bombs, with crews ready to go, in case warning should arrive that Soviet bombers were coming in. Still other measures, discussed below, were taken later.

INTO THE MISSILE AGE

Around the same time that many national security specialists were becoming concerned about SAC's vulnerability, the American public was becoming alarmed about the technological balance of power between the USSR and America generally. On October 4, 1957, the Soviet Union launched Sputnik, the world's first artificial satellite. This was followed within a few weeks by two more satellites that were much heavier than anything that the United States would be able to put into orbit for years. Flying around the planet about every ninety minutes, the Sputniks instantly became an immensely visible symbol, for nations everywhere, of Soviet technological prowess.

Americans were chagrined that a step of such great symbolic importance in human history should have been taken by another country, and disturbed again, as they had been at the time of the first Soviet atomic test, at what this might mean for the world balance. Throughout the West, Sputnik generated anxiety about overall American technological leadership, of which the "space race" instantly became the premier symbol. This anxiety was to go on for years, and to become a source of major shifts in U.S. government policy, including the institution of large-scale government loans and fellowships for students and the allocation of much larger sums for scientific research. The anxiety was renewed in 1960 when the Soviet Union launched the first man into orbit, Yuri Gagarin. It declined only when the United States regained clear leadership in strategic weapons in the 1960s (as discussed in the next chapter) and finally vanished when America landed a man on the moon.

What disturbed national security analysts and the U.S. government more than Sputnik, however, was the discovery by American intelligence some months earlier that the Soviet Union had tested a prototype long-range missile. It appeared that the USSR, not the United States, was going to be the first to deploy the Intercontinental Ballistic Missile, or ICBM.

Missiles that could fly very rapidly over intercontinental ranges were not a new idea. Nazi Germany had actually begun preliminary work on designing one, called the A-10, toward the end of World War II. Both Russia and America had continued this research during the cold war (both using German scientists who had defected or been captured at war's end), and the United States had two ICBM models under development in 1957, the Atlas and the Titan. But neither was ready yet to be test flown. If the Soviets were now test-flying a prototype ICBM they must be ahead of the United States in missile technology. The American development program could be, and was, accelerated somewhat but there was a limit to this. There seemed to be no way to avoid a situation, several years ahead, when the Soviets would be *deploying* operational ICBMs, and the United States would not yet have its missiles ready. There would be, as it came to be called, a "missile gap."

This danger was the source of the most urgent concern of many specialists about the vulnerability of American strategic forces. The possibility that Soviet *missiles*, not bombers, might suddenly strike SAC bases with little or no warning could hardly be discussed publicly. American intelligence information about the Soviet missile programs was, and had to remain, highly classified. Wohlstetter's article on "The Delicate Balance of Terror" only hints at the greatest danger; explicitly, it discusses bomber attacks. But Soviet ICBMs could fly over the North Pole far faster than bomber aircraft—the missile flight time is only about half an hour—and in this period the United States had no radar for spotting their approach. It seemed frighteningly possible that in the near future the Soviet Union might be able to destroy practically *all* of the American strategic force before it could be launched. It was this possibility above all, not just the mutual vulnerability of each side's bases to bomber attack, which could be written and talked about publicly, that inspired the most intense concern about U.S. vulnerability.

Certain steps could be and were taken to try to blunt the danger. The United States pressed ahead at the fastest possible pace with a new radar system called BMEWS, for Ballistic Missile Early Warning System, and this system did go into operation not long after the Soviet ICBMs began to be deployed. BMEWS could provide about fifteen minutes warning of an incoming missile strike, and SAC's "ground alert" was improved to the point where a substantial number of bombers could be airborne in that time. Beyond this, the United States put a small fraction of bombers on "air alert" during the period of maximum risk. This meant that a certain number of bombers, with bombs aboard, were kept *in the air* at all times, ready to fly to the Soviet Union on command. Although very expensive, it was one way to ensure that even a surprise missile strike that destroyed all SAC bases could not catch every bomber.

The anxiety of government officials and national security analysts over the potential missile gap assumed that the Soviet Union would push its development of ICBMs as rapidly as possible, and deploy as many missiles as it could as soon as it could. This was the only prudent assumption to make, since the Soviet Union would be in the most advantageous position it had ever been in, by far, it if could deploy a considerable number of ICBMs at a time when the United States still had none. But in fact the Soviet leaders decided *not* to manufacture many of the earliest, "first-generation" ICBMs. These missiles were primitive and unreliable, technically inferior to the first-generation

American ICBMs still under development. The Kremlin leaders decided to concentrate their technological resources (at that time still relatively scarce) on developing a better, second-generation missile and manufacturing it in quantity. During the time around the turn of the decade when the United States had not yet deployed any ICBMs, the Soviets deployed only about fifty of their earliest missiles.*

But this was not known in the West until 1961. The limitations of Western intelligence did not make it possible to find this out any sooner. The Kremlin, knowing this and no doubt being aware from its own intelligence of the anxiety in Western military circles, decided to play its seeming advantage to the hilt—as America had a few years earlier in the heyday of Massive Retaliation.

THE MISSILE GAP BECOMES A PUBLIC ISSUE

Not long after Sputnik was launched, Premier Nikita Khrushchev began publicly boasting that strategic superiority was passing to the Soviet Union. Indeed the Kremlin now undertook, and continued until 1962, a constant and systematic campaign of deception, in all its public statements concerning the East-West military balance. Taking advantage of the opportunities offered by a totalitarian society for manipulating information, high Soviet civilian and military officials released a steady stream of public declarations that "long-range rocket forces" were entering the Soviet arsenal in quantity, and that the USSR had surpassed the West in ability to devastate an enemy's homeland. These Soviet declarations were widely reported in the Western press and generated increasing public concern. The apparent lag in American missile capabilities generally, and not the specifics of U.S. strategic vulnerability, was what the public understood by the phrase "the missile gap," which became popular for awhile.

The intention behind the Soviet campaign of deception seems to have been to neutralize (at least) the advantage that strategic superiority had given the United States in the cold war. For years America had used strategic (Massive Retaliation) threats to try to deter the Communist powers from making gains in the international competition. Now the Soviets began to use claims of their strategic superiority to back their own cold war tactics.

---

*The figure of about 50 Soviet ICBMs in this period is given in nearly all public sources. Daniel Ellsberg, who has had access to relevant classified information, has stated in print that the actual number of Soviet ICBMs deployed, to early 1962, was four. In Daniel Ellsberg, "Introduction: Call to Mutiny," in E.P. Thompson and Dan Smith, eds., *Protest and Survive* (New York and London: Monthly Review Press, 1981).

In 1958 and 1959, and again in 1961, the USSR created severe crises in Berlin, in another attempt to drive the West out of its enclave inside East Germany. Although these efforts ultimately failed, they involved not only intense and sustained diplomatic, but also military maneuvers, including a famous confrontation between Soviet and American tanks at "Checkpoint Charlie" in Berlin in 1961. No shots were fired, but at this and several other points during these crises there was a real risk of war. And the Soviets did succeed, in August 1961, in permanently dividing East from West Berlin by erecting a wall between them, thereby closing the escape hatch that tens of thousands of people had used to escape East Germany.

Increased Soviet belligerence in Europe, as well as the constantly trumpeted claims of military superiority and the impact of Sputnik, all fed anxieties in the West. Knowing as we now do that this period was weathered without war and without too much damage or danger, political or technological, to the West, we tend to forget how strong the worries were at the time. Boasts that the Soviets now had military supremacy were delivered repeatedly and authoritatively from the highest levels of the Moscow government, including the premier himself, and the Soviets' renewed cold war aggressiveness suggested that they really believed it. Continuing Western failure in the space race, first to orbit satellites nearly as heavy as the later Sputniks, and then to place a man into orbit, seemed to be evidence that the USSR was indeed superior in the all-important field of rockets.

The phrase "the missile gap" became a shorthand label, not simply for the fact that the Soviets claimed to have long-range missiles and the United States did not, but for this entire mood of anxiety and threat. American missile inferiority seemed to be the source and core of the danger, but the larger fear was that primacy in the world competition might indeed have passed to the Soviet Union. In the presidential election of 1960, the missile gap became a major issue, which Senator Kennedy used to attack the "inadequacies" of the Republicans' stewardship of U.S. security.

Even before the presidential campaign, though, the American public was becoming acutely conscious, for the first time, of the strategic military balance. The difference between missiles and bombers, the importance of the technological balance between America and Russia, the power of the strategic forces of the two sides, and related topics were part of the general conversation and awareness of Americans around the turn of the decade. Never before had strategic military issues been so much in the forefront for such a sustained period, nor were they to be again until the early 1980s. As the decade of the 1960s opened, national security was probably the American people's leading concern.

SUMMARY

The period from the mid-1950s to the early 1960s represented one of the most significant eras in the evolution of American national security affairs from the onset of the cold war to the present. Soviet strategic power grew from the very modest level of the early 1950s to the point where the Kremlin leadership could credibly claim to have achieved superiority over the West. And in the same period, the shift from bomber aircraft to long-range missiles as the primary strategic technology introduced new complications into the military calculus, particularly since this shift occurred at slightly different times and in slightly different ways for the two superpowers.

These developments jointly made possible, and demanded, a fresh strategic analysis. Specialists at the RAND Corporation and elsewhere argued, with increasing vigor and clarity as the decade advanced, that the current U.S. strategic doctrine of Massive Retaliation was becoming outdated. As Soviet forces grew, the threat was becoming less credible, and SAC bases were becoming more vulnerable to the possibility of a Soviet preemption. The full development of these arguments created a body of thought that became the core of "national security affairs" considered as a field of study. The nature and requirements of "first-strike" and "second-strike" capabilities, and related ideas developed in these years continue to be central themes for the field today.

Flexible Response was put forward as an alternative "doctrine" (in a loose sense of the term) emphasizing deterrence operating on different levels. Nuclear forces at the strategic or tactical levels should be relied upon to deter, not conventional attacks, but only opposing forces of the same kinds. More U.S. conventional forces, and "multiple options" for deploying and using them, should carry the burden of deterring conventional attacks.

Above all, said theorists in the emerging new field of national security, the danger of a "delicate balance of terror" must be forestalled by both the United States and the USSR taking measures to make their strategic forces relatively secure. If the superpowers could "ride out" strategic attacks and retain enough forces to strike back, then deterrence could remain stable, and dangerous pressure to preempt anytime war threatened would be removed. Securing American bombers as much as possible against a Soviet missile strike was especially urgent during the time that the Soviets claimed, and intelligence information and events in the "space race" seemed also to suggest, that the USSR was deploying ICBMs while America as yet had not. Steps to make SAC bombers, or at least some of them, less vulnerable were taken promptly, even while the larger debate and concern waxed at the beginning of the 1960s over the real validity of the Soviet claims and the true extent of the dangers they suggested.

FOR FURTHER READING

Brodie, Bernard. *Strategy in the Missile Age*. Princeton: Princeton University Press, 1959. Probably the leading statement of the concerns and concepts developed in the new field of national security in the late 1950s, and especially of the ideas of Flexible Response, by one of its major architects.

Horelick, Arnold, and Myron Rush. *Strategic Power and Soviet Foreign Policy*. Chicago: University of Chicago Press, 1966. A scholarly analysis of the Soviet campaign of strategic deception of 1958–62.

Kahan, Jerome H. *Security in the Nuclear Age: Developing U.S. Strategic Arms Policy*. Washington, D.C.: The Brookings Institution, 1975. The first three chapters of this work provide a detailed, moderately technical history of American strategic policies from 1953 to 1974. Subsequent chapters analyze that history.

Kaufmann, William W. "The Crisis in Military Affairs." In *World Politics*, Vol. 10, pp. 579–603. Formally a critical review of Kissinger's *Nuclear Weapons and Foreign Policy*, this essay was an important public statement of the then-developing ideas of Flexible Response, by another of its major architects.

Smith, Bruce L.R. *The RAND Corporation*. Cambridge, Mass.: Harvard University Press, 1966. A scholarly history and assessment of the main American "think tank" for national security in the 1950s and early 1960s.

Synder, Glenn. *Deterrence and Defense*. Princeton: Princeton University Press, 1961. An important analysis of deterrence, oriented more toward the logic of international politics and less toward the specifics of a given era of weapons technology, than much of the material written in this period.

Wohlstetter, Albert. "The Delicate Balance of Terror." In *Foreign Affairs*, Vol. 37, pp. 211–234. The classic statement of why secure, second-strike forces are necessary for stable deterrence.

7
The Second Era of American Military Superiority

When the Kennedy administration took office in January 1961, it immediately asked Congress for an additional allocation of money for defense, beyond the regular defense budget for that year. The money was spent partly to increase U.S. conventional forces, as suggested by the Flexible Response doctrine that now became policy. But a good deal of it was spent to accelerate programs (described below) that would give America a more secure, second-strike strategic force. Further conventional improvements and a continued higher level of strategic effort were also built into planning the regular budget for the next fiscal years. The result was a surge in defense spending during the Kennedy administration, which Kennedy had said would be necessary while he was still a candidate for the presidency.

Within ten months of the inauguration, however, the Kennedy administration was making public declarations that the United States was not—and actually had never been—significantly inferior to the Soviets in strategic weapons. In fact this was conceded off the record only a few weeks after Kennedy took office. The missile gap, about which there had been so much public concern, and which had been such an issue in the presidential election, was turning out to be unreal. A serious gap in missiles had never existed.

This revelation came so soon after the election, furthermore, that it raised political suspicions. Because the issue had been so useful to Kennedy in the campaign (which he won narrowly) cynics now suggested that Kennedy and his advisers had known or guessed all along that there was little or no missile gap. Later many critics of the Pentagon were also to accuse the administration of having used a fictitious missile gap as an excuse to increase defense spending, which (they charged) it had wanted to do anyway for other reasons, such as domestic politics or Keynesian "pump-priming" of the economy. Both these ideas have been gradually accepted by many people in the years since, and it is often taken for granted now that Kennedy cynically manipulated the missile gap issue. In fact, what occurred was more complicated and considerably different. Because the missile gap period was such a dramatic moment in the evolution of American national security, and has been so widely misunderstood, let us pause on it for a little longer.

We recall that for the informed public the missile gap meant the general comparison between the sizable missile forces the Soviet government claimed to have and the absence of American ICBMs; whereas for many specialists it meant (at least primarily) the narrower and more specific problem of the vulnerability of U.S. bases. Responsible officials in the Eisenhower administration were a good deal less concerned in the late 1950s about the general comparison than most of the *public* critics because they had secret intelligence information that painted a much brighter picture. The administration was unwilling to reveal the reasons for its confidence, because most of the critical information was derived from a very secret source—aerial photographs. In those days before "spy in the sky" satellites, the United States had an airplane, the U-2, which flew so high that Soviet air defense had not been able to shoot it down. These planes were flying over the USSR regularly, and their photographs showed clearly that, despite the bombastic claims being made in Moscow, the USSR in fact had *not* yet deployed any significant number of ICBMs. This could not be revealed in Washington because the secret overflights of the Soviet Union were illegal and very sensitive, as proved in May 1960, when the Soviets finally shot down a U-2 piloted by one Francis Gary Powers. Moscow turned this into an immense international incident, attempting to embarrass the United States as much as possible, and going so far as to call off at the last minute a planned summit conference between Khrushchev and President Eisenhower.

The validity of the Soviet claims, however, was not what most concerned the national security specialists, who had access to the classified intelligence information and who were critical of the administration's policies in the *private* debate then raging. They agreed that, so far as the immediate present was concerned, the Soviet claims were greatly exaggerated. What they worried about was the prospect of Soviet ICBM deployments in the near future. The aerial photographs could reveal missiles actually deployed or sites being prepared for missiles, but could not reveal the number of ICBMs being manufactured, or already built and in storage. Estimates of the Soviet manufacturing capacity suggested that many more ICBMs could be under construction than the USSR had yet deployed. It would be quite possible, and given the Kremlin leaders' habit of deception, all too plausible, for them to deploy only a few missiles at first to be photographed by U-2s, while storing many more away secretly. These might then be deployed quickly at some point, in a bid to acquire a first-strike capability against American strategic bases. This was the critics' real concern until May 1960. The U-2 flights were canceled after Powers was shot down, and thereafter scanty information was available about *actual* Soviet deployments too, which was even more troublesome. Little of this leaked into the public discussion of the missile gap, but within the community of those privy to the classified information it was the near future, not the present, that was so worrisome—until the late spring of 1960, when the present became uncertain also.

Meanwhile the United States was rapidly pushing the development of the first "spy in the sky" satellite, called Samos. A satellite, part of whose orbit passed over the Soviet Union, could take photographs almost as useful as those of a U-2, and could not be shot down. In later years both the United States and USSR came to rely heavily on photographic and other kinds of intelligence-gathering satellites (which have become highly sophisticated) for monitoring each other's military deployments. But even pressing at the fastest possible pace, the first Samos satellites could not be launched until early in 1961.

Between the last U-2 flight and the first Samos photographs, therefore, there was a lapse of some nine or ten months. During this time Washington lacked "hard" evidence about Soviet missile deployments.

It happened that this intelligence lapse coincided with the 1960 campaign for the presidency. Kennedy and his advisers had legitimate reason, therefore, to express their worries (and no photographs could dispel the possibility that the Soviets were secretly storing more missiles than they were deploying).

During the fall and winter other intelligence, less reliable than photographs, filtered into Washington suggesting that the Soviets were probably not deploying many more missiles than were already known. It was on the basis of this intelligence that Kennedy's new secretary of defense, Robert McNamara, mentioned at an off-the-record press briefing, not long after entering office, that a real missile gap had not yet materialized. The timing of this about-face, then, was to a considerable degree an accident of how and when intelligence was received, not a product of political cynicism. Some indications had arrived during the fall but they were not definite, certainly not as early as October when the political campaign climaxed.

Indeed the evidence was still far from conclusive; others within the administration believed McNamara spoke prematurely. But the Samos satellites were launched over the next several months and by the late summer of 1961 their photographic coverage of the USSR was comprehensive enough that the administration could be confident that only a small number of Soviet missiles had been deployed. Under the pressure of the intense Berlin crisis that summer, Kennedy decided that the time had come to call the Kremlin's bluff of "strategic superiority." A defense spokesman gave a public address in October revealing the truth about the strategic balance in considerable detail. The missile gap, in the sense of a period of serious public anxiety in the West, now faded away. Thereafter Soviet propaganda did not stop, but its claims of superiority were couched in general terms and in ways that tacitly acknowledged the American revelation about the true balance.

THE AMERICAN STRATEGIC BUILDUP

When the Kennedy administration entered office determined to improve the American strategic posture, it took several steps at once. The ground alert that SAC had already begun was upgraded, to the point where almost half the bomber force was constantly ready to take off on about fifteen minutes notice. The administration pushed deployment of the first-generation Atlas and Titan ICBMs, the first of which were now beginning to enter the strategic force. The ICBMs had to be deployed at launch sites above ground, however, because the technology of constructing hardened underground silos for missiles had not yet been perfected. These early ICBM sites were every bit as vulnerable to Soviet attack as bomber bases, and hence contributed little to a secure second-strike force, although they did multiply the Soviet targeting problem. Of greater long-term significance than these developments was the administration's acceleration and expansion of U.S. programs for second-generation missiles.

Work had begun in the late 1950s on these missiles, which were improvements over their predecessors in many ways, but one above all — they used solid rather than liquid fuel. The Atlas and Titan missiles could not be kept fueled at all times; they had to be filled with liquid fuel after the command to be ready for launch. This was a time-consuming and somewhat difficult procedure. Solid-fuel missiles, on the other hand, have their fuel prepacked, in a stable form that lasts a long time. They are always ready and can be launched on very short notice. Though perfecting the solid-fuel technology was more difficult, the decision (made by the Eisenhower administration) to shift to solid fuel in the next generation of missiles was to give the United States a considerable advantage over the Soviet Union, which developed this technology much more slowly, and indeed still does not use it in many missiles.

Two solid-fueled missile programs had begun in the 1950s. One was America's second-generation ICBM, called the Minuteman. So named because it could be fired on about one minute's warning, the Minuteman was procured in large numbers by the Kennedy and Johnson administrations. It was designed from the outset to be launched from hardened underground silos, and after it became available in quantity the Atlas and most of the Titan missiles were gradually retired from the ICBM force. A few Titans were retained, however, and put in underground silos, because the Titan can carry a heavier warhead than any other American missile. In the jargon of the trade, the Titan has a larger "throw weight," and for this reason fifty-four of these missiles were kept in the American arsenal for a long time. Only in 1981 was it announced that they would be phased out.

The other solid-fueled missile was the Polaris, designed to be carried in submarines. Launching missiles from below the ocean's surface was a concept developed in the 1950s (and never yet improved upon) as a solution to the challenge of making strategic forces secure. Submarines are difficult to locate if they cruise submerged and if they do not have to come to the surface to fire their missiles. Officials and analysts both inside and outside the Eisenhower administration agreed that if all the necessary technologies could be developed, "submarine launched ballistic missiles," or SLBMs, could give the United States a highly secure second-strike capability, and the attempt was pursued with a high priority.

The development of the Polaris SLBM and of the submarine (also called Polaris) to carry it, proved to be one of the most successful research and development programs in postwar American history. With relatively few setbacks, the complicated technical problems involved were solved one by one, and the first Polaris submarines came "on station" in 1961, a remarkably rapid schedule. The first Polaris missiles had only an "intermediate" range of 1,500 miles or so; they were later replaced with improved models having a longer range. In the 1970s, these were replaced again with a new SLBM called Poseidon that had an intercontinental range. Each enlargement in range meant that more targets could be reached, and more importantly, that the submarines would have a much larger ocean area in which to hide. Since a rotating portion of the submarine fleet must be in port at any one time, longer range also meant that in a crisis, the submarines in port could be sent to sea and reach their cruising areas quickly.

By now, the strategic forces deployed by the United States, followed later by the Soviet Union, had become so diverse that it is useful to display information in the form of tables. Table 1 indicates the two sides' strategic forces as of October 1962. Similar tables later in the book give parallel data for other times.

When McNamara became secretary of defense he used some of the supplementary funds requested from Congress to accelerate the Minuteman and Polaris programs. The Kennedy administration was also faced with choices about how many of these missiles to deploy and was inclined, now and over the next several years, to create a comparatively large force. Ultimately one thousand Minutemen would be deployed, and forty-one Polaris submarines carrying sixteen missiles each, or a total of 656 Polaris missiles. With the fifty-four Titans, this added up to a strategic missile force of 1,710 ICBMs and SLBMs, although this total was not reached until the second half of the 1960s. This number, approximately decided upon while Kennedy was still president, was to remain the same well into the 1970s, although the quality of the forces (in reliability, accuracy, range, payload, and other factors) was improved steadily.

Decisions about the numbers of missiles to build had to be made relatively early since years would pass between the time of decision and the actual entry of many of these missiles into the operating

Table 1.   American and Soviet strategic forces as of October 1962

	Soviet Union	United States
ICBMs	75 (approx.)	100 Minuteman I (approx.)
		90 Atlas
		36 Titan
		226
SLBMs	0	144 Polaris missiles carried by nine Polaris submarines
Long-range bombers	70 Bears	600 B-52s (approx.)
	120 Bisons	750 B-47s (approx.)
	190	1350

Notes: Bear and Bison are NATO code names. The Bear was a propeller-driven heavy bomber; the Bison was a lighter bomber with four jets, somewhat less capable than the B-47. The B-47s were being rapidly phased out at this time.

All Soviet ICBMs were at very vulnerable above-ground launch sites. So were the U.S. Titans and most of the Atlases. The Minuteman I missiles were in hardened underground silos. The Minuteman I force was being rapidly expanded at this time; eight months later, in July 1963, about 450 were deployed.

Source: Institute of Strategic Studies, London: The Communist Bloc and the Western Alliance: The Military Balance 1962–63.

forces. When this magnitude was decided upon, analysts still were expecting a large Soviet deployment to show up on spy satellite photographs before long, and the decision was guided by a desire to at least equal the reasonable maximum that the USSR was likely to deploy. The years of inflated propaganda claims, and the more aggressive turn in Soviet foreign policy that had accompanied them, suggested that it would be unwise to allow the USSR again to achieve even an appearance of superiority.

Through approximately the first half of the 1960s, however, the Soviets did *not* deploy many ICBMs. Apparently they experienced technical difficulties in perfecting their second-generation missiles; by the beginning of 1965, for instance, they still had only about 200 ICBMs.* At

---

*The reader should recall that while this number was small compared to the American ICBM arsenal of the day, it represented tremendous destructive power if used in a first strike. Just ten percent of the force could have wiped out twenty American cities if all missiles reached their targets. All 200 could have almost annihilated the United States.

this time, too, the Soviets had not yet developed any SLBM forces; nor did they have a jet bomber of intercontinental range. Though later in the decade Soviet forces were to expand markedly (and continue to thereafter), in the early to mid-1960s American analysts remained pleasantly surprised by a continuing low level of Soviet intercontinental striking power, compared to U.S. power. (The USSR did build up its intermediate range forces aimed at Europe.)

This meant that the current U.S. strategic program was creating, rather unexpectedly, a growing *American* numerical superiority in the strategic competition. The Soviet Union's missile bluff earlier, the strong American reaction, and the Soviets continuing into the 1960s to deploy only a few ICBMs, all combined to create a situation that neither Washington nor, probably, Moscow had anticipated. Numerical strategic superiority was passing back to the United States. Even though the U.S. buildup was cut back slightly from what had been planned at one time, and the United States later withdrew some intermediate-range missiles that had been stationed at vulnerable, aboveground sites overseas, the balance in missile forces began to run heavily in America's favor. And this did not count the huge U.S. advantage in strategic bombers, nor the "tactical" aircraft carrying nuclear bombs stationed overseas and on aircraft carriers.

The first half of the 1960s was also the time when the United States was beefing up its conventional power, as Flexible Response counseled. Improvements in airlift, sealift, and communications, upgrading of the combat effectiveness of army and marine corps divisions, and expansion of these "general purpose forces," as they now came to be called, were creating a range of conventional options that the country had never previously possessed. The total surge in American military power, including general purpose as well as nuclear forces, in the early 1960s added up to the greatest peacetime military buildup that any nation had undertaken in a short period anytime in the twentieth century.

At this time, too, the United States was still ahead of the USSR in the numbers and kinds of nuclear weapons for tactical use; and contributions of various kinds of forces from the NATO allies were increasing. Although on paper NATO was still unequal to the Warsaw Pact in total number of troops, the Kennedy administration became confident that even in Europe the real balance of power was not disadvantageous to the West. In short, the return of strategic superiority was being accompanied by an increasingly favorable position over the military spectrum as a whole.

In this partly accidental, partly deliberate fashion, the period of the early to mid-1960s became a second era of American military superiority. The Kennedy administration, at first concerned that a missile gap might be appearing or about to appear, and later believing quite reasonably that the Soviets would begin a large missile deployment soon, took steps to increase American strategic power greatly. When the expected Soviet missiles did not materialize for some years, these steps proved to be considerably more than had been necessary at the time. There was a missile gap in reverse. For the second time in the history of the cold war, American officials found that they were coming to possess marked strategic superiority. Also for the second time, this was less planned or intended than it was a reaction to fears about sudden advances in Soviet power.

FURTHER CONCEPTUAL DEVELOPMENTS

On the first occasion, ten years earlier, superiority had led to the doctrine of Massive Retaliation. But the critics of that doctrine were now in power. Any new intellectual or policy departures would certainly begin from the perspective of Flexible Response. The essence of that perspective, creating multiple options, was something that many in the administration now became interested in extending to nuclear war strategy.

Indeed, the entry of missiles in quantity into the U.S. arsenal led to an important new concept, and the superiority they conferred soon led to more. The arrival of missiles had brought the United States three kinds of strategic offensive forces—ICBMs, SLBMs, and bombers. (The bombers were now mostly B-52s. The older and smaller B-47s were being phased out; later another small, but fast and advanced bomber, the FB-111, was added in modest numbers.) The concept now evolved that the United States would need this "triad" of forces indefinitely.

Under the triad doctrine, each of the three should be able *independently* to impose unacceptable damage on the Soviet Union. The United States would have hedges against any Soviet surprise attack. If one or even two legs of the triad were somehow destroyed in such an attack, the third could still retaliate. Knowing this, the Soviets would be completely deterred.

Furthermore, planners recognized that each element in the triad had particular advantages and disadvantages. Bombers are vulnerable until airborne, and some would be lost to Soviet air defenses, but they can be recalled after launch (as missiles cannot) and B-52s can deliver a heavy payload accurately. In the 1960s ICBMs were more secure, but not perfectly so: even a hardened silo cannot withstand a direct hit. The SLBMs are most secure of all but not as accurate as ICBMs or bombers (although this will change in the late 1980s). Also, the difficulty of communicating with submerged submarines makes their missiles hard to use flexibly. Only a simple "go/no go" message can be sent them from a hardened communications source; any more complicated message requires communications that are vulnerable to attack. Maintaining all three systems would provide the advantages of each and would yield the greatest flexibility in nuclear options.

This concept of a permanent triad of forces became part of official U.S. defense doctrine in the early 1960s and has remained so since. Although the strategic environment keeps changing, maintaining the triad has become part of the bedrock of U.S. defense policy. The continuing need for all three components has sometimes been challenged by defense critics, especially recently, as underground silos have seemed more vulnerable to highly accurate missile strikes. But, at least to date, preserving the triad has remained axiomatic in official U.S. planning.

As the growing American missile superiority of the early 1960s joined the already existing superiority in bombers, some further ideas evolved that have also remained important. A distinction now developed in the *purposes* for which the strategic offensive forces might be used. Clearly their basic function was, and always would be, deterrence of a Soviet attack on American cities. It was now an accepted principle that this deterrence rested on the capacity of secure, second-strike forces to devastate the Soviet Union. This capacity was now termed the "assured destruction" mission for U.S. forces. Deterrence of World War III ultimately rested on the Soviets knowing with assurance that their society would suffer nearly complete destruction if they attacked American cities. McNamara defined the necessary level of destruction as the death of one quarter of the Soviet population and the destruction of one half of Soviet industry. Since the quarter killed would include a high proportion of the country's educated people and skilled laborers, and the industry destroyed would include most of the heavy industry, rebuilding would take generations.

In the military jargon the cities and industrial districts on both sides came to be called "countervalue targets." To threaten them was to counter what each side most valued. One part of American forces was assigned the assured destruction mission against Soviet countervalue targets. As a generalization, it has been primarily the SLBM component of the U.S. triad that has received this mission. The SLBMs are the most secure, and are not accurate enough for other targets. But other U.S. forces have also had this mission in part. The assured destruction mission remains the core objective of U.S. strategic forces today.

But the United States was now coming to have much more strategic power than was needed for the assured destruction mission. Attention turned to the possibility of using the rest of the forces for another purpose—to reduce the damage that America and her allies might suffer in the event a war actually occurred. In principle, damage might be reduced in either of two ways: the traditional defensive way, for instance by shooting down incoming bombers; but also offensively, by attacking Soviet nuclear weapons before they could be launched. During McNamara's tenure as secretary of defense, which lasted through most of the Johnson as well as Kennedy administrations, both avenues were pursued. (The defensive avenue will be discussed later.)

Trying to reduce damage by *offensive* means was now termed the "damage limiting" mission for U.S. forces. Soviet bomber bases were vulnerable to U.S. missile attack, and in this period the limited Soviet ICBM force was still deployed above ground or in only semihardened silos, and was vulnerable also. So were Soviet intermediate-range missiles aimed at Europe and Japan, as well as tactical air bases and other military bases and sites of all kinds. In the strategic jargon all these targets were now called "counterforce targets." To attack them was to counter the opponent's forces (which were not an ultimate value in the same way as cities). A substantial part of the growing U.S. strategic forces was soon being assigned the damage limiting mission against Soviet counterforce targets. The strategy that emphasized striking counterforce targets, usually *before* any cities might be attacked, was called a counterforce strategy.

This is complicated enough to be worth recapitulation. The possible targets on each side were now divided into two categories: countervalue targets (mainly cities) and counterforce targets (military targets, especially strategic targets such as bomber bases and missile sites). To each of the two categories of targets a mission was assigned: the assured destruction mission against countervalue targets and the damage limiting mission against counterforce targets. At any given time, either mission could be emphasized by assigning more forces to it, which would mean less for the other mission unless the total size of one's forces was increased. The strategy of making counterforce strikes while holding back the assured destruction forces was called a counterforce strategy, or sometimes, controlled response. In the early 1960s this was increasingly emphasized in Washington as American superiority grew.

Secretary McNamara first announced this strategy in a classified address to the NATO defense ministers, delivered at a meeting in Athens early in 1962. A "sanitized" version of the same address (i.e., a version with classified information removed) was given publicly in Ann Arbor, Michigan, in June. McNamara argued that an announced policy of refraining from striking countervalue targets early in a nuclear war, while retaining strong assured destruction forces in reserve to do so if necessary, should give the Soviets a powerful incentive not to attack U.S. cities either. The secretary held out an image of nuclear war in which both sides might practice "city avoidance" (or a "no cities" policy) and concentrate on counterforce strikes on each other's weapons. He indicated that changes were being made in U.S. war plans in the hope of making this kind of less destructive conflict possible, should World War III ever occur. (The master plan for U.S. operations in a general nuclear war is called the SIOP—pronounced "sigh-op"—for Single Integrated Operations Plan.) The damage limiting (counterforce) mission was to occupy a prominent place in the SIOP for some years, and indeed was never entirely removed from it.

By this time the distinction between assured destruction and damage limiting missions as alternative, and to a degree competing, strategies had been bruited about for several years by national security analysts. Advancing technology was opening up more and more complicated strategic possibilities, requiring further theorization. Perhaps the ultimate in doctrinal elaboration appeared in a book by Herman Kahn, *On Thermonuclear War*, which gained Kahn fame and notoriety for awhile. Depending upon the assumptions one employed about the nuclear forces on each side, and how they were changing over time, almost any number of conceptual variations regarding nuclear war could be developed, as Kahn showed in that and succeeding books. However, the most lasting conceptual contributions of this period remained the basic distinctions between the assured destruction and damage limiting missions, and between offensive damage limiting (counterforce) and defensive damage limiting.

Some specialists were to question the counterforce strategy on the moral grounds that it seemed to imply that the United States would have to be the one to begin an atomic war. But this was not necessarily the case. American war plans at this time supposed that a sudden Soviet strike—the classic "bolt from the blue"—was highly unlikely because the Kremlin knew the U.S. assured destruction capability was secure. If nuclear war came, it would come through the escalation of a war in Europe (or perhaps elsewhere around the Soviet periphery). Although no one could have a clear idea in advance about how an escalation "scenario" might develop, it seemed most likely that nuclear weapons would be used tactically in the local theater first. If the arena in which nuclear weapons were being used then widened, it would probably extend into the USSR itself. At this point there might well be opportunities for the United States to make counterforce strikes on vulnerable Soviet missile forces, strikes that might not represent a great extension of what would already be occurring.

This was a frightening, bizarre, and extremely unpredictable image of how World War III might progress, but something like this seemed among the least unlikely possibilities. A counterforce strategy against the Soviet homeland under these circumstances would not mean "beginning a nuclear war." It would already be nuclear. Many specialists did not think it immoral to disarm partially an enemy who was already using nuclear weapons and who presumably had begun the war, and thereby reduce the devastation the war would cause. During the era in the 1960s when the U.S. enjoyed strategic superiority, counterforce remained a major component in the SIOP.

THE CUBAN MISSILE CRISIS

However, a strategy to partially disarm the opponent was a strategy in some conflict with the concept (discussed in the previous chapter) of *each side* enjoying secure, second-strike forces. The conflict was not complete since even the most optimistic counterforce advocates did not believe that the Soviet second-strike capability could be entirely removed, and they expected a large Soviet missile buildup soon. Nonetheless, the more effective the counterforce effort might be in the meanwhile, the more the Soviets might find, or at any rate feel, the security of their deterrent to be threatened.

Something like this may have been part of the motive for the most risky gamble either side has taken since the East-West conflict began—the clandestine deployment of Soviet missiles into Cuba in 1962. The Cuban regime had been a Soviet ally ever since Fidel Castro had seized power in 1959, and the Kremlin leaders now determined on the bold step of trying to smuggle missiles onto the island and bring them to operational readiness before the United States knew they were there. Having repeatedly given assurances that offensive forces would not be introduced into Cuba—and continuing these assurances while in the very act of doing so—the Soviets started shipping scores of missiles and their nuclear warheads starting in the late summer. These were intermediate- and medium-range missiles (specifically, with ranges up to 2200 and 1100 miles respectively) of types that the Soviets could manufacture and deploy in quantity, as they were already doing in Europe.

The Kremlin leaders probably hoped that nothing worse than another cold war diplomatic crisis would ensue when Washington discovered the deception, preferably after the missiles were fully installed. But they must have recognized the possibility of an intense military crisis something like the one that did occur, and chose to accept the risk. A successful missile deployment in Cuba would have gone far toward reversing what otherwise must have seemed a slipping, perhaps even dangerous, world position. Their four-year campaign to further their political ends by claiming strategic superiority had been called as a bluff—and worse, had generated a strong American reaction that was creating a real missile gap in reverse. (See Table 1 page 109 for the strategic balance in October 1962.) An intense effort to dislodge the West from Berlin the previous year had failed, and they probably knew (as the West did not) that their ICBM forces at home would not be greatly enlarged for years yet. Washington had also revealed that it knew the location of missile sites in the USSR precisely enough to target them, and was actively implementing a counterforce strategy designed to do exactly that. The situation may have seemed quite threatening to Khrushchev and his advisers. Successfully deploying missiles into Cuba would have been at a minimum a political and propaganda coup, a deterrent to what was now a preponderant West, and an opportunity to reverse the unfavorable trend in the cold war and redress the general balance of power.

Probably we will never know the exact mixture of the Soviet leaders' motives. In any event they chose to gamble on a clandestine Cuban deployment, and their hope that the first missiles might be in place before the United States discovered them was almost realized. American reconnaissance of the island (again by U-2 aircraft) was hampered by bad weather and other factors, and U.S. intelligence was not sure the missiles were there until early October, when the first of them were close to operational readiness.

The crisis that ensued brought the world—analysts and historians agree—closer to World War III than it has been anytime before or since. President Kennedy threw a naval blockade around the island to halt all missiles still on their way, and insisted that those already there be dismantled and removed at once. He reacted so sharply because he and his advisers believed that a sudden shift in the world balance of power would be dangerous both to peace and to the West. If the Soviets were allowed to strengthen their hand so greatly through such an aggressive act, other aggression could be expected to follow soon. There might also have been a damaging shift in Soviet, allied, and neutral perceptions of American resolve. Furthermore, Cuba is very close to the United States. Missiles launched from there would strike their targets in the United States with very little warning time. In other ways too, if Cuba were allowed to become a Soviet armory the military threat could soon become severe. If action were to be taken it would have to be immediately, because once the first missiles were operational, any attack on them or on the many that would follow might provoke their immediate launch.

Had Kennedy's demand not been met, his next step would have been strikes by U.S. Air Force tactical aircraft against the missile sites before they could be finished. However, the sites were being constructed not by Cubans but by Russians, some of whom would be killed. The reaction in Moscow might be drastic. Options for a retaliatory Soviet move against Berlin, or a strike against some vulnerable American missiles located overseas not far from Soviet territory, or simply a militant defiance of the blockade, were anxiously studied in Washington over the succeeding days. There were several paths by which the crisis could have escalated, perhaps rapidly, to outright fighting and perhaps even to a general war. But Soviet ships en route to Cuba did respect the blockade, and after some negotiation Khrushchev backed down and agreed that the missiles already in Cuba would be removed. Thirteen days after the crisis erupted it was over. Kennedy is said to have remarked that during part of the time he personally thought that the odds of a nuclear war were one in three.

This is not the place for an analysis of the Cuban Missile Crisis, on which there is now a large literature. But it is worth remarking that its occurrence at a time of Western military superiority may have had much to do with its resolution, as well perhaps as with Soviet motives for risking it in the first place. The United States did discover the missiles before they were ready to launch, which meant that the highly favorable world balance of forces had not yet changed. If escalation toward a general war had ensued the Soviets might have been in a difficult military position. America also had almost absolute supremacy in the local theater. Because Cuba is so close to the United States the naval blockade could be made very tight, and air strikes, plus other options if necessary, could have been carried out without doubt as to the outcome. The possession of both complete local and considerable global advantage played a large, perhaps crucial, role in the United States' success in securing its demands. Another intense crisis, occurring elsewhere under today's less advantageous conditions, might not permit a similar Western victory.

A DEFENSE AGAINST MISSILES?

Although the Soviets' effort in Cuba to leapfrog their way cheaply into the strategic lead was turned back, American specialists knew that it would certainly be only a matter of time before Soviet nuclear striking power would increase in the ordinary way: through building up a force of ICBMs and, no doubt, SLBMs. How much time might be uncertain, but that it would occur was not, and the destruction those forces could inflict would be greater than anything America had ever faced. Only under certain circumstances might it be reduced somewhat by way of the counterforce strategy, and then only with great uncertainties in the midst of a highly destructive nuclear conflict. In no case could this offensive form of damage limiting eliminate the Soviet ICBM or bomber threat entirely, nor the coming SLBM threat much at all. Could damage limiting by *defensive* means help make the American people more secure?

In this period the U.S. air defense system was brought to the highest level of capability it has ever reached, before or since. Analysts expected that against a Soviet bomber threat that was not increasing much in quantity or quality, it might prove fairly effective, if it were not badly damaged by Soviet missile strikes arriving first. The more serious threat would be the missiles. Might there be some method for supplementing the air defenses with a missile defense?

The U.S. Army, which shared responsibility with the air force for defending the fifty states against attack from the sky, believed that there was. Since the mid-1950s the army had been experimenting with ways to extend its successful Nike series of antiaircraft missiles into a capability for shooting down incoming missiles (or to be exact, their warheads, known technically as "reentry vehicles"; the main body of the missile does not fly the whole distance). By the early 1960s the army was testing prototypes of a new Nike, the Nike-Zeus, for this mission. But Secretary McNamara's analysts concluded that the Nike-Zeus system would be expensive, and not effective enough against the large number of missiles the USSR was expected to have before long. To use a term that was now coming into vogue, the system would not be "cost effective." Nike-Zeus was never deployed.

The army was already moving on to the next generation of technology for AntiBallistic Missiles, or ABMs. By the middle of the decade it was proposing the deployment of a new ABM system called Nike-X, and this one was more attractive. Nike-X consisted of radars more advanced than anything that had existed before, a new generation of computers, and not one, but two new missiles: a large one called Spartan and a smaller but extremely fast one called Sprint. The concept of Nike-X was that Spartans would be fired early, soon after incoming Soviet reentry vehicles were first spotted and before they entered the earth's atmosphere. Many would be destroyed; those that escaped would be allowed to fall into the atmosphere and then intercepted, more or less at the last minute, by Sprints. The atmosphere itself would help to identify decoys, which the Soviets might include along with the real warheads; decoys behave differently in atmospheric flight and hence could be spotted by the radars and computers.

The system looked so effective that for some years in the middle 1960s analysts debated whether its high cost might be worth it. The ABM question, and Nike-X in particular, was one of the main subjects of discussion among national security specialists during those years. But McNamara and his staff concluded that deploying Nike-X on a large scale, to try to provide a roof for the whole nation, would be too expensive. Depending on just how big a system was built, it would cost from forty to a hundred billion dollars (in 1983 dollars), and even in the largest size could not promise anything close to a leakproof defense.

For years Secretary McNamara fought a battle within the government to prevent a large ABM system from being deployed, while much of the uniformed military, led by the Joint Chiefs of Staff, pressed President Johnson to "defend the country" against the Soviet missile threat. Repeatedly, and in the end successfully, McNamara argued that it would always be cheaper for the Soviets to build more missiles, and better decoy devices, than it would be for the United States to beef up the ABM system further to counter them. A competition could begin in which the USSR could add more and more to its missile forces and the United States more and more to its ABM system. At each stage in the race the new increment of threat would be cheaper for the USSR than the extra ABM defense would be for the United States. Down that road lay bankruptcy.

A smaller version of the ·system might be another matter, however. Nuclear war scenarios could be conceived in which the Soviets might fire only a few missiles. There was also the unlikely but perhaps not impossible case where a single crazed Soviet commander might fire the handful of missiles under his command without authorization. More important than these contingencies was the fact that the Chinese were now beginning to test long-range missiles, though they probably would not have a large number of them for many years. A small and not too expensive ABM system for the United States that could deal with these kinds of limited attacks might be worth having, whereas a huge ABM system that tried to cope with everything the Soviets could do was not. In July 1967 the Johnson administration announced that it had decided to deploy this kind of small system. Based on the Nike-X technology, it would be called by another name, Sentinel, to distinguish it from the full-scale ABM deployment that many voices were calling for, but which McNamara insisted was imprudent.

However, this was the time of the Vietnam War and of the antiwar movement it inspired. The Johnson administration, feeling pressures from its right to give the country some kind of missile defense, did not fully anticipate the reaction that its announcement would inspire on its left. Although the immediate outcry was not great, pressure on Congress to postpone or cancel Sentinel built up, especially after citizen groups discovered that missiles and radars for the system would have to be located in populated areas of the country. Nobody wanted Sentinels next door, and sentiment in "the great ABM debate" turned more and more against the system.

When the Nixon administration entered office in 1968, it scuttled Sentinel and came up with another ABM system, using most of the same technology in another way. Its system, called Safeguard, would be designed, not to provide a "thin" defense of the whole country against small attacks, but a "thick" defense against even large attacks on a limited part of the country—the areas where American ICBMs were deployed. The Soviet Union was now expanding its offensive missile forces rapidly, and many analysts were beginning to predict a time, not far off, when the USSR might be able to attack American ICBM silos with a large number of warheads. The Nixon administration believed that the Safeguard system could shoot down a high percentage of these, thereby protecting the ICBMs. The administration also expected public objection to locating ABMs in populated areas to become irrelevant; Safeguard would be positioned near the missiles it protected, which were already located in the least populous parts of the country. (If this "point defense" system for a few selected points proved successful, the administration planned to enlarge Safeguard later into a thin "area defense" of the whole nation, like Sentinel.)

But the public ABM debate did not die down. Critics of the Pentagon and of high defense spending, having succeeded in defeating Sentinel, were not about to accept Safeguard easily. They kept up a drumfire of criticism, questioning its expense, its real effectiveness, and the possibility that the Soviet threat to the ICBM silos was being exaggerated. Aided by the antiwar, antimilitary mood that was cresting at that time in American politics, they succeeded in delaying Safeguard in Congress for a while, and in halting its area defense version entirely.

By the end of the 1960s the whole question of ABM systems was becoming deeply involved in the negotiations that had begun between Washington and Moscow to limit both sides' strategic forces. As a separate issue, the public ABM debate faded. (The SALT negotiations are discussed in a later chapter.) The Nixon administration continued to fund the development of the point-defense verison of Safeguard for several years, partly to strengthen the American bargaining position in those negotiations. But the system was never actually completed, and the final SALT I treaty included a tight limitation on any future ABMs. In the years since, both superpowers have continued research on very advanced technologies—such as energy beams—that might someday be turned into a different kind of missile defense.

THE SECOND ERA OF U.S. SUPERIORITY PASSES

In the latter half of the 1960s the long-awaited buildup of Soviet missile forces finally arrived, and when it did, it developed rapidly. Technical problems were now solved, hardened underground silos were built, and for several years Soviet missile production exceeded even the "worst case" predictions offered by U.S. intelligence. In a little over a year, from the end of 1964 to 1966, the number of Soviet

ICBMs deployed jumped from about 200 to 340, and the following year it doubled, to 730. By late 1968 the Soviet ICBM force was reaching parity with the U.S. total of slightly over a thousand. That same year Moscow began to deploy SLBMs in submarines somewhat comparable to the Polaris. Table 2 indicates American and Soviet strategic force totals at the end of the decade.

The rapidity of this buildup may have been inspired partly by the Soviets having been "humiliated," as they later said they experienced it, in the Cuban Missile Crisis. They believed that their humiliation had been made possible by American strategic superiority and were determined, as they were to reiterate many times, to ensure that it did not happen again. In addition Khrushchev, who had tried to limit military spending in favor of developing the Soviet economy, departed as party chairman late in 1964. His successor, Leonid Brezhnev, favored larger defense budgets and a more rapid attainment of military equality, at least, with the United States.

As the Soviet threat grew, the Johnson administration backed off from its previous interest in damage limiting strategies and gave increasing emphasis to the assured destruction mission. Although counterforce was not entirely abandoned, it could promise less and less as Soviet forces (especially SLBMs) developed. The administration reoriented its attention toward ensuring that a sizable second-strike force would always remain secure, and as certain to fulfill its mission as human design could make it, no matter how large the Soviet forces might grow and under the worst conceivable wartime circumstances.

Table 2. American and Soviet strategic forces at the end of 1969

	Soviet Union	*United States*
ICBMs	1,200	1,054 (1,000 Minutemen and 54 Titans)
SLBMs	230	656 (41 Polaris submarines each carrying 16 missiles)
Long-range bombers	150 Bears and Bisons	540

Note: At this time the Soviet totals of both ICBMs and SLBMs were rising rapidly. American totals were constant, although substantial qualitative improvements were being made in the American missile forces.

Source: Institute of Strategic Studies, London: Strategic Survey, 1969.

Now Washington gradually accepted the principle that meaningful and lasting superiority in strategic weapons was probably no longer attainable, and that the better course would be to ensure that no inferiority could develop again, as at times in the past it had seemed to. A rough parity would suffice, and might remain stable.

For some twenty years the United States had shifted back and forth between sudden fears for its security and almost equally sudden discoveries of unexpected superiority. Twice the United States had gone through a complete cycle: first from atomic monopoly through the anxieties of NSC-68 to the superiority of the early 1950s; and again from Massive Retaliation through the missile gap fears to the superiority of the early 1960s and counterforce. As the second era of superiority passed, analysts and policy makers preferred to avoid both the trough and peak of a new cycle, and to focus on stability instead.

Toward the close of his long and controversial tenure as secretary of defense, Robert McNamara stressed repeatedly the need to maintain deterrent stability. America's assured destruction capability against the Soviets was secure and could be kept secure indefinitely; so could the Soviet assured destruction capability against the United States. It would become increasingly expensive and futile for the United States to strive for continuing superiority against an opponent who clearly was willing, and now was able, to match U.S. forces. An era of unchallengeable mutual deterrence had arrived, the secretary argued. Mutual Assured Destruction (MAD) would become the common policy (and soon the acronym MAD passed into the language). The two superpowers, to save money and relieve tensions, should leave their forces in that posture and explore ways to limit the growth of their armories, and if possible reduce them.

When the Nixon administration entered office it too accepted the desirability, or at any rate the necessity, of permanent parity with the Soviet Union in strategic forces. The principle of "sufficiency" would guide its defense decisions, it announced. In practice this meant that the security of the assured destruction forces would be maintained carefully, and U.S. strategic power would not be allowed to become inferior to the Soviet, numerically or in other ways. But no major strategic advantage would be sought. (One exception to this will be discussed later.)

The principles of "Mutual Assured Destruction" (MAD) and of accepting strategic parity rose rapidly to prominence in the U.S. national security literature in the second half of the 1960s; and for a period of some years, it appeared that debate over strategic doctrine was largely a thing of the past. Later some of the ideas of the 1960s would be revived, but for a while, stability in the balance of the superpowers' forces was accompanied by stability in doctrine.

The strategic side of American national security, on which the last several chapters have focused, thus changed character in the late 1960s. The preceding years had witnessed an enormous burst of theoretical creativity. This period has been discussed in some depth in this book because so many basic ideas were developed then. Nothing so conceptually fundamental has happened since.

The shift from bombers to missiles as the basic offensive technology, and the differences East and West in when and how this shift occurred, had called forth a wave of ideas about strategic deterrence under differing conditions, and about how nuclear wars might be fought between superpowers with somewhat disparate forces. But late in the decade the two sides' strategic armories came more to resemble each other, both in character and in size. The concepts were now well in hand to describe a situation of stable parity and to analyze how to maintain it; new conceptual advances were not needed. In the following years the armories grew greatly in power, but another, comparable shift in basic offensive technology did not occur; a new wave of strategic thinking was not demanded.

By the end of the 1960s some of the national security theorists who had played prominent roles during the era of conceptual flowering (for instance, Herman Kahn and Thomas Schelling) partially or entirely left the field to work on other kinds of problems. The strategic questions that now arose were usually not interesting to theorists, for issues of doctrine were usually not at stake. Many analysts shifted their focus to arms control, a topic that had been growing in importance for years and now was moving to center stage. To this story the two following chapters are devoted.

SUMMARY

The early and mid-1960s represented the culmination of the fresh wave of strategic analysis that had first appeared a few years earlier. A burst of conceptual inventiveness that had begun with the first-strike/second-strike distinction, the vulnerability concern, and Flexible Response, carried on to develop a variety of new ideas.

If the Soviets had deployed ICBMs on anything like the schedule that was expected early in the decade, there might have been less of this continuing inventiveness. The already well-established principle of secure second-strike forces would probably have evolved quickly into the ideas of Mutual Assured Destruction and sufficiency. But the Soviets did not, and these ideas and the plateau of stability they represented were reached only a few years later.

Instead the period of conceptual creativity continued as national security specialists explored the possibilities in strategic superiority. The Kennedy administration's large deployment of the U.S. second-generation missiles, Minuteman and Polaris, created for a few years a marked U.S. strategic advantage. Improvements suggested by Flexible Response in the conventional forces also enhanced the U.S. position. Undoubtedly the overall global advantage as well as complete local supremacy contributed greatly to the successful resolution of the Cuban Missile Crisis.

Many of the analysts who had developed Flexible Response now became interested in extending its approach into the field of nuclear warfare and finding multiple options there as well. While a portion of U.S. strategic forces would always remain committed to the assured destruction mission, American superiority was making it possible to attempt damage limiting missions with the remaining forces. For a while it appeared that a strategy of counterforce (controlled response) could reduce the destructiveness of a nuclear war; deliberately holding back assured destruction strikes on Soviet cities might encourage the Soviets to do the same and make possible a "no cities" war. Additional damage limiting by defensive means—improved air defense and possibly antiballistic missiles (ABMs)—also seemed attractive for a while.

The fast-paced Soviet missile buildup that began about the middle of the decade caused the Johnson administration to reverse priorities. Damage limiting objectives were not removed from the SIOP altogether but Secretary McNamara began arguing that the era of Mutual Assured Destruction (MAD) was rapidly arriving, and that neither a continuing effort to retain superiority in offensive forces nor deployment of an extensive ABM system would be cost effective. First one, then another small ABM system was approved by Washington, but public resistance halted the first and limited the second to a token deployment. By the end of the decade the USSR was rapidly reaching strategic parity, and the Nixon administration had opted for a policy of merely maintaining a "sufficiency" of U.S. strategic forces.

Strategic parity now became a lasting feature of the superpower balance. Concepts for analyzing and maintaining this balance were already well in hand; the theoretical inventiveness that had been demanded by the earlier surges of strategic advantage back and forth was no longer needed. The great era of creativity in strategic studies now came to an end. By the end of the decade the specialists' primary attention was turning to other aspects of American national security, especially the fast-developing area of arms control.

FOR FURTHER READING

Abel, Ellie. *The Missile Crisis.* Philadelphia: Lippincott, 1966. Perhaps the best-known introduction to the Cuban Missile Crisis written for the popular audience.

Allison, Graham T. *Essence of Decision.* Boston: Little, Brown & Co., 1971. An extremely influential analysis of the Cuban Missile Crisis, and presentation of three major "models" by which governmental decisions may be explained.

George, Alexander L., and Richard Smoke. *Deterrence in American Foreign Policy: Theory and Practice.* New York: Columbia University Press, 1974. Chapter Fifteen presents an analysis of the Cuban Missile Crisis; the ten preceding chapters are analyses of most of the other major cold war crises.

Kahn, Herman. *On Thermonuclear War.* Princeton: Princeton University Press, 1961. An encyclopedic elaboration of the many conceptual and policy possibilities that arose in the 1960s as missile technology evolved.

Kaufmann, William W. *The McNamara Strategy.* New York: Harper and Row, 1964. A detailed, quite readable account of the defense policies of the Kennedy administration by one who, as an important consultant to Secretary McNamara, had influence in their formulation.

Kennedy, Robert S. *Thirteen Days.* New York: Norton, 1969. A moving account of the Cuban Missile Crisis, written by the president's brother and cabinet member, who shared responsibility for its resolution.

Levine, Robert. *The Arms Debate.* Cambridge, Mass.: Harvard University Press, 1963. A lucid description and assessment of the various schools of strategic thought that flourished in the period from the mid-1950s to the mid-1960s.

8

Security Through Arms Control

If one nation (or group, or organization, or person) feels hostile toward another, there are in the abstract two fundamental ways for the threatened party to find security. One is for it to become, and to remain, at least as able as its opponent to use force, and hence able to defend itself or make threats in return. The other is for *neither* party to have forcible means available, and hence for neither to be able to convert hostile feelings into a real threat. The first way offers some security but leaves open the possibility of a competition for power, and also the possibility that one side or the other sometime will use the force available to it. The second way offers more true security *if* both parties can be really confident that neither can use force. Then one

127

side's hostile feelings for the other may create regret in the other, but not fear or insecurity.

In the real world of nations as in the abstract, security may be sought by either of these two approaches. The conventional approach, which is the first (and often the only) one that most people think of when they think of national security, is for a nation to increase its military power. The other approach is for all nations to decrease their military power. A high degree of security for all could be achieved if everyone's power were reliably reduced to low levels through disarmament. Security might also be improved for all if everyone's power were reduced somewhat—partial disarmament—or if nations were to forego increases in power they would otherwise seek. These last two possibilities are now called "arms control."

This second approach to national security is so different from the conventional one that some specialists (and some of the public) do not regard it as part of "national security affairs" at all, but as a different topic entirely. The majority of specialists, though, would probably agree with the viewpoint being suggested here—that security simply means security, and depending on circumstances either approach may be a valid means to the goal of real national security. Arms control and disarmament are potentially just as much part of achieving security for a nation as arms buildups.

Indeed, an unarmed or largely unarmed world would be a far more secure place than the quite dangerous one in which we actually live. Since many Americans think of this as a visionary ideal—a dream of a distant, Utopian future—rather than an image of national security, it bears repeating: *The national security of the United States* would be incomparably greater in a world in which *no nation*, including the United States, possessed significant military power. (Here "significant" simply means that any country will always want to retain enough police and national guard forces to deal with crime and internal disturbances.) Quite apart from other advantages in living in such a world, the American people would be more secure than they have been any time in the recent past—including times when the United States enjoyed strategic superiority—or than they would be in any future world of armed powers and superpowers.

This greater form of security would only be realized, however, if the United States, and every nation, was quite sure that every other nation really was unarmed; and this would require a degree of mutual cooperation among nations that so far has seemed completely unattainable. Conceivably this cooperation might take the form of creating some supranational entity, like a strengthened United Nations organization, which would police every country's military potential for the benefit of all. Or perhaps it might simply take the form of some kind of mutual inspection scheme among the nations themselves. All variations on these ideas would require in one fashion or another more joint action among countries for their common security than they have yet been able even to attempt. In a world in which many countries, not limited to the Communist ones, are widely believed to be (and may well be) interested not only in security but also in aggrandizement, it is especially hard to see how this kind of attempt could succeed. It is partly for this reason that the goal of an unarmed world has seemed so idealistic.

In the absence of the necessary cooperation, the United States, like other countries, has largely fallen back on the conventional approach of pursuing national security unilaterally. Or to be more exact, the United States in the years since World War II has pursued security unilaterally, while *also* making increasing attempts to mitigate the costs and dangers involved by pursuing arms control efforts. The United States has also proposed from time to time partial and even complete disarmament. How this approach of trying to decrease arms has gradually been added to the overall U.S. effort to improve its security is the subject to which we now turn.

EARLY HISTORY

Less than a year after Hiroshima and Nagasaki, the United States proposed a plan whereby the United Nations would assume control of all atomic energy and the United States would destroy its stockpile of atomic bombs. Bernard Baruch publicly unveiled the plan that subsequently carried his name in an address to a UN commission in June 1946. The previous winter the United States, Canada, and Great Britain had agreed that atomic energy would be transferred to United Nations control; a high-level U.S. State Department committee and a consultative group, headed respectively by Dean Acheson and David Lilienthal, had been created to find a way to do it.

As described in an earlier chapter this was the period in which America and its allies hoped and expected that the United Nations would become the protector of the world's collective security. It was not surprising, therefore, that the three powers that had shared (to a degree) in the development of atomic energy decided to turn over its control to the United Nations. It was not even particularly surprising that the Acheson-Lilienthal Report concluded that the U.S. atomic stockpile could be safely destroyed once the strict plan the report proposed for UN control had been implemented, although both at the time and afterwards this feature was advertised by Washington as highly generous. Sanctions by which the plan could be enforced were omitted from the Acheson-Lilienthal Report but added by Baruch himself before the plan was submitted to the United Nations.

Under the Baruch Plan, an international authority associated with the UN would have exclusive ownership and management of all atomic materials everywhere in the world, from initial mining of ores through research, manufacturing, and building of installations such as power generators. The only exception would be research for peaceful purposes, which individual countries could carry out under the authority's licensing and inspection. Other inspectors would watch all over the world for illicit activities involving atomic energy, and the authority would have the power to impose penalties on any violators without the Great Power veto that could immobilize the Security Council. This was a remarkably radical scheme, even for that brief period when American hopes for peace and collective security were pinned so completely on the UN; it amounted almost to a limited form of world government for atomic energy matters.

The Baruch Plan was so far reaching, indeed, that some scholars and observers have wondered if the Truman administration anticipated from the outset that it would not be accepted by the USSR or other countries, and perhaps even preferred that outcome. Its seeming generosity was also much reduced by the fact that the plan would have had the indirect effect of preserving forever the American monopoly on atomic bomb technology. Knowledge of that technology, once held by the United States, could not be eliminated or forgotten and the authority would prevent any other country from conducting the research that could reproduce it. Although the United States would not retain any actual weapons, if the system broke down it could build new ones quickly and no one else would be able to.

For these and other reasons the Baruch Plan was soon pronounced unacceptable by the USSR. The following year the Soviets offered a counterproposal involving inspection only of predesignated atomic facilities, and leaving enforcement to the UN Security Council, where Moscow enjoyed a veto. This obviously would open the door to clandestine development of weapons by the Soviet Union, and under these circumstances Washington was not about to give up its nuclear arsenal. An impasse had been reached. Although both plans remained on the table for some time, serious discussion of controlling atomic weapons now waned (along with belief in collective security generally) while international tensions waxed into cold war.

In 1949 the Soviets exploded their first atomic bomb. Truman responded by ordering the development of the hydrogen bomb. Throughout the Korean War and for several years thereafter, there was little effort by either superpower to rein in this new technological competition. Both sides, having seen their original disarmament plans rebuffed, were inclined to turn their attention in the other direction and explore what the powerful, rapidly evolving strategic technology of the day could offer toward security. In 1952 the United Nations consolidated several negotiating bodies into a single Disarmament Commission, and later tried to encourage more meaningful discussions by creating a smaller subcommittee of just the powers that were involved with atomic energy, but various proposals and counterproposals aired in these and other forums were not (and probably were not expected to be) taken very seriously.

A partial exception was President Eisenhower's "Atoms for Peace" proposal, offered in a speech to the UN General Assembly in 1953. He suggested that the nuclear powers transfer some fissionable materials to an international organization that would supervise their use by various countries "for peaceful purposes" such as research, power generating, etc. This was initially rejected by the Soviet Union, even though it was not really a disarmament proposal. But in a modified form the idea later bore fruit in the International Atomic Energy Agency, which has played an important role both in promoting nuclear development and in helping to maintain controls on the spread of nuclear materials around the world.

It is not much of an exaggeration to suggest that from the onset of the cold war until the mid-1950s the nuclear powers produced disarmament schemes primarily for propaganda and diplomatic purposes, and only secondarily, at best, from a real desire to find ways of reducing arms. Quite early it became clear that the Soviets would always resist Western proposals that included inspection of military and weapons-production sites within the USSR; they regarded inspection as a potential method for spying. The United States and its allies sometimes focused less on trying to find imaginative ways around this problem than on picturing the Soviets to world public opinion as intransigent. There was also a more genuine dilemma: the West, to ensure that the USSR's closed society would not hide cheating, had to emphasize verification in some form; while the Soviets, fearful of SAC's growing bomber fleet, felt that maintaining secrecy about the location of many of their military sites made a knockout blow by SAC less feasible.

Meanwhile Moscow saw disarmament negotiations as an arena for driving wedges between the United States and its allies. Britain developed atomic weapons in the 1950s and France was not far behind; and there were some differences in viewpoint among the three Western powers about disarmament issues that the Soviets tried to exploit. Moscow also tried over the years to reap full propaganda benefit from American refusal to state that the United States would never be the first to use atomic weapons in a new war. A "no first use declaration" was something that the USSR, inferior in nuclear weapons but superior in number of troops deployed, found easy to offer; the United States was in the opposite position and felt it could not. Finally, from time to time both sides produced complicated schemes, often involving conventional as well as nuclear force reductions, that predictably would be hard to be implemented, or even negotiated. On the whole they probably were not intended to be.

By the mid-1950s the superpowers began turning their attention back toward exploring disarmament seriously. The rapidly evolving strategic technology was not offering more security but less, as hydrogen bombs and long-range bombers multiplied on both sides, and trying to find an alternative to the arms race was becoming more attractive. In 1955 Eisenhower appointed a special assistant to the president for disarmament and offered an "Open Skies" proposal whereby aerial reconnaissance would be substituted for on-the-ground inspection. The next year the United States also suggested a mutual cutoff in producing fissionable material. For their part the Soviets, in May 1955, produced a disarmament plan which, for the first time, came a considerable distance toward the Western viewpoint and seemed to be a geniune attempt to propose terms that might be negotiable. For about two years around mid-decade it seemed that there might be real opportunities for finding agreement on some form of disarmament. By 1957 some of the bargaining was being pursued energetically and privately, out of the propaganda limelight.

But the differences among the four powers proved too great. No agreement could be reached, and then changing technology brought the opportunity to an end, and the moment was lost. The Soviets rejected both the Open Skies proposal and the fissionable material cutoff, except as possible elements in a larger plan for abolition of atomic weapons. The United States was moving in the opposite direction. Though earlier it too had proposed, at least formally, various plans in which all atomic weapons would be scrapped, Washington was now coming to think such plans unrealistic. By this time so much fissionable material had been produced that all of it could never be tracked down and accounted for. Any nuclear nation could hide away enough for a few bombs and then, when everyone else had disarmed, build the bombs quickly and be supreme. Even something as far-reaching as the Baruch Plan might not prevent this now.

Other ideas were tried. For instance, the Soviets were interested in a ban on atomic test explosions, but France, which wanted to be able to conduct its own tests, was not. A "Rapacki Plan," named for the Polish diplomat who championed it, called for both sides to pull back military forces from central Europe, where they faced each other. Several variations on this concept were explored, but they all raised complications for the internal relations within the two alliance systems, and were abandoned. Combining these and various other ideas into new packages was also discussed to little avail.

Even so the atmosphere seemed sufficiently promising to warrant further attempts. In May 1957 the United States produced a memorandum outlining an overall bargaining position close enough to Soviet views that productive negotiations might have followed. But a diplomatic error caused it to be shown to Soviet diplomats the same day it was first revealed to the British and French. The allies were indignant, the memorandum was withdrawn, and a less forthcoming one written later with allied agreement. Moscow seized on this to accuse the West of retreating from real interest in disarmament and refused to continue the current series of negotiations.

Actually it was Soviet attitudes that were changing. The USSR was now testing ICBMs and starting its campaign of claiming strategic superiority. Previously Moscow had accepted a degree of disadvantage by negotiating alone with three Western powers, but now it announced that henceforward it would negotiate with the West only on a basis of parity—one-to-one with the United States or with allies from both sides represented. This meant that the diplomatic process had to begin over again almost from the beginning.

The new missile technology was also creating a new and less favorable context for disarmament. For example, American proposals for schemes to make surprise attack impossible had presupposed that attacks would be made by bombers, and were now rendered irrelevant. And as the decade advanced, attention in Washington shifted more and more to the "missile gap"; until this could be closed there would be little serious pursuit of disarmament. The post of special assistant to the president for disarmament was abolished late in 1957.

In fact disarmament, as opposed to arms control, was now a dying topic, at least so far as the real agendas of the superpowers were concerned. Although Premier Krushchev proposed a plan for "general and complete disarmament" in 1959 and President Kennedy also proposed one in 1961, probably neither leader expected his proposal to be negotiated seriously. Plans for extensive disarmament had been floated for a decade and had proved implausible even in a simpler military environment; they seemed even more so in a technological context that was changing rapidly and becoming more complicated. It was also acknowledged universally by now that some bombs could be hidden beyond the ability of any verification scheme, however strict, to forestall or uncover. No far-reaching disarmament plans have been brought forward by the superpowers in the years since.

ARMS CONTROL COMES OF AGE

Ironically, it was also during the late 1950s that public pressure for disarmament mounted. Large numbers of people awoke to what specialists already knew: the superpowers now had enough nuclear weapons to devastate each other's homelands wholesale. A disarmament movement arose, similar in some ways to that of the early 1980s, though smaller.

For more than a decade the United States had been spending large sums of money on strategic weapons and had developed an enormous arsenal, yet at the end of this time America and its allies were much *less* secure than they had been at the beginning, because the Soviets had done the same thing. From this grim fact one could draw either of two general conclusions, the choice between them governed basically by one's view of the stability of the Soviet-American deterrent relationship. The same choice and logic apply equally in the 1980s.

One possibility was to conclude that something had to be done quickly to lessen the ever-growing danger that these arsenals posed. In the late 1950s, some intellectual and political elements in Britain and America, that had paid little attention to security questions previously, initiated a campaign to turn government policy in the direction of disarmament, even if this might pose other risks. Most extreme was a radical and noisy, but short-lived, "ban the bomb" movement, some of whose members accepted the slogan "better red than dead." More moderate opinion included belief in some less total form of unilateral disarmament by the West, and/or a desire for much greater Western concessions to obtain mutual disarmament with the Soviet Union.

Some scholars, scientists, and others who advocated this viewpoint educated themselves in national security affairs and became, at least for a while, an active and significant voice within the field. Some of the conceptual richness that was flowering in strategic studies around this time derived from the contributions of these advocates. One well-known concept they offered, for instance, was "minimum deterrence." Under this doctrine the United States would divest itself unilaterally of most of its strategic forces but retain, say, 200 secure missiles to deter the most' blatant forms of Soviet aggression, and negotiate further reductions thereafter. (Later the minimum deterrence school changed its name to "finite deterrence," thereby suggesting that other positions implied potentially infinite military demands.)

The thread running through this entire range of opinion, including its extremes, was an underlying conviction that the Soviet-American deterrent relationship could not remain stable forever. Sooner or later the arms race would lead to a nuclear Armageddon, just as arms races in the past had nearly always culminated in wars. Hence drastic steps should be taken if necessary to halt the strategic competition as soon as possible and—if nuclear weapons could not be abolished altogether—at least to reduce the two sides' forces to the point where, if deterrence did fail and war ensue, the destruction would not be complete.

The other general view of the deterrent relationship was that it could indeed remain stable, if not forever, at least for a long time during which much might change. This was the opinion of the majority of analysts in the late 1950s and has remained the mainstream view within the field since. The majority of national security specialists in America have always been more concerned with the adequacy of American efforts to deter Soviet attacks than with the long-term feasibility of deterrence per se.

Around the end of the 1950s the majority of specialists came to believe that when the vulnerable forces and "delicate balance of terror" of the time were replaced with secure, second-strike forces, the intense competition that had been fueling the arms race would moderate. They expected that, as each side came to feel more secure, the arms race could be reduced and controlled by degrees, and eventually the two sides' armories frozen. *After* the arms competition ended disarmament could begin, probably in gradual stages. In the meantime the emphasis should be placed on arms control rather than disarmament.

The development of this viewpoint coincided with the loss of official interest in extensive and complicated disarmament schemes. Both inside and outside the American and other Western governments, attention now shifted toward finding ways to slow down, channel, and eventually halt the arms competition. The choices that the United States made in its strategic weapons might be adjusted, so that not only defense needs but also possibilities for restraining the arms race might be enhanced. Through a mixture of wise American choices and new negotiations, Soviet weapons choices might also be influenced. A progressive arms control over the coming years would be far more effective in the long run than a fruitless search for grand disarmament plans.

This dominant viewpoint was developed in a burst of literature that began appearing about 1960. Many of the strategic specialists who, not long before, had been analyzing U.S. needs for more defense capabilities now began considering the need to control weapons. Investigating ways to mitigate the arms race brought a new dimension into national security analysis; one effect was to enlarge the scope of national security as a field. From this time on arms control was increasingly accepted as a vital goal by most of the community of national security analysts. Simultaneously some of the writers interested mainly in reducing arms began to acknowledge that the kind of analysis the strategists had developed could make a contribution toward stabilizing deterrence and the arms race.

Except for a minority of unilateral-disarmament advocates, a consensus gradually emerged over the following years that defense needs and arms control should be considered together in analyzing security issues. Naturally, individual analysts differed among themselves about the relative emphasis to be given one or the other, but defense and arms control considerations were increasingly assessed together in general analyses of American security problems.

The new wave of arms control literature in the 1960s produced a variety of ideas for restraining the arms race, a few of which bore fruit later in tangible Soviet-American agreements (mentioned below). Analysts started to examine, for instance, whether certain weapons that were now becoming possible, such as nuclear bombs placed into permanent orbit around the earth, might be forestalled. They also began to investigate whether some strategies and force structures might better lend themselves to control than others. For example, one of the arguments against the counterforce strategy and in favor of assured destruction only was that the latter strategy would be more conducive to U.S.-Soviet agreements to put a ceiling on strategic arms. "Force structure" means the quantities of various kinds of military forces and their overall configuration. A force structure that emphasized secure second-strike forces, for instance, would be conducive to arms control because it would discourage the opponent from deploying extra weapons in hope of gaining a first-strike capability.

The volume and sophistication of arms control thinking was also enhanced around this time by contributions from physical scientists. Some Western and Soviet scientists had begun meeting in 1957, and approximately annually thereafter, to explore arms control questions from their own perspective. Though not part of any governmental negotiation, these "Pugwash Conferences" (named after the first meeting site) before long were adding another useful impetus to arms control. Since both sets of scientists were in touch with their own governments, the conferences came to serve, to a degree, as an unofficial communications channel between East and West. And Pugwash provided a forum where new scientific possibilities (for instance, technical means for verifying that a clandestine explosion had occurred) could be explored and assessed free of diplomatic and other factors that affected official negotiations.

At the official level, too, arms control was now coming into its own. In 1961 President Kennedy created the Arms Control and Disarmament Agency, to provide a locus for the previously scattered study groups, offices, etc., involved with the topic. The State and Defense Departments and other agencies all had other goals as their primary missions. A separate agency that had arms control as its sole mission made possible a breadth and depth in the government's analysis, and in the development of negotiating positions, that had not been feasible previously. Furthermore, ACDA was not just an analytic office: though linked to the State Department it had the responsibility for negotiating with the Soviets on arms control. It was not long before it had some successes to show.

THE LIMITED TEST BAN TREATY

There is a melancholy tendency for the greatest advances toward the prevention of war to come only after a war or severe crisis has jolted people. The League of Nations was founded in the wake of World War I, the stronger United Nations only after a second global war.

The frightening Cuban Missile Crisis of 1962 had a similar effect.

Shortly after that crisis the American and Soviet governments agreed on the need for a new, high-speed form of communications between their capitals. Normal diplomatic channels were far too slow and formal for the nuclear missile age, and during the crisis Kennedy and Khrushchev had had to improvise awkward means for bargaining more freely and frankly—letters hand delivered by individuals, for instance. Something better was obviously needed, and the two governments established the "hot line" telecommunications link between Moscow and Washington.

Thanks to its appearance in films and other popular media, most people think of the hot line as a red telephone in the White House oval office, over which the president and the Soviet premier can talk in person. It is not. It is a teletype, because written communication was felt to offer less chance for misunderstandings, and it is housed in the Pentagon and in the Situation Room in the White House basement. The link is kept ready at all times, and on a handful of occasions since it was installed it has been used for real messages between the governments (e.g., during the 1973 Middle East war). Fortunately it has never yet had to be used in the situation for which it was designed—the kind of intense, fast-moving, very dangerous crisis in which the ability of heads of government to communicate quickly and candidly with each other might be crucial in finding a peaceful resolution.

A less direct but still more important byproduct of the Cuban Missile Crisis was the first treaty to come out of the long-standing East-West negotiations aimed at reducing arms. In August 1963 a Limited Test Ban Treaty was signed, outlawing nuclear explosions in the atmosphere, under water, or in outer space. (Continued underground atomic testing was permitted.)

Bargaining over some kind of ban or limit on testing atomic weapons went back to the mid-1950s, when this feature had sometimes been included as one element in larger proposals. Considerable pressure developed then, from both unaligned countries and the public in Western nations, for the superpowers to cease testing their bombs in the open air. Strontium 90 and other radioactive material was being spread throughout the world's atmosphere by these tests, and the fallout level was gradually rising all around the planet. No one knew just what the consequences might be for genetic defects, cancer, and other maladies but many scientists thought they might be ominous if radiation levels were not reduced.

In 1958 the USSR, after completing a long series of atmospheric tests, announced a unilateral moratorium. When the United States declined at first to follow suit and continued with its own testing, the USSR resumed also; then each imposed a moratorium on itself which lasted about two and a half years. Negotiation over some kind of test ban continued throughout this time, but each side linked its proposals to larger arms control plans that proved unacceptable to the other. Progress was also stymied by disagreement over whether each side could detect the other's underground tests by seismic evidence alone, without the on-site inspection that was anathema to the Soviet Union. When the Soviets resumed atmospheric testing in 1961, followed a few months later by the United States, the public outcry was even greater than before. Still the negotiators could not resolve their differences over underground testing, and the Soviets insisted that this kind of testing be included in any agreement whether its cessation could be verified or not.

After the Cuban Missile Crisis the pace of bargaining stepped up and the heads of state, Kennedy and Khrushchev, involved themselves personally in various ways. The Soviet leader made an offer to allow two or three on-site inspections a year within the USSR, but then angrily withdrew it, claiming he had been misled into believing that this was all the West would require. In June 1963 Kennedy delivered, at American University, one of his most famous speeches, devoted almost entirely to the need for both superpowers to cope more creatively with the perils of the arms race. Whether directly in response to this appeal is unknown, but Soviet policy now changed. Khrushchev indicated that the USSR would accept a limited treaty that banned testing in three environments and left aside the thorny problems associated with underground testing. Such a treaty was now negotiated quickly. The inspection question could be dropped because each superpower could verify by its own "national means"—primarily satellites—whether an explosion has occurred in the air, ocean, or outer space.

It is indicative of the strength of cold war attitudes at the time that the Limited Test Ban Treaty faced a difficult struggle in the U.S. Senate. The U.S. military had many plans for weapons tests to come, and a number of senators argued that the treaty would hinder the development of future American weapons by restricting necessary testing. Only after Kennedy promised that underground tests would continue vigorously was the agreement ratified.

Prior to the Senate's deliberations and even after this promise, the treaty's supporters hoped that it would have a real braking effect on the arms race. This hope has hardly been fulfilled, although it is impossible to be sure what extra weapons might have been developed, and how fast, in the absence of the treaty. Both superpowers discovered that in fact most of the weapons testing they had previously done in the air could be carried on with almost equal usefulness underground, and in the years since the treaty both of them (especially the United States) have carried on extensive underground testing almost annually. The development of weapons has proceeded rapidly and it is hard to see that the test ban has really had much effect on slowing the arms competition. China and France also refused to join in the treaty and have continued a modest number of atmospheric tests.

Even so the Limited Test Ban Treaty was one of the two great arms control achievements of the 1960s, because it largely stopped the spread of radioactive materials in the atmosphere. In the years since, we have forgotten how intense was the concern of physicians and biologists over the fallout; our having been able to forget is the proof of the treaty's great value. In spite of French and Chinese testing, worldwide fallout levels declined within ten years after the treaty, almost to the level of background radiation naturally present in the environment.

In 1974 the treaty was followed by a second agreement, the Threshold Test Ban Treaty, which extended the prohibition on atomic testing to underground tests of greater than a certain yield. The technology for seismic identification of underground blasts had improved in the intervening years, to the point where many explosions could be reliably detected at long distances. But this treaty was a disappointment to arms control specialists because the threshold was so high — 150 kilotons — that most weapons testing could still continue.

The 1974 treaty also allowed testing, without limit to the yield, of so-called "peaceful nuclear explosives" (PNEs) but a supplementary treaty in 1976 set the same threshold for those tests. PNEs are nuclear explosive devices arguably intended for large civil engineering purposes, such as digging canals. In technology they are hardly distinguishable from bombs. As of this writing neither the 1974 Threshold Test Ban Treaty nor the 1976 Peaceful Nuclear Explosions Treaty has been ratified by the U.S. Senate, although both Moscow and the executive branch in Washington have declared that they are abiding by both treaties.

A *comprehensive* test ban (CTB) continues to elude arms controllers. Seismic technology had improved sufficiently that in 1977 the United States, Soviet Union, and Great Britain began negotiations for a ban on all testing, including devices with yields below 150 kilotons.

Considerable progress was made, and at one point a treaty seemed almost within reach. But the talks were suspended in November 1980, in part because the Carter administration decided to give priority to the SALT II Treaty (discussed later) and did not believe it could command sufficient political support for both. In July 1982 the Reagan administration decided not to resume negotiations toward a CTB.

OTHER AGREEMENTS OF THE 1960s

The years following the Limited Test Ban Treaty of 1963 witnessed several other arms control agreements that in one way or another represented attempts to close off dangerous possibilities before they could develop. As soon as the test ban was signed, negotiations began for an agreement to keep nuclear weapons from being stationed in space. The resulting Outer Space Treaty, signed by the United States, the USSR, and other nations in 1967, prohibits placing any weapon of mass destruction into earth orbit, or onto the moon or other celestial bodies. A similar prohibition against placing these weapons on the ocean floor, the Seabed Treaty, was signed in 1971. In both cases neither superpower really wanted to extend the arms race into the new environment, for its own reasons of high cost and questionable effectiveness; but each faced the possibility that its opponent might do so, whereupon it might feel compelled to follow suit. A mutual agreement to close the door prevented an extension of the competition that no one desired.

Of the two agreements, the Outer Space Treaty especially has probably made a real psychological difference for Americans' and others' experience of security. At one time experts had feared that one or both superpowers might eventually place a number of nuclear bombs in permanent earth orbit, to be dropped on their targets in the event of war. The bombs might well have been visible to the naked eye, and the sight of nuclear satellites passing overhead every night would certainly have created a different and less secure atmosphere. In fact any American city can be destroyed as quickly by an ICBM launched from the Soviet Union as by a satellite's descent; but a psychological feeling of insecurity might have been much increased by a threat that was visible in the sky every night.

Earlier the Cuban Missile Crisis had had yet another positive by-product. Many Latin American nations reacted to it with a desire to prevent any second nuclear crisis from occurring in their region, and negotiations got underway at the UN for an international agreement to exclude all nuclear weapons from Latin America. Under the 1967 Treaty of Tlatelolco, the Western hemisphere from Mexico south was designated a "nuclear-free zone" in which there would be no testing, manufacture, deployment, or use of nuclear weapons, although nuclear facilities for peaceful purposes are permitted. Despite efforts to make the treaty acceptable to Castro, Cuba—the source of the first crisis—did not sign and remains outside the zone.

Unfortunately Argentina has not yet ratified this treaty, and until it does, Brazil, though a ratifier, is not legally bound by it. Argentina and Brazil both have potential to develop nuclear facilities, and there have been some indications that they might be retaining an option to develop weapons. Whether the treaty will succeed in keeping Latin America free of nuclear weapons permanently is still open to question.

The 1960s also saw progress on the troubling question of chemical and biological warfare, often abbreviated CBW. This is a realm of military technology where the possibilities can be as bizarre and frightening as those created by atomic weapons, and CBW has proved just as difficult to control. In 1925 most major nations joined in a Geneva Protocol, which banned the use, but not the development or stockpiling, of chemical and biological agents for warfare. (The American role in the protocol was curiously like its role in the League of Nations not long before: the United States was the prime instigator in its creation, then turned around and declined to ratify it.) There had been desultory interest over the decades in a better agreement, but a strong new impetus did not come until the United States used tear gas and chemical defoliants on a large scale in Vietnam. Opposition to these measures grew, and some feared that more deadly chemicals might follow. There was also a widely-publicized incident in 1968 in which 6,000 sheep died in Utah following the accidental release of some stockpiled nerve gas twenty-four miles away.

The domestic and international reactions led the Nixon administration, when it took office, to declare that it would consider itself bound by the Geneva Protocol in everything except tear gas and defoliants and would renounce biological weapons altogether. A UN disarmament group took up CBW, but negotiators soon ran into the usual impasse of Soviet refusal to allow inspection and Western refusal to make agreements without verification. However, the United States and its allies decided they could drop this requirement in the case of biological weapons because these weapons could not be made reliable without large-scale testing, which would probably become known internationally even without a formal mechanism to ensure it.

In 1971 the Soviets agreed to separate biological from chemical weapons, and the following year a convention prohibiting the development, production, and stockpiling of biological weapons was signed. In a sense this convention hardly affected American policy since the United States had already renounced the weapons; but the convention enabled the United States to maintain its renunciation by letting the West remain fairly confident that the USSR is not moving ahead in this field. Hence the convention may have headed off a technological competition in biological weapons. In 1974 the U.S. Senate ratified both the convention and (forty-nine years later!) the Geneva Protocol. Some efforts since the convention to extend arms control to chemical weapons have all floundered.

The four agreements just described all foreclosed possible avenues along which the arms race might have expanded. One other success of this kind should be mentioned even though it came earlier and was not the result of arms control negotiations. In 1957 scientists from all over the world had jointly studied Antarctica, and this cooperative venture, combined with the military irrelevance of the continent, led rapidly to an international agreement setting it aside. The Antarctica Treaty of 1959 prohibits any kind of military base or activity there and holds territorial claims (previously advanced by various nations) in abeyance for thirty years.

Several agreements were reached during the 1970s that are generally considered more minor. A Soviet-American "incidents at sea" agreement established rules governing occasions when the two sides' naval units are in close proximity. An "accidents" agreement provides that each government notify the other in the event of accidents that might involve a nuclear detonation, and of missile test flights in the other's direction. A "prevention of nuclear war" agreement obliges the two governments to consult with each other whenever there appears to be any danger of nuclear confrontation, between themselves or involving other countries.

THE NONPROLIFERATION TREATY

When the Limited Test Ban Treaty was signed in 1963, less than a year after the Cuban Missile Crisis, specialists were hopeful that other major agreements might be forthcoming at a fairly rapid pace. A number of measures to stabilize the arms race and prevent it from expanding into new areas might be achieved within a few years, they believed. Attention could turn then to the central problem of limiting and freezing the competition in strategic weapons. Many analysts were optimistic that each success would build trust and confidence that would make the next step easier, in a cumulative process that might proceed steadily and fairly swiftly.

In fact, progress was much slower. For instance, work began on an outer space agreement almost at once, but it was not achieved for nearly four years. Other agreements took longer still. And fewer agreements than had been hoped for could be reached at all.

By the end of the 1960s (or shortly thereafter, counting the seabed and biological treaties) the sum of what had been accomplished came to much less than had seemed reasonable to expect some years earlier. Although all the various agreements reached were valuable, they added up to only a modest restraint on the arms race as a whole. It was also almost the end of the decade before serious talks about limiting strategic arms became a reality, as will be discussed in the next chapter. In short, the net results of the first few years of arms control were somewhat disappointing. But those efforts did enjoy one more triumph during the decade. That achievement was the Nonproliferation Treaty of 1968.

In earlier years the danger that nuclear weapons would spread to additional countries was becoming more and more worrisome. Ten to fifteen years after Hiroshima, previously classified information about how nuclear explosions could be triggered and how bombs might be constructed was gradually diffusing into publicly available literature. Many countries were developing their scientific establishments, including physics laboratories, as a matter of national policy. Advancing technology was reducing greatly the cost of the facilities (once extremely expensive) needed to manufacture "weapons-grade" uranium or plutonium. All these trends meant that it was becoming steadily easier for a growing number of nations to build their own atomic bombs if they wanted to.

The prospects were genuinely frightening. It was difficult enough to feel much security in a world of three or four nuclear powers. If there were many more, atomic weapons would probably be *used* in some war. About three wars a year have occurred, on average, in the decades since World War II, nearly all of them involving countries that did not have nuclear weapons. But it seemed predictable that if more and more countries had them and warfare continued at any similar rate, before too long some cities would be destroyed, thousands or millions of lives lost, and the world's atmosphere polluted by bombs used in anger. If this happened once it might become easy for it to happen again and again. Analysts agreed that the best way—probably the only way—to prevent this would be to forestall the proliferation of atomic weapons.

It was impossible to know just how rapidly nuclear technology might spread, but shortly before his death President Kennedy said he feared there might be ten nuclear powers by 1970, and fifteen or twenty by 1975. Such a world, he said, would pose the "greatest possible danger" the United States could face. France had already become the fourth nuclear power with a successful test explosion in 1960; China's first test was to come in 1964; other nations were known to be close to the ability to explode a bomb. It would be impossible to clamp a lid on the diffusion of technical knowledge. To halt the spread of weapons the world's nations would have to come to an agreement on nonproliferation as a deliberate arms control measure.

This was an issue where America and the USSR shared interests in common, which made negotiation easier. Unfortunately it was also one where America and her NATO allies shared other interests that made nonproliferation negotiations more difficult. The Kennedy administration was sincere about wanting to halt proliferation and pursued negotiations with the USSR with this aim. But the administration was also sincere about wanting to strengthen the alliance, and thought that a good way to do so would be to give all the allies a degree of control over some NATO nuclear weapons. For years plans were pursued for a "multilateral force" of "mixed-manned" ships carrying missiles and atomic warheads, to which every ally would contribute some officers and men and over which each would enjoy some control.

The Soviet Union was strenuously opposed to nuclear sharing within NATO, especially if it meant any access to atomic weapons for West Germany, something to which Moscow has always been allergic in the extreme. The issue became hopelessly entangled with the nonproliferation negotiations since the United States kept making proposals that allowed an opening for alliance sharing, and the USSR was always anxious to reject just that. Finally Washington decided, toward the end of 1965, to drop its plan for the multilateral force, around which were gathering various other troubles as well. The main roadblock to an East-West agreement on terms for a nonproliferation treaty was now removed.

However, there was a delay of two more years, caused mainly by negotiations with non-nuclear nations who would naturally be expected to sign such a treaty and toward whom it would be, in a sense, directed. Although most of the nations of the world that did not possess nuclear weapons favored nonproliferation in principle, they were not necessarily ready to agree to the terms that the superpowers wanted. They pointed out that the treaty would perpetuate the current division of the world into nuclear "have" and "have not" nations; that was its point. The "have not" nations were being asked to give up something—the future possibility of becoming nuclear powers—while the "have" nations were giving up nothing. In return for their agreement the non-nuclear countries wanted, and to some extent got, other concessions.

The final Nonproliferation Treaty (NPT) stated, in what the superpowers regarded as its main articles, that the non-nuclear states signing were committed not to obtain nuclear weapons or the makings thereof, and nuclear states signing were committed not to provide them. Additional clauses promised the non-nuclear states help in developing nuclear energy for peaceful purposes and in obtaining facilities, and even peaceful nuclear explosives (PNEs), from the nuclear powers. A process for reviewing the treaty every five years and a twenty-five year time limit on it were added to give the non-nuclear countries greater leverage in the future.

Finally the superpowers promised to negotiate in good faith toward ending the arms race, halting all nuclear testing, and mutual disarmament. These last features amounted to a promise by the nuclear "have" nations that they would try to reduce, not widen, the gap between themselves and the "have not" countries. In fact only very limited progress has been made in the superpower negotiations, and the military disparity between them and most of the rest of the world's nations has grown in the years since.

Of the nuclear powers, France and China refused to sign the treaty, although France has said that it will abide by it. A distressingly long list of non-nuclear powers have also declined to sign the NPT, including Argentina, Brazil, India, Israel, Pakistan, Saudi Arabia, and South Africa. As of this writing Egypt has signed but not ratified it. All these countries are capable of building atomic weapons, in many cases rapidly; and several of them are just the "high risk" nations that arms control specialists had been most worried might "go nuclear," and most wanted the NPT to include.

India conducted an atomic test explosion in 1974 that it insisted was only a peaceful device, but as mentioned previously the technology for a bomb is almost identical. Most national security and arms control specialists have regarded Israel as a nuclear power for some time, although Israel is not known definitely to have conducted a test. Israeli technology is considered so good that Israel could have confidence its bombs would work without testing them, and at the beginning of the 1980s well-informed sources in London released an estimate that Israel possessed an arsenal of some 200 nuclear weapons. In September 1979 there was a mysterious flash of light off the South African coast which some analysts believe was a clandestine test by South Africa and Israel jointly; the two countries cooperate in other military matters.

Clearly the Nonproliferation Treaty has not halted the spread of military nuclear capabilities entirely. Even so, it was a major achievement. The world of "nuclear plenty" that President Kennedy feared has not yet even been approached, and many specialists remain hopeful that the number of nations possessing nuclear weapons can be held to not much more than the current total for a while yet. By its mere existence and prominence, and by the weight of the large number of countries that *have* signed it, the NPT has become a strong symbol of the worldwide desire to avoid the nightmare of many nations having atomic bombs. Certainly no country can be ignorant of this desire, and in this sense the NPT serves as a deterrent to proliferation even for countries that have not joined in the treaty.

SUMMARY

In the first flush of idealism over the prospect of collective security, the United States proposed to turn over control of atomic energy to the United Nations and destroy its stockpile of bombs. But the Soviet Union could not accept the implicit maintenance of the American monopoly this would have meant, as it could not accept other aspects of the Western conception of collective security. The brief time during which only one nation on the planet could build bombs passed without the world finding any bottle for the genie.

When the atomic arms race began the superpowers turned their attention to that competition and only years later made some sincere efforts to find ways to disarm. By then the difficulties had become too numerous and the fissionable material too plentiful. Onrushing military technology complicated the problems involved in any extensive disarmament beyond the ability and will of the major powers to find solutions, and any hope for early disarmament was abandoned.

Arms control became the substitute. The analysts of the early 1960s believed that when Washington and Moscow had made their strategic forces less vulnerable they would feel more secure, and would allow their competition in arms to moderate and eventually come to a stop. The task became defined as one of managing the arms race: insofar as possible, to foreclose the most dangerous possibilities, mitigate the costs and hazards along the way; and search for force structures that both sides would find satisfactory and would allow to become stable.

Success was only partial, even midwived by the world's frightened reaction to the Cuban Missile Crisis. The Limited Test Ban Treaty did stop the poisoning of the atmosphere, but it did not slow the arms race as much as its supporters had expected. Some other agreements along the way made useful, but not very extensive, contributions toward closing off fresh avenues of technological competition and closing geographical regions to atomic weaponry. The greatest success was the Nonproliferation Treaty, which probably did brake considerably the spread of nuclear weapons around the globe, although some important powers, both nuclear and non-nuclear, declined to join it.

On the whole the torrent of the onrushing arms race did not seem to be greatly affected by the arms control achievements of the 1960s. In that sense, the hopes that many had held for rapid step-by-step progress toward lessening the competition were at least temporarily disappointed. The greatest effort, the strategic arms limitation talks between East and West, were only beginning as the decade closed. Their outcome, to be described next, would prove the main test of hopes for arms control.

FOR FURTHER READING

Bechhoefer, Bernhard G. *Postwar Negotiations for Arms Control.* Washington: the Brookings Institution, 1961. An extensive history and analysis of arms control and disarmament negotiations in the late 1940s and 1950s.

Bull, Hedley. *The Control of the Arms Race.* New York: Praeger, 1961. A leading example of the new arms control literature that began appearing in the early 1960s, in which managing the arms race replaced disarmament as specialists' main focus.

Independent Commission on Disarmament and Security Issues (Palme Commission). *Common Security: A Blueprint for Survival.* New York: Simon & Schuster, 1982. An influential review, by a panel of high-level international experts, of the dangers posed by nuclear and other arms. Includes forty-four recommendations for arms control and related measures.

Jacobson, Harold K., and Eric Stein. *Diplomats, Scientists and Politicians: The United States and the Nuclear Test Ban Negotiations.* Ann Arbor, Michigan: University of Michigan Press, 1966. The premier scholarly history of the Limited Test Ban Treaty of 1963 and its background.

Schelling, Thomas C., and Morton Halperin. *Strategy and Arms Control.* New York: Twentieth Century Fund, 1961. Perhaps the leading work of the early 1960s synthesizing arms control considerations and the viewpoint of "classical" strategic analysis.

SIPRI (Stockholm International Peace Research Institute). *Armaments and Disarmament in the Nuclear Age: A Handbook.* Atlantic Highlands, N.J.: Humanities Press, 1976.

——*The Arms Race and Arms Control.* Cambridge, Mass.: Oelgeschlager, Gunn & Hain, Inc., 1982. Two basic reference works containing large amounts of factual information and analysis regarding arms control issues.

Stanford Arms Control Group: *International Arms Control: Issues and Agreements.* Second edition, edited by Coit D. Blacker and Gloria Duffy. Stanford: Stanford University Press, 1984. A standard textbook on arms control and disarmament in the post-World War II world, with emphasis on negotiations between the superpowers.

9
SALT

For a few hours in late June, 1967, President Lyndon Johnson and Premier Alexsei Kosygin met together in the previously obscure town of Glassboro, New Jersey. Kosygin was in the United States briefly to speak before the United Nations, and the two leaders took advantage of his presence to arrange a short summit meeting. Their conversation was mostly about limiting the strategic arms race, and their meeting led to the birth of SALT — the Strategic Arms Limitation Talks.

For about two years Robert McNamara and other U.S. national security officials had been publicly suggesting talks aimed at slowing and halting the superpowers' competition in strategic weapons. The time was rapidly approaching, they had concluded, when the United States and Soviet Union would each have large and secure second-strike forces — an ample assured destruction capability. Neither would be able to remove the other's assured destruction capability by any conceivable effort or action, then or any time in the foreseeable future. McNamara and others reiterated in many congressional and other

151

public appearances that when both superpowers reached this position, they would find the further accumulation of strategic weapons more costly than it could possibly be worth. If the arms race went on, the two sides would match each other's acquisitions and find, after spending large sums, that they had added nothing to their security or relative advantage. Hence the sensible thing would be for representatives of the two nations to sit down and find ways to halt the race on a basis of something like the current forces. Repeatedly this suggestion was also made privately to the Soviets through diplomatic channels. At the Glassboro summit Johnson suggested it again to Kosygin, and the Soviet leader agreed in principle.

However, there was an interruption before the two sides had completed their preparations for actual Strategic Arms Limitation Talks. The Soviet invasion of Czechoslovakia in the summer of 1968 made it impossible for the United States to start new East-West negotiations right away on any topic. To do so might have seemed as if the West did not much disapprove of the invasion. Hence it was 1969 before the SALT talks—as they are redundantly but almost universally known—actually got underway.

The most important arms control effort of our time, and the one that goes to the heart of the Soviet-American military competition, continued almost to 1980. Under a different name it resumed about three years later. By 1980, the SALT process had produced three agreements, two formal and one less formal. Most of this chapter presents the story of this effort over its first decade, and an outline of the agreements reached. Since both the negotiations and the agreements (especially the third) became quite complicated, all the details cannot be included here. A sketch of the main outlines of how the SALT process developed, and of the most important features of the agreements reached, is all that is feasible, and is sufficient for the purposes of this book.

SALT I

It took some two years for the Soviet and American SALT negotiators to settle on terms and definitions and to find enough of a common perspective on the arms race to be able to talk meaningfully about how to limit it. Gradually they turned to substance, and after some discussion agreed to handle offensive and defensive weapons in different ways. If mutual deterrence was to be maintained, the negotiators agreed, both sides would have to keep many offensive weapons, but strategic defensive weapons might be limited more sharply.

Each side's air defense against attacking bombers was already too large and too complicated to do much about. But neither side had yet built extensive defenses against missiles; an agreement might be reached not to do so. Such an agreement would be consistent with mutual deterrence, in fact would enhance it, since the essence of deterrence was that each side *should* be confident of its ability to destroy the other's cities. If each side knew the other were prohibited by SALT from trying to defend itself against missile attacks, then each could remain confident that its current *offensive* forces would be sufficient for an assured destruction capability. Further development and expansion of offensive forces would seem less desirable, and agreement to freeze them might thereby become easier.

An absolute prohibition against either side constructing Antiballistic Missile (ABM) systems was impossible because both had already begun to construct small ones. The Nixon administration was already building some of the components of Safeguard, the point-defense system it planned for U.S. missile fields. The Soviet Union, too, had long since begun work on ABMs. During the 1960s it had installed a small system around Leningrad and had started work on another, different system to try to protect Moscow.

However, neither side had yet started to build nationwide ABM systems. If these were prohibited, and the systems currently under construction were restricted from growing much larger, the overall capability of each side's offensive forces would not be much threatened. The USSR would know it could overwhelm a small Safeguard system, and the United States would know it could penetrate the systems around Leningrad and Moscow and destroy those cities. A prohibition on further ABM work should also be permanent, since otherwise the two nations would hold open the option of building larger offensive forces later, to be sure of penetrating possible expanded ABMs of the future. By 1972 the bargaining teams had agreed on the terms for an ABM limitation, and these became the permanent part of the SALT I agreement.

Offensive strategic weapons, discussed simultaneously, proved more complicated for the negotiators. Here both sides had large programs under way, as both were anxious to improve their strategic striking power. They had also created offensive forces over the years that were somewhat different in character as well as in size, and this made exact comparisons between them difficult. In the early 1970s the United States still had the 1,054 ICBMs it had had for some years: 1,000 Minutemen and fifty-four Titans. The Soviets, building rapidly, already had hundreds more than this. American missiles were more accurate; Soviet missiles carried larger warheads. The United States also had the forty-one Polaris submarines, carrying sixteen missiles apiece, that had been deployed in the early and mid-1960s. The Soviets were building submarines and SLBMs rapidly and had already exceeded the American totals, with more under construction. On the other hand the United States had hundreds of long-range B-52 bombers while the USSR had nothing comparable. Moscow also complained that American "tactical nuclear" or "theater nuclear" forces in Europe, the Far East, and at sea could strike targets inside the Soviet Union. These "forward-based systems," claimed Soviet negotiators, should be counted as strategic weapons also.

To reach an agreement on offensive weapons, the SALT I negotiating teams made some rough compromises. Ceilings were placed on how many ICBMs, SLBMs, and missile-launching submarines each side would be permitted, but the Americans agreed to set the Soviet ceilings higher to accommodate the extra Soviet forces in place or under construction. In exchange the Soviets agreed, for the time being, that no ceilings at all would be placed on American bombers or forward-based systems. Since neither side found this arrangement entirely satisfactory, a time limit of five years was put on it. It was expected that in that time the superpowers could negotiate a follow-on SALT II agreement that would fashion more permanent and comprehensive limitations.

The SALT I agreements were signed by President Nixon and Party Chairman Brezhnev on May 26, 1972 at a summit conference, the president making a trip to Moscow for the purpose. The permanent agreement restricting ABM systems was cast as a formal treaty; the five-year limitation on offensive missile systems was put in the form of an interim agreement, a less formal document that still carried the force of international law. The numerical ceilings and other particulars are indicated on the accompanying table. The agreements also created a Standing Consultative Commission (SCC) to arbitrate any misunderstandings or disputes in interpretation that might arise later, declared that further negotiations would proceed immediately, and included some other provisions.

When SALT I was submitted to the United States Senate for ratification, the Senate did not immediately give its approval. Many senators complained that the arrangement was unequal because the Soviets were permitted so many more ICBMs, SLBMs, and missile-launching submarines. The counterargument that this advantage was offset by the American advantage in bombers was not convincing enough to win the approval of two-thirds of the Senate. At this point Henry

**TABLE 3.   The SALT I Agreements
Signed in Moscow on 26 May 1972**

BY TREATY:
   The United States and Soviet Union are indefinitely prohibited from deploying ABM systems, except at two sites each containing no more than 100 intercepter missiles.*

BY INTERIM AGREEMENT:
   The United States and Soviet Union are limited for five years to the number of offensive strategic missiles deployed or under construction as of the date of the signing.** These numbers were as follows:

	ICBMs	SLBMs	missile-launching submarines
United States			
Deployed May '72	1,054	656	41
SALT I limit	1,054	710	44
Soviet Union			
Deployed May '72	1,618	740	56
SALT I limit	1,618	950	62

Within the overall limitation on missile forces, each side was allowed freedom to substitute newer weapons for older, and was allowed "freedom to mix," trading fewer ICBMs for more SLBMs or vice versa, within certain limits. The Soviets could not deploy any more large ("heavy") ICBMs than were already deployed, about 300. No limitation was set upon long-range bomber aircraft, or upon short-range missiles and aircraft that the United States maintains in Europe, Asia, and aboard navy vessels.

*In 1974 this was modified to one site each, containing the same number of intercepter missiles.

**To be exact, ICBMs but not other forces were limited to the number deployed or under construction as of July 1, 1972.

Jackson, a senator expert in national security, proposed a compromise. He sponsored an amendment declaring that no *future* SALT agreement would be ratified by the Senate unless it embraced a principle that Jackson called "essential equivalence." The two sides' strategic forces would have to meet this standard, including an overall numerical equality in strategic delivery vehicles. With this stipulation the Senate ratified SALT I.

   The Jackson amendment left "essential equivalence" only partly defined, which left some room for interpretation in the next round of SALT negotiations. It also imposed a requirement on the American bargaining team that might not be easy to carry out. In the complex calculus of strategic power, "essential equivalence" might not find auniversally agreed meaning. For instance, how was equivalence to be determined between the larger yields of Soviet missile warheads and the greater accuracy of American missiles? Various complicated formulas were discussed among specialists, who tried to sum these and other considerations together into an overall total, but no formula proved entirely satisfactory. Meanwhile, a new technological development was appearing that was to make the whole challenge of strategic arms control more complicated and difficult.

MIRVs

Up to this time, nearly all strategic missiles had carried a single warhead each. One rocket booster was required to loft one reentry vehicle (RV) to its target. Or, in a slight variation, a few American missiles in the late 1960s carried three warheads each. These "multiple reentry vehicles" were delivered to the same target area and were designed to explode only a short distance from each other.

But by the end of the decade American weapons scientists were well along in creating the technology for delivering RVs to *separate* targets. One rocket booster could launch a "bus" that would carry the RVs and then detach them at various times in the flight trajectory, launching them in different directions. Their targets might be separated by hundreds of miles. This new strategic weapon was named the MIRV, for Multiple Independently-targetable Reentry Vehicle.*

The arrival of MIRVs proved to be a watershed in the evolving Soviet-American strategic relationship. In some ways the impact of this technology turned out to be almost as great as the impact a decade earlier when the technology of long-range missiles had first arrived. MIRVs permitted the superpowers to increase greatly the destructive power they could fling at each other, at a bearable economic cost. Having many thousands of missile warheads had been prohibitively expensive as long as one had to purchase a whole missile for every warhead. It became quite affordable when one missile could carry many RVs. This way of multiplying one's striking power proved so advantageous that by the end of the 1970s single-warhead strategic missiles made up only a fraction of each side's missile forces.

---

*MIRV is pronounced to rhyme with *curve*.

The United States, which developed MIRV technology ahead of the Soviet Union, did so originally as part of the search for an answer to ABMs. During the 1960s, as the Leningrad and Moscow ABM systems were being built, U.S. national security analysts worried that the Soviets might decide to build a "thick" nationwide ABM system. With only 1,710 missiles in the American arsenal, it was conceivable that such a system might be able to shoot down most or all American warheads. The U.S. assured destruction capability, the whole basis of deterrence, might be threatened.

It was true that the United States was also developing sophisticated "penetration aids" for its warheads, which would assist them in getting through a large Soviet ABM system to their targets. In the late 1960s some American missiles were already being equipped with early versions of these devices, but something more was wanted. In a sense, MIRVs were developed as the ultimate penetration aid. Unlike decoys that were tricked up to look something like a warhead to the enemy's radar, MIRVs really were warheads and the enemy would be compelled to try to shoot down every one, thereby exhausting his supply of intercepter missiles in his ABM system. (This is called "saturating" his ABM system.)

The United States publicly announced in November 1966 that the Soviets were building an ABM system around Moscow, and announced simultaneously the development of a new American missile to counter it. The new missile was called Poseidon, and it would replace the older Polaris SLBMs carried in submarines. Why Poseidon was an effective counter to a Soviet ABM system was not made completely clear at this time. What was announced was only that the Poseidon had a considerably longer range than the Polaris, which meant that American submarines could cruise in waters much farther from the Soviet Union (and hence from Soviet antisubmarine warfare forces) and still strike their targets.

The real reason Poseidon was being built as a counter to a Soviet ABM system, and was announced in conjunction with the revelation of the Moscow system, was that Poseidon would carry MIRVs. Ten MIRVs aboard each Poseidon missile would overwhelm any feasible Soviet ABM system. A secondary reason for developing Poseidon was that it would more than balance the rapidly growing Soviet SLBM force, the eventual planned size of which was not, of course, known to the United States. American defense planners of the 1960s were counting on Poseidon to maintain the U.S. assured destruction capability indefinitely.

About the time Poseidon was announced, the United States also began developing a new, MIRVed version of the Minuteman ICBM, called Minuteman III. Carrying three MIRVs each, 550 Minuteman III missiles would ultimately be deployed, replacing the old Minuteman I missiles that dated back to about 1962. (The other 450 missiles in the Minuteman force were Minuteman IIs, a modernized and improved version of the missile, first deployed in the mid-1960s. The Minuteman II carries only one warhead.) The Minuteman III and Poseidon both completed development and began to enter U.S. silos and submarines in the early 1970s. In the following years they became the backbone of the U.S. strategic force, carrying between them some 90 percent of the bombs and warheads the United States had targeted on the Soviet Union. The USSR began deploying MIRVs several years later, in the mid-1970s.

The arrival of MIRV technology made the Soviet-American strategic relationship more difficult and troubled, for at least two reasons. One is that MIRVs on ICBMs pose a danger to the stability of the strategic balance: under some circumstances they might make it too tempting for one side to try to destroy the enemy's ICBM silos. Back in the era of single-warhead ICBMs, either side had to use up a missile for every enemy silo it wanted to attack, even if it assumed 100 percent reliability and accuracy in its ICBMs. This is called a one-to-one "exchange ratio." With this exchange ratio either side would use up its own ICBMs at least as rapidly as it could destroy the other's silos, and under these conditions there was little or no temptation to strike.

But with, say, three MIRVs on each missile, three enemy silos might be destroyed for each missile expended (again assuming the ideal condition of 100 percent reliability and accuracy). With a three-to-one exchange ratio, only a third of one's own ICBMs would be used up in attacking *all* the enemy's silos. Of course, reliability and accuracy are far from ideal in fact. But when the USSR began deploying ICBMs that carried eight MIRVs each in the 1970s, American analysts worried that the Soviets might calculate they could make up for reliability and accuracy deficiencies with sheer numbers of warheads. A number of Soviet warheads striking near each American missile silo would be likely to destroy most U.S. ICBMs. No doubt the Soviets also were worried earlier, when the United States began deploying three-warhead MIRVs on Minuteman III missiles that were known to be more accurate than Soviet missiles.

What MIRVs really do, in creating favorable exchange ratios, is make it more tempting for *each* side to strike the other's missile fields. In this way they tend to re-create, with respect to ICBMs only, a situation something like the "delicate balance of terror" that was developing in the late 1950s. With favorable exchange ratios, as with vulnerable above-ground missile and bomber bases in the earlier period, each side perceives a great advantage in striking first and an equally great risk in waiting—a temptation to strike that could be important in a crisis.

Fortunately none of this applies to the SLBM forces that each side also maintains. The assured destruction capabilities of these forces greatly reduce either's temptation to preempt. Exchange ratios are not thereby rendered irrelevant, however, because the proportion of ICBMs to SLBMs is substantially larger in the Soviet arsenal than in the American. The Soviets therefore tend to feel that they have proportionally more at risk in the MIRV era than does the United States.

A second reason why the arrival of MIRV technology has made the Soviet-American strategic relationship more troubled is that it practically guarantees that each side will deploy a large number of warheads. Even if one or both did not want to, they are almost compelled to because of the way their intelligence systems operate.

The superpowers carefully watch each other's testing programs for missiles. When the United States conducts tests, Soviet observation ships gather near the American test ranges in the Atlantic and Pacific Oceans. Sophisticated American satellites and electronic observation posts close to the Soviet borders watch Soviet missiles, which are launched over a test range stretching from the western USSR to Siberia. When either side tests a missile the other observes the number of warheads that impact. The largest number that any missile is *seen* to carry becomes the number the observing nation assumes the missile always *will* carry, because there is no way to count individual MIRVs once missiles are deployed in silos or submarines. Each side knows from its reconnaissance satellites the number of launchers the other possesses. But it cannot count the number of MIRVs on each missile. So it must assume that every missile is carrying the maximum number.

Since each side knows the other makes this assumption, each usually does not even bother to test missiles carrying much less than the maximum feasible number of warheads. In this way the largest number of MIRVs that each missile might carry usually becomes the number they *do* carry. Thus strategic forces tend to grow larger than they might otherwise.*

---

*In a few cases, several MIRV packages with somewhat different numbers of MIRVs have been tested. The opponent may remain uncertain which deployed missiles contain which packages. But it remains true that neither side, having tested a MIRV package with many MIRVs, bothers to design or test a package containing only a very few MIRVs.

Another consequence of the fact that MIRVs cannot be counted like launch vehicles was a challenge that the SALT process proved unable to meet. This event was important enough to pause on for a moment.

A TRAGEDY OF TIMING

As it became clear in the late 1960s that MIRV technology could be successfully developed, many national security specialists realized, and were disturbed by, its arms control implications. They understood that once a MIRVed launch vehicle had been tested there would be no way for SALT to place a ceiling on the number of MIRVs deployed, short of the maximum that could be carried by whatever number of launch vehicles either side deployed. The number of warheads that each side would be aiming at the other was about to rise meteorically.

If this new round in the arms race was to be avoided, SALT would have to stop the technology of MIRVing while the MIRVed missiles were still in the testing stage. Neither side would dare trust its security to missiles that had not been thoroughly tested. If the testing of MIRVed missiles could be halted, the whole of MIRV technology could be "frozen" before it fully materialized. Each side would remain limited to single-warhead missiles, and each side's arsenal would probably not grow much larger than it already was. But if MIRV technology could not be prevented from being fully tested, there would be no later chance to halt a huge growth in each side's destructive power.

There now occurred what seems, especially in retrospect, to have been a real tragedy in timing. The SALT I Treaty signed in 1972 successfully limited both sides' ABMs to small systems that could easily be penetrated. The principal justification for the United States having taken the lead in developing MIRV technology was therefore removed. MIRVs had been developed in the first place as the ultimate answer to ABMs, but ABMs were no longer a threat. Furthermore, the Soviets had not yet developed MIRVs, so the United States did not need them simply to keep up in the arms race. There really was no need for MIRVs in the American arsenal of 1972.

Unfortunately, the United States had begun testing its MIRVed Poseidon and Minuteman III missiles in the late 1960s, and started deploying the missiles at the beginning of the 1970s. Once it had done so, the Soviets understandably refused to make any agreement that would forbid them to have MIRVs also. Moscow was not about to accept a permanent technological inferiority. Thus the opportunity to stop MIRVs in the testing stage was missed, and the stage was set for a MIRV race in which both sides deployed, at great expense, many thousands of warheads in the following years. Thanks to MIRVs, the number of separate atomic warheads that each side can rain down on the other has increased from between one and two thousand as SALT was getting under way, to nearly ten thousand in the early 1980s.

The justification offered by the United States government for completing the test programs and deploying MIRVs was that in 1970 there was no way to know that in 1972 the Soviets would agree to a satisfactory limit on their ABM systems. The Defense Department was faced with the possibility of the Soviets enlarging and strengthening their ABM, which at some point would threaten the American assured destruction capability.

On its own terms this justification cannot be refuted. However, many national security specialists believe that the U.S. government did not make a serious, sustained effort in the period around 1970 to grasp the arms control opportunity that presented itself. American testing of MIRVs could have been halted for a period while SALT negotiators explored a permanent test ban combined with an ABM treaty. There is disagreement about just how interested the Soviets were in a MIRV test ban, but apparently they *did* at times express an interest in preventing MIRVs from entering either side's forces. Perhaps a package agreement, restricting ABMs and halting MIRV tests, could have been successfully hammered together.

Such an agreement might have had the very positive effect that was originally hoped for SALT. It might have effectively halted, at least for awhile, the strategic arms race at one "plateau" of technology. A precedent, and an arms control momentum, might have been created for banning tests of other new strategic technologies, and perhaps the entire strategic arms race could have been greatly slowed down. Instead the opportunity was lost.

As a practical matter this tragedy of timing may have been inevitable. The Poseidon and Minuteman III test programs were proceeding successfully and with a very high priority. Thousands of people, billions of dollars and huge organizations were committed to pushing them as rapidly as possible. Halting or greatly slowing programs with such an enormous momentum, because of a *chance* that an arms control accord might halt them altogether, is one of the most difficult things a government could try to do. On the other hand, it was well known in Washington at the time that the United States was some years ahead of the USSR in MIRV technology.

In any event, by the time the SALT I agreements were signed it was too late to halt MIRVs. In the negotiations the Soviets refused to consider any ban on MIRV testing once the United States had completed its tests, and without a test ban there could be no way to limit numbers of MIRVs, only numbers of launchers. The issue of MIRVs was left out of the SALT I agreements altogether, and deferred for the next round of negotiations.

THE VLADIVOSTOK ACCORDS

The assumption behind the five-year duration of the SALT I Interim Agreement had been that within that time the superpowers would reach a second agreement that put more extensive restraints on their strategic forces. Arms control specialists hoped for progress in several areas. Though MIRVs could no longer be limited directly, a distinction could be formally made between those launch vehicles that were capable of carrying them and those that were not, and separate limits set for each category. It was hoped that the limit on MIRVed vehicles might be set quite low. Beyond this the overall ceiling on missiles might be reduced. SALT I had permitted a total of 1,764 American and 2,568 Soviet missiles, numbers considerably greater than needed for assured destruction in the absence of major ABM systems. A still more ambitious hope was that at least a little progress might be made on limiting qualitative advances, an elusive goal that demands explanation.

The superpowers are constantly making qualitative improvements in their strategic capabilities. A weapons system is not purchased in quantity and then allowed to remain static over its deployed lifetime. Major and minor improvements are introduced, both in the weapons themselves and in related systems. To take Polaris as an example: as time passed the original Polaris missiles were replaced with several later models, each better than the last; these in turn were equipped with newer and newer types of warheads; and the submarines were made quieter and improved in other ways. Another example is the SRAM air-to-surface missile, which was added to the B-52 and FB-111 bombers. Each aircraft carries several SRAMs in addition to its "gravity bombs." By firing SRAMs, each aircraft can destroy more (and more widely scattered) targets and does not have to fly over heavily defended targets.

Some qualitative improvements do serve arms control as well as military objectives. Making submarines quieter, for instance, or missile silos "harder," makes the weapons more secure from attack. It has been axiomatic since the late 1950s that secure forces represent a "second-strike capability," do not arouse temptations toward preemption, and hence add to stability in Soviet-American relations. On the other hand, many qualitative improvements make weapons more potent. The weapons may become as much more dangerous to a potential enemy as adding to their numbers would be. Curbing such improvements becomes an arms control objective. One obvious example of this kind of development is improving the targeting accuracy of missiles, something the superpowers have been working on continually (as will be discussed further in a later chapter).

Finding ways to limit such qualitative improvements is a far more difficult task for strategic arms control than setting numerical ceilings on forces because, with a few exceptions, neither side can verify whether the other may be making some improvement that it agreed not to make. Satellites and other "national means of verification" (as they are euphemistically called in the SALT agreements) can count silos and submarines but cannot reliably observe the improvement of a weapon. Without this ability to verify unilaterally, the superpowers cannot have confidence that any agreement reached will be honored, and therefore are unwilling to make agreements about limiting qualitative improvements.

It is partly for this reason that even if the arms control process eventually succeeds in setting fixed ceilings on the numbers of all types of strategic weapons, this would not end the arms race. Improvements could go on and on. In addition, the superpowers are constantly engaged in scientific research that might lead to wholly new weapons in the future, and it seems that no agreement restricting this kind of qualitative advance could be verifiable either. For example, in recent years both the United States and USSR have invested heavily in research on lasers and particle beams, in the belief that either or both technologies might eventually yield whole new ("star wars") types of weapons. This kind of work is as much part of the strategic arms race as building a new missile, but here the verification issue is so difficult that negotiators have not even begun to grapple with it. Scientific research leading to qualitatively new weapons and to improvements in existing systems presents verification difficulties so great that arms control specialists do not understand, even in the abstract, how these aspects of the arms race might be verifiably limited.

Though a complete halt to the arms race, and a reduction of current forces to fairly low levels was and is the ultimate goal for strategic arms control, specialists would have been pleased if the next agreement after SALT I had merely set a low ceiling on MIRV launchers and made some reduction in overall ceilings. When negotiations resumed an attempt in this direction was made. But the talks got bogged down in issues that had been sidestepped earlier.

The Soviet negotiators again raised the matter of U.S. strategic bombers and "forward-based systems." SALT I had placed no ceiling on bombers, which, from Moscow's viewpoint, left the United States free to increase its bomber forces without limit if it chose. And nothing had been said about American nuclear forces at sea, in the Far East, and especially in Europe, which the Soviets correctly pointed out had a significant capability against the Russian homeland.

The American team regarded bombers as a negotiable issue, but the latter question threatened to tangle the talks hopelessly. Whatever these forces might be able to do against the USSR, their primary mission, and the reason they were deployed, was to deter and if necessary defend against attacks on Western Europe, Korea, or other areas near the USSR. The Soviets *also* kept theater nuclear forces in Eastern Europe, the Soviet Far East, and elsewhere, which these U.S. forces were intended to balance and neutralize. (Because of happenstance of geography, these Soviet forces do not "accidentally" threaten the United States itself, as the equivalent American forces do the USSR, because the United States is too far away.) From the American viewpoint, then, the U.S. "forward-based systems" should be seen in the context of the equivalent Soviet forces and not as a strategic issue.

Furthermore, the American forces in Europe could scarcely have been brought into SALT without also bringing in the nuclear forces that Britain and France maintain. The Americans argued that the complications would be endless. The Western powers had quite a variety of bombers and missiles that could carry atomic weapons. Some could easily reach the Soviet homeland, some barely could, some could if they were moved, and some could not at all. Equal complications applied to the variety of bombers and missiles the Soviets kept in Eastern Europe and the western parts of the USSR. Furthermore, once the European nations became involved they would assert their own point of view. For them even relatively short-range weapons on both sides were "strategic" because they could strike European homelands and cities. Indeed, the term "Eurostrategic" was coined during the 1970s to name all those weapons that were not strategic from the American viewpoint, but were partly so from the Soviet perspective and entirely so for Europeans.

The American team at SALT argued that to open this Pandora's box would delay the talks endlessly. Separate negotiations should be undertaken to limit weapons in Europe. The Soviets were reluctant, although later these negotiations did begin, as will be described below.

As bargaining continued through 1973 and into 1974, the two sides eventually reached a compromise. The next SALT agreement would *include* U.S. bombers (as the Soviets wished) in exchange for *excluding* the forward-based systems (as the Americans wished). The U.S. bargaining team found it easier to make this compromise because it was constrained by the "essential equivalence" requirement of the Jackson amendment. The next SALT treaty taken to the Senate would have to include numerical equality in launch vehicles, and since the Soviets were not about to scrap already-deployed missiles if the United States did not, the only reasonable way to achieve this would be to count American bombers. An agreement began to take shape that set an equal overall ceiling not too far from what the Soviet ceiling had been before, and included American bombers to make the forces roughly equal.

When Richard Nixon stepped down from the presidency in August 1974 and was succeeded by Gerald Ford, the new president found, as many of his predecessors had, that he and Soviet Party Chairman Brezhnev wished to meet in person to take each other's measure. The two leaders met in November at a brief summit conference in Vladivostok, the largest city in the Soviet Far East. They took that opportunity to put their names to the main outline of a new SALT agreement. The president and chairman approved the compromise and agreed upon numerical ceilings for all strategic launch vehicles and for vehicles carrying MIRVs. Though details remained to be negotiated, they announced that a SALT II Treaty would be completed by the summer of 1975.

Details of the Vladivostok agreement are shown on the accompanying table. Though specialists and commentators withheld their full reactions until the final treaty could be completed, the informal reaction of many was dismay at how high the limits were set. Especially were they distressed at the very high limit on MIRV launchers. If, as seemed likely at the time and did in fact later come to pass, most of these launchers would carry eight or ten warheads each, the superpowers could deploy some ten thousand warheads under this "strategic arms limitation" agreement! Indeed, the USSR could deploy

TABLE 4. The Vladivostok Accords

In November 1974 President Ford and Secretary Brezhnev announced the following agreement:

A SALT II agreement will be reached no later than early summer 1975, limiting the United States and Soviet Union to the following totals of strategic offensive weapons:

	Strategic launch vehicles	Vehicles carrying MIRVs
United States	2,400	1,320
Soviet Union	2,400	1,320

The SALT II agreement will be in force until 1985, and before it expires the two powers will begin seeking reductions in their forces. There is no limitation upon the United States' forward-based systems.

many more than this, since the missiles it then had under development (and has since deployed) are much larger than American missiles and therefore can be modified to carry many more warheads.

The numerical limits set at Vladivostok also gave evidence of having been chosen to require no cutback of existing programs. The overall total was within 10 percent of the Soviet overall total permitted under SALT I; the slight reduction required could be accomplished painlessly by phasing out older missiles, which would be done anyway. Even more strikingly, the MIRV launcher total was set very close to the number of MIRV launchers already deployed or being planned in 1974 for U.S. forces (Poseidon plus Minuteman III, plus a new system to be described later). Furthermore, no commitment was made at Vladivostok that the superpowers would try to negotiate reductions in these huge forces soon—only that they would begin to do so before 1985. Under pressure, Secretary of State Henry Kissinger did announce later that SALT III negotiations aimed at force reductions would begin promptly after completion of SALT II. But the fact remained that the Vladivostok levels were so high that even a considerable reduction would leave the superpowers' forces much larger than they had been before the SALT process started.

SALT II

When President Ford and Chairman Brezhnev made their Vladivostok agreement they were sincere in announcing that it would provide the basis for a SALT II Treaty to be completed almost immediately. For a while both governments genuinely expected that a final treaty would follow within six months, or a year at most. The compromise that had been struck, exchanging the inclusion of heavy bombers for the exclusion of forward-based systems, seemed to clear away the main sticking points and leave only details to be cleared up in final bargaining. In the wake of Vladivostok President Ford was confident that he would be signing a SALT II Treaty well within the time that he remained in office.

But this did not happen. Negotiations dragged on and on, and almost another five years passed before a SALT II Treaty was finally signed — one rather different from the Vladivostok agreement. And that treaty was never ratified by the U.S. Senate.

In the months following Vladivostok the negotiating teams discovered two new issues that proved just as contentious as the previous ones had been. One was a new weapon called the cruise missile, to be discussed in detail in a later chapter. In the mid-1970s the United States was well ahead of the USSR in beginning research and development on cruise missile technology, and the Soviets began demanding that any cruise missiles having ranges longer than 600 kilometers (about 375 miles) be counted as "strategic launch vehicles" and come under the limit for those vehicles. The United States saw the cruise missile as a different kind of weapon altogether and refused.

The other issue was a new Soviet bomber. For a long time the Soviets had remained content not to compete with the United States in long-range bombers. They had good short-range bombers that could be used against Europe or China, but had chosen not to build a modern jet long-range bomber comparable to the American B-52 or FB-111. In the 1970s they reversed this choice and developed a sophisticated jet bomber, which, in NATO parlance, was code-named the "Backfire." Capable of supersonic speeds, the Backfire began to enter service in the Soviet Air Force just about the time Ford and Brezhnev were meeting in Vladivostok.

The Soviets maintained that the Backfire was not a strategic bomber like American bombers because its unrefueled range was not sufficient for it to fly from the USSR to the continental United States and return. The American negotiating team countered that in every other respect the Backfire had the characteristics of a strategic bomber, and that its range could easily be extended by in-flight refueling from tanker aircraft. This was a technique long used by the United States to give its strategic bombers a truly intercontinental range;

though it had not yet been used by the Soviet Union, it could be developed quickly. As an alternative, Backfires could also fly to Cuba and land at Castro's air bases after they had bombed American targets. The United States therefore demanded that Backfires be counted as "strategic launch vehicles" and come under that limit. The Soviets reiterated that the Backfire was not a strategic bomber and refused.

Ultimately the Backfire question was to be partially sidestepped in the SALT II agreement, and cruise missiles limited only for a short while. But in the period following Vladivostok these issues deadlocked the negotiations. The Soviets gave no ground for a considerable time, and as 1975 stretched into 1976 the Ford administration found that it could not either, for domestic political reasons. Conservative opinion in America wanted no SALT concessions. Even making none, Ford just barely won the Republican nomination from Ronald Reagan.

Jimmy Carter entered office in January 1977 determined to complete a SALT II Treaty quickly, and within two months sent his new secretary of state, Cyrus Vance, and a negotiating team to Moscow to try to break the deadlock. Vance made two offers, either of which, if accepted by the Soviets, might have led rapidly to an agreement. One was to leave both Backfire bombers and cruise missiles out of SALT II altogether, deferring them for later negotiations, and conclude a treaty approximately on the basis of the force ceilings agreed on at Vladivostok. The other, and more radical, offer was to include both the Backfire and cruise missiles in a revised agreement, with numerical ceilings on both. In this proposal, the overall ceiling on all strategic vehicles would also be lowered substantially, and fairly low limits would also be placed on the number of MIRVed ICBMs and the number of so-called "heavy"—that is, large—ICBMs.

The Soviets rejected both offers: one for representing nothing new, the other for being *too* new. The first was essentially a resurrection of the Vladivostok understanding, now two and a half years old. That had become unacceptable to the USSR, mainly because of Soviet fear of the American lead in cruise missile technology. The other called for something Moscow thought unfair. It placed restrictive limits on ICBMs but not on SLBMs. ICBMs made up a considerably larger proportion of Soviet forces than SLBMs, whereas SLBMs were a more important part of American forces. Hence this proposal would have a more restrictive effect on the Soviets than on the Americans. Also, only the Soviets were building ICBMs large enough to count as "heavy" by the SALT definition, so this feature too would discriminate against them. Moscow rejected this proposal and its companion even as possible starting points for discussions.

The Kremlin leaders might have been more forthcoming, but they were already angry with the Carter administration and wished to demonstrate their displeasure. The new administration had violated the usual protocol in these matters by releasing information publicly about the offers it would make before communicating them privately to the Soviets. Carter had also begun his term with a very vigorous campaign against human rights violations around the world, including explicit attacks on Soviet human rights practices. Moscow was offended.

Though Vance's trip failed, neither side wanted to discontinue the regular SALT negotiating process. Several months later the American negotiating team brought up his second concept again, in a compromise form. They proposed that cuts in the overall ceilings be included in SALT II and not (as the Soviets preferred) postponed for SALT III, but now the magnitude of the suggested cuts was limited to ten percent. This time the Soviets agreed at least to discuss the issue, and something like it survived into the final treaty.

The interim agreement that had been part of SALT I was due to expire in October 1977, its five-year formal duration exhausted. As the expiration date approached, however, first the United States and then the Soviet Union announced that they would continue to observe its limits, as long as the other did also and the SALT process continued. Over the preceding months, too, some significant progress was made in SALT II. Another year and a half of bargaining over the particulars was yet to come, but the superpowers reached an understanding on the structure of a SALT II agreement. A "three-tiered" framework would treat different issues in different ways. A treaty would use the Vladivostok ceilings as a basis and would include a formula for sublimits on certain kinds of forces. Some of the most contentious issues would be handled by making only a short-term agreement about them. And there would be guidelines for reductions to be negotiated later. This general outline was released publicly. Some public debate now got underway, and continued sporadically, about whether the Senate should ratify such a treaty.

During the following year American negotiators agreed to a further compromise in the reduction of overall ceilings. The 2,400 limit would be reduced, not ten percent, but only to 2,250, and only after the beginning of 1982. This would give the USSR time to phase out some of its older missiles, as it planned to do anyway. Other details of the limitations formula were worked out by the end of the year, and final terms were agreed upon in the spring of 1979. President Carter and Chairman Brezhnev met in Vienna and signed the agreement on June 18.

SALT II was a complicated agreement with many provisions; the most important are presented in the accompanying table. Like SALT I, the second agreement included both a formal treaty and a less formal document, this time called a protocol. The treaty extended through 1985, the protocol only through 1981 (a period of only about thirty months following the date of agreement). In addition to the numerical limits listed, the treaty also limited both sides to deploying only one new type of missile, specified that neither side would interfere with the other's ability to monitor performance by spy satellites or other means, reaffirmed the 1972 ABM Treaty, and included a number of other provisions as well.

Cruise missiles were included in the short-term protocol and hence, by 1981, were unlimited again. (There are certain not very restrictive technical limitations on cruise missiles in the treaty as well.) The negotiators created a separate mechanism to handle the issue of the Soviet Backfire bomber. In an exchange of letters the two superpowers stated that Backfires would not be based in the Soviet far north,

TABLE 5.   Most significant provisions of the SALT II Agreements
Signed in Vienna on 18 June 1979

BY TREATY (to expire at the end of 1985):
  (1) The United States and Soviet Union are limited to an aggregate of 2,400 strategic launch vehicles each (ICBMs, SLBMs and heavy bombers) until the end of 1981. From then until the treaty expires they are limited to an aggregate of 2,250 each.
  (2) Until the treaty expires the two superpowers are limited by three sub-limits within these overall ceilings. They may not deploy more than 820 launchers of MIRVed ICBMs; not more than 1,200 launchers of MIRVed ICBMS and MIRVed SLBMs; and not more than 1,320 launchers of these MIRVed missiles and heavy bombers equipped with long-range cruise missiles.

BY PROTOCOL (to expire at the end of 1981):
  (1) During the protocol period the superpowers are barred from testing or deploying mobile ICBMs.
  (2) During the protocol period they are barred from deploying cruise missiles with ranges longer than 600 kilometers (about 375 miles).

where their limited range would be least handicapping, and that their manufacture would not be accelerated beyond its current rate, estimated by the United States at about thirty per year. The formal SALT II Agreement also included, as planned, a joint statement of principles to guide the negotiation of reductions in the next stage of the SALT process.

The Carter administration submitted the SALT II Agreement to the Senate in the summer of 1979. It was highly controversial and the administration promised a strong campaign to win its approval. That fall SALT was one of the main topics commanding the Senate's attention. But in December the USSR invaded Afghanistan; the reaction in the United States was severe. Leading Senators declared that there was no possibility of SALT's passage, at least for the time being. Early in 1980 the administration withdrew the agreement from active Senate consideration.

Later that year Carter campaigned for reelection, in part on the basis of his arms control record, reaffirmed his commitment to the SALT II Agreement, and pledged to resubmit it to the Senate. Ronald Reagan opposed it, and after his election and inauguration announced that he would not resubmit it, and would instead reopen negotiations with the Soviets.

The debate over SALT II had lasted with greater or lesser intensity for some three years, from 1977, when its main terms became known, until the Afghanistan invasion. The scope of this book cannot do justice to the debate, which was as complicated as the agreement itself. In general, opinion divided into three main camps. A small group of senators and others regarded SALT II as a caricature of real arms control. Its protocol was so short-lived, the limits set by the treaty so high, and the room permitted for other force expansions and qualitative improvements so great, that to this group it seemed to accomplish little control at all.

A much larger body of senators, most arms control specialists, and many national security analysts supported SALT II. Many of them viewed it as flawed, and acknowledged that it had limited significance in restraining the arms race, but felt that it should be ratified for the sake of whatever restraint it did provide, and as a means of keeping the SALT process alive. This group saw rejection by the Senate as a threat to the whole future of the Strategic Arms Limitation Talks, something too important to be risked.

A third large group of senators, joined by many national security specialists and most of the conservative wing of American opinion, opposed the agreement. This group believed that it restrained the

United States too much and/or the Soviet Union too little, and challenged whether the United States would really be able to verify, by its own means, the USSR's compliance with many of the important provisions of the agreement. There was also doubt whether the agreement really lived up to the spirit of the Jackson amendment's requirement of "essential equivalence," because most Soviet missiles are much larger and can carry many more MIRVs than American missiles.

After withdrawing SALT II from Senate consideration, the Carter administration announced that it would honor the terms of the agreement, although not legally bound to do so, so long as the Soviet Union did so also. The Soviets then made a similar announcement. After entering office the Reagan administration also said it would abide by the treaty—the protocol having by then expired—even though Reagan had opposed it earlier. (The new negotiations that administration opened will be discussed later.) As of mid-1983 it seemed likely that the terms of the SALT II treaty would be respected until its expiration in 1985, even though it remains unratified.

SUMMARY

The Strategic Arms Limitation Talks became the centerpiece of American efforts toward arms control after they began at the end of the 1960s. For specialists in national security and arms control, as for the American public, SALT became the main hope for braking and halting the arms race. If the continual increase in the nuclear destructive power of the two sides could be reversed in our time, SALT would be the means by which it would be done.

Although the process of getting the talks underway seemed lengthy at the time, the first agreement was achieved in about three years. The SALT I treaty, which is still in force, limited the two sides' ABM systems to quite low levels. The accompanying interim agreement set, as ceilings for the next five years, the numbers of missiles deployed or under construction at the time of the May 1972 signing. These agreements represented a considerable arms control achievement. Unfortunately they were negotiated just as strategic technology was taking another major step. MIRVs were tested and perfected by the United States before a SALT agreement banning their testing could be hammered out, and thereafter no way could be found to prevent MIRVs from entering both sides' armories.

If a SALT II agreement setting a limit on MIRV launchers could have been reached very quickly, it is possible that the limit might have been set quite low. But contention over bombers and forward-based systems delayed the next understanding for over two years. When President Ford and Chairman Brezhnev met in Vladivostok in November 1974, they underwrote a successful compromise on those contentious issues, but also underwrote a MIRV launcher limit that many specialists found distressingly high. The Vladivostok accords allowed the two sides each to deploy some ten thousand strategic warheads.

There was even greater delay in what was supposed to be a rapid translation of these accords into a formal SALT II Treaty. New contentious issues, domestic American political considerations, hastily formulated policies of the Carter administration, and other factors held up any understanding about the outlines of a new treaty until 1977, and the final terms of the treaty itself until June 1979. Before the Senate had finished debating the very complicated SALT II agreements, the Soviet invasion of Afghanistan made early ratification impossible; the Reagan administration did not resubmit them to the Senate. By that time the moderate limits set in the very short-lived protocol had expired anyway. Meanwhile the SALT II Treaty again "limited" offensive forces for about five years to high levels roughly equal to what the superpowers already had deployed or under construction.

A survey of SALT as a whole suggests that, with one important exception, the effort accomplished little, if any, real limitation on the strategic arms race. The 1972, 1974, and 1979 SALT agreements ratified approximately the size and composition of the strategic forces the two sides had deployed or under construction at the time each agreement was reached. While SALT may have braked the arms race to some degree, it specified as "limits" roughly the developments that were occurring anyway, and thereby sanctioned them. If the arms race is visualized as something like a freight train speeding down the tracks, then the SALT process is best visualized as something running *alongside* it. SALT has not succeeded in getting out in front, as it were, to push in the opposite direction and thereby slow it down significantly.

The one important exception to this generalization is the first agreement ever reached in the Strategic Arms Limitation Talks, the ABM treaty. Most specialists think it is quite possible that the superpowers might have built much larger ABM systems in the 1970s had this treaty not forestalled them. But even this true strategic arms limitation may not last. In the 1980s lasers based in space are attracting defense planners as a technique for destroying ballistic missiles. In March 1983 President Reagan devoted part of his famous "star wars" speech to a plan and appeal for the United States to develop space-based missile defenses. There is talk of terminating the ABM treaty, or interpreting it as not applying to energy-beam systems. More than a dozen years after the Glassboro meeting, strategic arms continue to multiply.

FOR FURTHER READING

Foreign Policy Association. *SALT II—Toward Security or Danger?* New York: Foreign Policy Association, 1979. This short pamphlet presents a good introduction to the SALT II debate, presenting both positions fairly.

Lehman, John F. and Seymour Weiss. *Beyond the SALT II Failure*. New York: Praeger, 1981. Essays analyzing SALT II, and the Soviet-American strategic relationship generally, by authors who represent the viewpoint that favors a buildup in American strategic forces and is skeptical of arms control.

Newhouse, John. *Cold Dawn: the Story of SALT*. New York: Holt, Rinehart and Winston, 1973. An "inside" history of how the SALT I Treaty and Interim Agreement were negotiated, based heavily on confidential interviews with participants in the negotiations.

SIPRI (Stockholm International Peace Research Institute). *World Armaments and Disarmament: SIPRI Yearbook 1980*. London: Taylor and Francis, Ltd. 1980. Chapters Six and Seven contain a comprehensive statement of the SALT II Agreements, and a lucid assessment of them from the viewpoint that favors much stronger limitations on the arms race.

Talbott, Strobe. *Endgame*. New York: Harper, 1979. Another "inside" history, comparable to Newhouse's, of the SALT negotiating process. This one covers the 1977–79 period when the SALT II Agreements were being hammered out.

Wolfe, Thomas W. *The SALT Experience*. Cambridge, Mass: Ballinger Publishing Co., 1979. An analytical history of SALT from its beginnings in 1969 through nearly the final details of SALT II, written by a leading analyst of Soviet military policy.

10
The
Soviet
Buildup

We recall that in the late 1960s and early 1970s, American strategic doctrine stressed "sufficiency" in forces and stability in deterrence. Twice in twenty years the United States had found itself, not entirely intentionally, with strategic superiority, and twice the Soviets had caught up. Now a "plateau of stability" had been reached. Each side had ample capability to destroy the other's cities. Neither side could stop such an attack. Neither side could stop it defensively, because effective nationwide ABM systems had not yet been built. Neither side could stop it offensively, with counterforce strikes on the other's missiles, because the ICBMs now were hardened in silos and the SLBM-carrying submarines could not be located.

Much of the original motive behind SALT was an effort to formalize and freeze the "plateau of stability." First, the stalemate of Mutual Assured Destruction would be made permanent and explicit. The ABM treaty, SALT's main triumph, represented essentially a Soviet-American agreement that the two sides would remain defenseless against each other permanently. Effective ABM systems would never be built. Neither side would be given any reason to doubt that its forces could readily destroy the other's society.

The arms control thinking of the day held that this treaty, in turn, should set the stage for imposing fairly low limits on offensive forces because neither side would have any need for more. Missiles would not be needed for counterforce because limiting damage to one's homeland this way was no longer possible. And missiles would not be needed to penetrate defenses because each had now agreed not to have defenses. Each side would have no use for missiles other than those needed to be sure of destroying the other's society. The weapons were so destructive that this could not be a very large number, so both sides should be able to agree on limiting offensive missiles, at some not-very-high ceiling. In a nutshell, this was the theory of SALT.

Several rents might eventually have appeared in this tapestry, but the first and greatest was MIRVs. Once MIRVs were deployed, first on the American side, then on the Soviet, the total number of warheads on both sides began rising rapidly. But earlier, in the most optimistic years of the SALT process, U.S. negotiators hoped that they would be able to set fairly low ceilings that institutionalized the rough parity then existing. In fact, the SALT I Interim Agreement did something like this for ICBMs and SLBMs.

At the time this agreement was first being negotiated, around 1970, the *overall* balance of forces was still noticeably unequal. The United States was still ahead in many important ways. Its improved Polaris and Minuteman II missiles were qualitatively superior to their Soviet counterparts. MIRVs would be arriving soon, while the Soviets would not have them for some time. They also had no jet bombers capable of reaching the United States, but the United States had many B-52s and FB-111s targeted on the Soviet Union. In Europe the Warsaw Pact was superior to NATO in numbers of troops deployed and certain other categories, but the overall disparity between the two alliances was not great. The U.S. Navy was still unquestioned mistress of the Mediterranean Sea, indeed of all oceans except the immediate territorial waters of the USSR.

During the decade following, all this was to change for the worse from the American perspective. The Soviet Union mounted an enormous, unrelenting buildup across the entire range of military power. Though the total size of the Soviet economy remained only about half that of the United States, year after year Moscow's defense expenditures substantially *exceeded* American expenditures. The burden on the Soviet people was tremendous: by the beginning of the 1980s the Soviet economy was stagnating in many areas. But Soviet military capability was immensely greater than it had been ten years earlier. In many ways it now equaled American capabilities, and in some respects exceeded them.

THE SOVIET STRATEGIC BUILDUP

During the 1970s the USSR produced four new ICBM models. One was not a success and was never deployed in quantity. The other three missiles are all much larger than any American missile. In NATO terminology they are called the SS-17, SS-18 and SS-19. The SS-18 in particular is huge. Its throw weight is seven times that of the most powerful American missile, the Minuteman III. Where the latter carries three MIRVs, the SS-18 carries eight, every one of which has a much larger yield than the Minuteman MIRVs. (More data are given on the accompanying table.)

Technically, the Soviet decision to build very big new ICBMs was more a confession of weakness than a statement of strength, though psychologically and politically the effect was the opposite. The Soviets had to build large missiles, and new ones, because the older ones were too small to carry the large MIRV vehicles the Soviets were obliged to design. They had not mastered the technology of miniaturization, so both their warheads and their bus for carrying them were necessarily larger. This in turn required a much larger missile to carry the size and weight.

By contrast the Americans had succeeded in designing, from the beginning, a much smaller bus and warhead. The MIRV package for ICBMs fit onto the existing American ICBM, the Minuteman; the MIRV package for SLBMs fit onto the Poseidon missile, which in turn

TABLE 6.   American and Soviet strategic forces as of mid-1975

	Soviet Union	United States
ICBMs	1,618 (includes about 70 new SS-17, SS-18, SS-19 missiles)	1,054 (includes 550 Minuteman III missiles)
SLBMs	784 in 75 submarines	656 (includes 400 Poseidon missiles) in 41 submarines
Long-range bombers	135 Bears and Bisons	463 B-52s and FB-111s

Notes: Data for Soviet long-range bombers do not include about 25 Backfire bombers deployed as of this time. The American FB-111 is technically a medium-range bomber, but acquires long range with aerial refueling, a technique long practiced and perfected with FB-111s.

Source: International Institute of Strategic Studies, London: The Military Balance, 1975–76.

fit inside the same submarine tubes as the old Polaris missile. But this early U.S. technical triumph later came to seem almost a liability, when some Americans were frightened by the sheer size of the Soviet missiles and the fact that they were new.

At sea there were comparable Soviet improvements. At the beginning of the 1970s the Soviet Navy was still deploying a fairly primitive SLBM, roughly comparable to America's first Polaris missile, with a range of only about 1,750 miles. By mid-decade a new fleet of submarines, called Deltas in the West, were carrying a new, much-improved SLBM with a range of almost 5,000 miles. The table gives additional data.

By the end of the 1970s yet another SLBM was entering the Soviet forces. This one had about the same 5,000-mile range but carried MIRVs. And a colossal new model of missile-carrying submarine, called the Typhoon in the West, was under construction. The largest submarine ever built, the Typhoon apparently is intended to be able to remain at sea for long periods of time.

During the decade of the 1970s the USSR also began deploying the Backfire bomber in quantity, as discussed in the previous chapter. Although the Backfire is not, on balance, as capable a bomber as the United States' B-52 or FB-111 bombers, improved with advanced electronics and standoff missiles, the Backfire also does not have to face nearly as difficult an air defense system as American bombers must face.

There were other improvements in the Soviet strategic posture as well. Some of the ICBM silos were "superhardened," making them invulnerable to anything but an almost direct hit. The USSR also continued work on a civil defense system. While programs for creating shelters and stocking them with provisions had been abandoned in the West by the mid-1960s, the Soviets chose to continue and improve their similar program, and their plans for evacuation of Soviet cities in a crisis. Exactly how effective this civil defense program would prove in a real war is a matter of debate among Western analysts.

Much of this strategic buildup was predictable and in that sense undisturbing. But the number of models of missiles, their size, and the pace of their development and deployment exceeded Western expectations. Western leaders naturally were disturbed when the Soviet strategic effort proved to be greater than Western intelligence had anticipated. Toward the end of the 1970s the Carter administration revealed that Moscow had begun work on a group of four more strategic missiles—the fifth generation—and a new long-range strategic bomber. Later the new bomber was given the name "Blackjack" in the West.

Once the MIRV era was launched it also became predictable that both superpowers would end up deploying large numbers of warheads. But some American officials had believed in the late 1960s and early 1970s that it would take the USSR longer to develop and deploy MIRVs than it actually did. Here too the Soviet strategic drive exceeded expectations. And the large size of Soviet missiles meant that, if and when the Soviets mastered the miniaturization technology, the USSR could deploy many more MIRVs than the United States could, on the same number of launch vehicles. Barring a long-lasting negotiated limit on total numbers of warheads, the United States could eventually face a tremendous disadvantage, missile for missile.

THE SOVIET BUILDUP OF GENERAL PURPOSE FORCES

More disturbing to many in the West than the Soviets' strategic improvements was their vast buildup of general purpose forces during the 1970s. In aircraft, in short-range missiles with nuclear warheads, in armor, in ships—in fact, in most kinds of military equipment—new models were introduced; and in many cases Soviet production rates exceeded American production of similar items. By decade's end the Soviet Army, Navy and tactical Air Forces were equipped, in many categories, with more weapons than their American counterparts. And, in striking contrast to past eras when Soviet weapons were often inferior, the new ones were often equal and occasionally superior to American weapons.

In important respects the disparity was becoming vivid. By the early 1980s the Soviet Air Force had about double the number of tactical aircraft as the USAF. Most of these were recent models, and they could deliver a variety of nuclear as well as conventional bombs. The production rate of new Soviet aircraft was faster than of new U.S. planes. From 1974 to 1982 the USSR manufactured over 6,000 military aircraft of all types; the United States about 3,000.

The Red Army, which has always emphasized armor, had almost four times as many armored personnel carriers (APCs) and over four times the number of tanks as the U.S. Army by the early 1980s. Both APCs and tanks were at least equal to their American equivalents in quality. The Soviet production rate of new models during the 1970s was about five times the U.S. production rate in tanks, over three times the U.S. rate in APCs, and eight times the U.S. rate in artillery.

These kinds of numerical superiority did not necessarily confer the same ratio of real superiority; their true significance was a matter for debate among American national security analysts. A significant fraction of Soviet air and ground forces — from a fifth to a quarter depending on what exactly is counted — are deployed for possible conflict with China, and perhaps should be excluded from direct comparison with U.S. forces. Also, the comparisons become more complicated and more controversial if Warsaw Pact and NATO forces, rather than Soviet and American, are compared. Nor does one necessarily have to match forces directly. It may be less important to compare the Red Army's tanks with Western tanks than with Western antitank weapons, which are numerous, effective, and much cheaper than tanks.

Finally, in modern warfare a technological edge makes an enormous difference. In the 1982 war in Lebanon the Israelis, using sophisticated new tactics and a combination of their own and American advanced technology, completely destroyed late-model Soviet air defense systems deployed by Syria with almost no losses to the Israeli forces. In critical factors like tactical air defense, air battles for air superiority, and defense against armor, the United States continued to hold an advantage, thanks to its superiority in electronics and related technologies. All this said, however, the disparities in air and ground forces between the USSR and the United States became worrisome to American specialists during the 1970s and thereafter.

The growth of Soviet naval power was at least equally disturbing, especially in its implications. A ship-building program begun in the 1960s began yielding a modern, expanding Soviet Navy able to operate far from the USSR. As recently as the time of the Cuban Missile Crisis the Soviet naval force had been, except for submarines, mainly a coastal defense arm. Now it was becoming a true "blue water navy," capable of projecting Soviet power almost anywhere around the globe. During the decade of the 1970s, for instance, the USSR kept about twenty ships in the Indian Ocean and conducted naval exercises as far away as the Gulf of Mexico, on America's doorstep. Soviet naval power in the Mediterranean grew to the point where the U.S. Sixth Fleet could no longer be confident of retaining control of that sea in the event of war.

In total striking power the U.S. Navy remained superior because the Soviet Union did not deploy large aircraft carriers capable of making major attacks at distances of hundreds of miles. But its production rate was such that in 1973 the Soviet Navy, for the first time, passed the U.S. Navy in numbers of major surface ships. Submarines were also built at a consistently faster rate than in America. By the close of the decade the Soviets had almost half again the total number of combat ships—surface and submarine both—as the United States had. Three aircraft carriers, smaller than American carriers, were also at sea or under construction. With these the USSR could deploy "naval infantry" in amphibious and helicopter operations similar to those first made famous by the U.S. Marines.

For U.S. national security analysts this great naval buildup raised serious questions about the Kremlin's long-term goals. The USSR does not need a large blue-water navy for maritime "defense" in the usual sense. Unlike the United States, Europe, and Japan, it does not depend heavily on shipping for oil and other resources, nor for reinforcing allies in wartime. It is hard to think of motives other than expansionism that account adequately for the increasing Soviet ability to deploy large forces far from home for long periods. The amphibious capability especially suggests that the Kremlin may be visualizing military intervention in parts of the world where Soviet power has hitherto been absent.

The Soviet military buildup in its entirety was all the more impressive because it was the product not of a sudden surge but of a steady, sustained effort. Year after year the USSR increased its military expenditures, at a roughly constant five percent rate of increase. This sustained effort began, in fact, not in the 1970s but in the mid-1960s, after Brezhnev replaced Krushchev as the party secretary. A few years passed before it was widely noticed in the West. Krushchev had preferred to limit military spending in favor of building the Soviet economy. Blamed for the humiliation of the Cuban Missile Crisis, he was replaced by a leader determined to build up Soviet military might. The constantly increasing military effort continued throughout Brezhnev's term, and preliminary evidence suggests it will continue thereafter. The real meaning of that effort, however, was a matter of some disagreement among national security analysts in the West—a disagreement that deserves more attention.

THE AMERICAN REACTION TO THE SOVIET BUILDUP

At all times there is a spectrum of opinion, corresponding vaguely to the left-right dimension of political attitudes, among American national security and arms control specialists regarding the best policy options for the United States. To describe this spectrum fairly is not easy. The "dove" versus "hawk" terminology so popular during the Vietnam era has often been resisted by specialists, who see their policy positions and rationales as containing too many offsetting ingredients for such simple descriptions. Nor does the difference always come down to a choice between more arms control or more weapons. For instance, many of those who usually favor larger defense expenditures also favor arms control, given the right conditions. Perhaps the best way to characterize the spectrum of opinion is in terms of *which risks* a particular analyst or group emphasizes in any given situation: the risks that may be posed by adversaries enhancing their power, or the risks (and costs) posed by continuing and perhaps accelerating the arms race. Thus nearly all specialists may favor negotiating some kind of new strategic arms control treaty, for instance, but some will emphasize the risks in failing to find strict treaty conditions that constrain the USSR, and some will emphasize the risks of delaying or losing the treaty out of a search for stricter conditions.

During the 1970s almost the entire spectrum of U.S. national security and arms control specialists became concerned about the buildup in Soviet military power, but it was viewed with more alarm by some than by others. Toward one side of the spectrum, analysts tended to find explanations for it that emphasized Soviet motives other than aggressive ones. Possible motives included Moscow's fear of China or other possible enemies, Soviet reaction to American choices (such as MIRV), the great influence of Soviet generals and heavy-industry bureaucrats in Kremlin decision making, and the sheer exploitation of technical possibilities. Toward the other side analysts stressed the increasing dangers the USSR could, in fact, pose to the United States even if the military expansion might indeed result partly from other motives. As the momentum of the Soviet arms drive continued, some of these specialists became increasingly vocal and organized.

Best known was a group called the Committee on the Present Danger, formed in 1976 to promote popular support for an answering increase in American military power. The committee was headed by Paul Nitze, who had been a principal member of the U.S. negotiating team for SALT I and, many years earlier, one of the principal architects of NSC-68. Later Nitze and the committee assumed the leadership of those opposed to the SALT II agreement, both during its final stages of negotiation when its main outlines were known, and afterwards when the Carter administration submitted it to the Senate.

Also in 1976, considerable publicity was generated for the so-called "Team B Report," which expressed alarm about the Soviet buildup. Team B was a group of national security specialists, some of them shortly to be leaders of the committee, and all sharing its viewpoint. George Bush, then director of the CIA, formed the team and invited it to challenge the regular annual CIA estimate of Soviet capabilities.

This annual review and certain other major intelligence reviews are known as "National Intelligence Estimates," or NIEs. They form the basis for much official national security planning. Previously the CIA had come under some criticism for underestimating the USSR's power and it decided to respond by opening its data, and the regular, "Team A," interpretation thereof, on a highly classified basis to a group of critics who could form their own judgment.

The Team B Report was itself classified but its main conclusions were leaked to the press. The Kremlin leaders do believe a nuclear war could be fought and won by the USSR under advantageous circumstances, said Team B, and are driving toward the advantage necessary either to defeat the United States or force it to back down in crises. These conclusions (and the team's assessment that the Soviet Union had already achieved a significant degree of superiority) were later reviewed by the CIA's own analysts and rejected, at least so far as that time period was concerned. But in the following years the exact extent and character of the Soviet buildup remained a subject of intense discussion among U.S. national security specialists.

Much of the debate revolved around differing estimates of Soviet military expenditures. The official defense budget published by the USSR is a fiction; in actuality expenditures are considerably higher, exactly how much being a matter of estimate. A CIA figure commonly cited holds that over the ten-year period of the 1970s the Soviet Union spent on its military forces about $300 billion *more* than the United States spent. Analysts of the "present danger" viewpoint have suggested that the difference may be even greater, and strongly advocate that the United States close the gap.

Specialists taking the opposing point of view argue that some of the Soviet expenditure represents money wasted—on an air defense system, for instance, that the United States can penetrate—and some of the expenditure goes to forces deployed against China. For these and other reasons these analysts reject the idea that the United States should have to match Soviet expenditures. The United States, they argue, is in a quite different position from the USSR and should plan its forces on the basis of its own needs and goals.

These analysts also challenge the validity of the estimates themselves. Normally the figures are derived by calculating how much it would cost the United States to develop the same forces. This is misleading, they argue, because many of the components cost more in America than in the Soviet Union. This is especially true of manpower: American military personnel are much better paid than their Soviet counterparts, and *American* pay scales are used in calculating what it would cost to reproduce the USSR's forces in America. These analysts argue that if one examines what personnel and other components actually cost the Kremlin, the real difference between Soviet and American military expenditures is much less, though still not negligible. Specialists on the opposing side reply that other inaccuracies creep into any effort to calculate the Kremlin's "actual" costs, and pricing Soviet forces in terms of what they would cost in America is really the fairest method. The debate is unresolved and, due to the differences in the structure of the American and Soviet economies, may be unresolvable.

EUROPEAN NUCLEAR ISSUES

The Soviet military buildup included the development of a particular missile, called the SS-20, that was later to have enormous political and policy consequences. To understand how this aspect of the Soviet buildup took on such importance in the American experience, it is necessary to summarize, in the remainder of this chapter, the problem of nuclear weapons in European strategy. Let us approach the question by examining briefly the historical context out of which it developed.

From the beginning of NATO, America's allies in Europe have been concerned to make sure that the United States would be thoroughly involved in any major European conflict. We recall from an earlier chapter that a primary function of the U.S. troops stationed there is to serve as a "trip wire" or "plate glass." No major Soviet invasion can occur in central Europe without involving them; once they are involved the United States could not avoid full-scale participation in the war. For many Europeans this "political" function, and not their fighting capability, is the main role these forces play; whenever suggestions are put forward in America for reducing the size of the force, Europeans react mostly by questioning whether the overall U.S. commitment is declining, not by questioning the purely military consequences.

Naturally, the point of this troop deployment is deterrence. If the Soviets know they will have to fight not just Europeans but Americans too, they may be much less likely to attack. But from the European perspective the mere presence of U.S. troops in quantity may not be enough. The Soviets must also be convinced that they cannot win simply by defeating the combined NATO forces, American and European, on the ground.

In the early 1950s there was a brief effort to accomplish this by enlarging the ground forces. At a conference in Lisbon the allies set targets for the numbers of troops they would commit, targets intended to weld together a combined army large enough to cope with the Soviets. But the "Lisbon force goals" never came close to being met. Meanwhile nuclear weapons for tactical use were being developed by the Americans. Soon NATO adopted a strategy that any Soviet attack would be repulsed with atomic weapons. High levels of ground forces would not be needed.

At the end of the 1950s and for a while thereafter, the United States deployed at bases in Europe some missiles, called Thor and Jupiter, capable of striking within the Soviet Union and carrying nuclear warheads. And the Soviet Union deployed missiles, called by NATO the SS-4 and SS-5 (plus a few SS-3s), capable of striking almost any target in Western Europe, and also of carrying nuclear warheads. Gradually both sides also deployed various kinds of shorter-range missiles. In the 1960s, after the Thors and Jupiters became vulnerable to Soviet attack, they were withdrawn. The SS-4s and SS-5s remained, and continued to grow in number to over 600.

When the Kennedy administration came to office in 1961, Robert McNamara's civilian analysts launched a new assessment of the balance of European forces. On the one hand the Soviets were now deploying nuclear weapons for tactical use also; the United States would not be able to resort to them easily. On the other hand, the new analysis indicated that Soviet conventional capabilities were less than had been thought; a defense of Western Europe using only conventional forces might be possible after all. At least the attack might be held off for some time, during which negotiations might end the war. Alternatively, a small number of nuclear weapons might be used by both sides, and then negotiations ensue. Flexible Response became the U.S. strategy.

NATO adopted Flexible Response in 1967, but from the European viewpoint it was done at American insistence. The Europeans were not entirely comfortable with a strategy that supposed there would be a period of fighting and then a negotiated settlement. Whether the fighting involved large conventional forces only, or included some nuclear weapons, the damage would be suffered mostly by Europeans—Eastern and Western both. It was all too easy to visualize an outcome where the United States and Soviet Union both emerged from the war relatively undamaged, while Europe lay in shambles.

Behind this discomfort lay a long-standing and more basic disagreement over the nature of deterrence, which has continued. The Europeans have always believed that the Soviets would be most surely deterred by the threat that their own homeland would be destroyed. Hence they have always favored policies, such as Massive Retaliation in the 1950s, that seemed most certainly to pose that ultimate threat. Since abandoning Massive Retaliation, the Americans have believed that under some circumstances, the Soviets might not find credible the threat of Armageddon. All-out Soviet invasion is not the only possibility. Under some conditions the Soviets might calculate that NATO would never launch a global holocaust to prevent some small loss.

The Americans reason that the Soviets would be more surely deterred from this kind of attack if they knew that they could be defeated "in theater" by some combination of conventional and (if necessary) a few nuclear weapons. NATO would not be immobilized by its own reluctance to launch an all-out war. The Europeans respond that preparing for a limited engagement might make it too easy for the two sides actually to get into one, precisely on the assumption that it *could* be ended without a holocaust. They reason that if any attack seems likely to turn into a holocaust, there will be no attack at all.

The Europeans accepted Flexible Response under pressure, but many of them have interpreted it differently from the Americans ever since. The Americans want to emphasize policies that assume that, in a European war, nuclear weapons would be used later, if at all, and in small rather than large numbers. For instance, they favor building up sizable stocks of ammunition and other supplies for fighting conventionally. If that capability is in place, the threat to fight locally will be credible, and the Soviets will be deterred.

The Europeans want to emphasize policies that imply that nuclear weapons would be used soon and devastatingly. For instance, they favor long-range weapons that effectively "couple" theater nuclear war to all-out war. If in a European war such weapons began to destroy the Soviet homeland, the Soviets would have to attack the United States or risk losing. If the "coupling" is in place, the Soviets will run no risks at all. They will be deterred.

The running differences over the interpretation of Flexible Response and the role of nuclear weapons has not been the only strain within NATO over the years. In 1967 the French, who had been distancing themselves for some time, withdrew from the alliance in order to have a freer hand to pursue an independent foreign policy. About the same time the U.S. Senate became interested in reducing the American troop commitment. For years the U.S. forces in Europe had numbered roughly 300,000, but the feeling grew in the Senate that a smaller force could symbolize the U.S. commitment to NATO as well as a larger one, and would be much less expensive. Senator Mike Mansfield began proposing resolutions calling for reductions because the Vietnam War was such a drain on American resources. When that war wound down other reasons appeared: the Senate was eager to reduce the swollen defense budget, and East-West crises, once frequent over Berlin, had ceased in Europe.

As this impulse gradually gathered senatorial adherents, the Nixon administration negotiated "burden-sharing" agreements whereby the allies paid some of the costs of maintaining the troops in Europe. Even so, by 1973 sentiment in the Senate was growing so strong that the administration was able to secure a majority vote to continue the usual troop level only by arguing that a unilateral reduction would hinder arms control negotiations.

NATO and the Warsaw Pact entered into negotiations that year for reducing the numbers of troops on both sides. Called "Mutual and Balanced Force Reductions" (MBFR) in the West, the negotiations dragged on fruitlessly. The Soviets would not agree to the Western concept of "balance" and omitted this word from their name for the talks. Beginning from a situation in which the Pact had significantly more troops under arms, the Soviets wanted equal *cuts*, which would leave their margin of superiority relatively more important. The West demanded differential cuts down to equal final *levels*. Later, a major disagreement arose over what forces actually exist, with the Soviets insisting both that the West was overstating the Warsaw Pact troop totals and that French forces should be counted on the NATO side. For these and other reasons too numerous and complicated to detail, the two sides have never yet (by the time this book was written) been able to reach an agreement, though they continue to talk.

Another rift opened within the Western alliance in the wake of the October 1973 Mideast War. Many Americans were angered that, with the important exception of Portugal, the NATO allies had refused the United States permission to overfly their airspace or use NATO bases in the effort to resupply Israel. This time the Senate assembled a majority behind the idea that the European allies should compensate the United States for any balance-of-payments costs in maintaining the American troops. The Pentagon was required to reduce the troop level by the same percentage as any shortage in the European compensation. The NATO allies had no choice but to agree to "offset" payments covering the U.S. balance-of-payments costs.

After MBFR got underway, however, Senate interest in unilateral reductions waned. The Soviet military buildup also contributed to this, and to the strength of NATO. In the mid-1970s political cohesion among the allies increased as the alliance felt challenged by the increasingly obvious buildup in the quantity and quality of weapons the Soviets could bring to bear against Europe. Some of the allies now increased their military commitments.

NATO also explored whether advanced conventional technology could help restore the balance. Precision-guided munitions (PGMs) were becoming available that could offer very high accuracy ("one-shot/one-kill") against many kinds of targets. Especially important was a new generation of antitank guided missiles (ATGMs) which offered a way to counter the huge Soviet tank force without NATO having to deploy an equal number of tanks.

New nuclear technology was appearing too. American weapons scientists perfected an "enhanced radiation weapon," popularly called the neutron bomb. Properly employed, this weapon could kill over a fairly wide area by prompt radiation, but blast and fire damage would be less than many nuclear weapons would produce, and fallout would be minimal. Proponents argued that the weapon would be ideal for the European theater because damage to the allies' own towns and territories would be reduced, and within hours NATO forces could reoccupy areas where the weapons had been used.

A lengthy debate ensued within NATO over this concept. Skeptics wondered, for one thing, if once again the Americans had come up with a way to fight a nuclear war confined to Europe. The bomb seemed inhumane to others, and encountered objections from the left wing of the Labour Party in England and the Social Democratic Party in West Germany, both then in office.

But the new weapon did seem to be an effective answer to the threat implicit in the Warsaw Pact buildup, and it fit in with European ideas about resorting to nuclear weapons early in any war. After considerable pulling and hauling the allies approved a neutron bomb deployment.

Meanwhile the NATO debate was being accompanied by another in Washington. Arms control advocates argued that, precisely because the weapon did seem so effective against conventional attack, it would be too easy and tempting to resort to it. In the event of an intense crisis involving low-level fighting, NATO might start using the weapon too soon. The Soviets could not be expected to distinguish, in the confusion of battle, between enhanced-radiation and other nuclear weapons. They would respond with their own nuclear strikes and the conflict would quickly escalate to all-out war. In 1978 President Carter decided to "defer" production of the weapon.

EUROSTRATEGIC MISSILES

From the perspective of some Europeans, Carter's withdrawal of the neutron bomb made it all the more important to find an answer to what seemed the most vivid threat of all—the Soviet SS-20. This new missile was first deployed in 1976. Easily moved from one site to another and quickly launched, the SS-20 was MIRVed with three accurate warheads per missile. Its range was sufficient to reach any target in Western Europe from launch sites within the USSR.

Initially the Americans, and some Europeans, were not particularly disturbed by the SS-20. Clearly it was a modernization, and probably a replacement, for the old SS-4s and SS-5s, which were being phased out as the SS-20s arrived. The older missiles were somewhat primitive, and if anything it was slightly surprising that the Soviets had waited so long to deploy a new missile. Though many of the SS-4s and SS-5s could also reach any Western European target, the Europeans had never been especially exercised about them.

The Soviets themselves also seemed to look on the SS-20 simply as a modernization of essentially the same capability they had had for a long time. As the SS-20s were deployed the Soviets launched neither threatening propaganda nor any "peace offensive." They drew no attention to them, nor to the other new, shorter-range missiles that they (like NATO) deployed from time to time as technology improved.

But some Europeans felt that the SS-20 was a serious new threat. Its relative mobility, quick launch time, good accuracy and MIRVs made it much more capable than anything the Soviets had ever had. And NATO had nothing that was at all comparable. The Americans had long ago withdrawn their primitive Thors and Jupiters. They did keep in Europe some Pershing I missiles, but these also were older, and did not have the range, quick launch, or other features of the SS-20.

In fact NATO had no missile at all in the category that was now being called "long-range theater nuclear forces" (LRTNF). These are weapons with ranges from 1,000 to 5,500 kilometers. Weapons with ranges from 200 to 1,000 kilometers are called medium-range TNF, and those of less than 200 kilometers short-range TNF, or "battlefield nuclear weapons." Both NATO and the Warsaw Pact have missiles in the latter categories, and both have aircraft able to carry bombs more than 1,000 kilometers. But NATO had no LRTNF missile, at least none launched from the ground.*

Since it is generally assumed that at least some of the long-range forces on both sides are targeted against cities, LRTNF have also come to be called "Eurostrategic" forces. Strategic targeting means targeting against cities, and the term Eurostrategic means forces on both sides that are based in Europe and so targeted.

This complicated nomenclature has helped to foster some confusions. Strategic *targeting* always means targeting on cities and this is

---

*Certain Poseidon missiles aboard U.S. submarines are assigned to the NATO commander for targeting, but these are not usually counted as part of NATO's forces, even by the Soviets.

often confused with strategic *forces*—be they Eurostrategic forces or other Soviet or American strategic forces. But as noted earlier, these forces can also be used against military targets—bases, airfields, missile sites, and other military targets in rear areas, or even forces on or near the battlefield. Conversely, some of the American, Soviet, NATO, and Warsaw Pact aircraft that are usually called "tactical" aircraft can deliver bombs against cities in Western Europe, Eastern Europe, and the western USSR. Strategic or tactical targeting should not be confused with the forces that are used.

Another confusion is sometimes engendered by the fact that NATO has had no long-range or Eurostrategic missile, but Britain and France both do. The British have sixty-four missiles, carrying three warheads each, on four submarines. (In addition to these SLBMs they also have long-range bombers carrying nuclear bombs.) The French have eighteen land-based missiles plus eighty SLBMs carried on five submarines. (They also have long-range "nuclear capable" aircraft.) All of these forces are targeted primarily on the Soviet Union and primarily against cities.

Understandably the Soviets have always wanted to count these forces in discussions of NATO's and the Warsaw Pact's Eurostrategic capabilities against each other. But NATO has always taken the position that it cannot do this, because the British and French forces are not available to NATO. They are national forces that probably would not be used until Soviet missiles were striking (or Soviet forces invading) the British or French homelands. Besides, France is not a military member of NATO. Thus NATO could find itself engaged in nuclear warfare in central Europe without being able to call on these forces at all.

In short, when the Soviet SS-20s were first deployed NATO had nothing comparable to turn to—neither from Britain and France, nor from America. The United States did have something roughly comparable under development: the Pershing II. This missile would carry only one warhead, but a very accurate one, and it would have a range comparable to the SS-20. The United States was also developing ground-launched cruise missiles (GLCMs), a new kind of missile that will be discussed in the next chapter. When some elements of NATO, especially in West Germany, and now also in some quarters in Washington, grew concerned about the Eurostrategic threat in the late 1970s, U.S. weapons scientists were able to promise these systems in the near future.

Other members of NATO, for instance the Belgian and Dutch governments, thought these weapons unnecessary and were more interested in seeking arms control agreements with the USSR. Debate within the alliance culminated in a meeting in December 1979 at which it was decided to try both policies. The "two-track" decision, as it became known, called for the United States to seek an arms control agreement with the Soviets that would make a Pershing II and GLCM deployment unnecessary. If those negotiations failed, then NATO would deploy the Pershings and GLCMs.

The decision was readily understandable as a product of the concern of many military and diplomatic elements within NATO. They were concerned that the SS-20 might eventually be used to intimidate Western Europe if nothing comparable were deployed by NATO. And some Europeans wanted to increase the "coupling" between any potential European war and all-out strategic war. Pershing IIs and GLCMs deployed, controlled, and launched by Americans, and striking within the USSR, would certainly be answered by Soviet strikes on America. But the "two-track" decision did not (and could not have) taken into account the popular reaction that ensued in Western Europe, and subsequently in America. We will return to that story below.

CHINESE NUCLEAR FORCES

Brief mention should be made of the strategic nuclear capabilities of the Peoples Republic of China (PRC), which at some times have been considered seriously as part of the nuclear threat to the United States. For example, one of the arguments put forward in the late 1960s by advocates of the Sentinel "thin" ABM system was that Sentinel, although nearly useless against the Soviet Union, would be able to protect the United States against a small number of Chinese missiles. At that time the PRC was in the earliest phases of testing long-range missiles.

By the beginning of the 1980s, the PRC had deployed about fifty intermediate- and about fifty medium-range ballistic missiles, and about ten ICBMs, all aimed at targets in the Soviet Union. It was just beginning to deploy another ICBM whose much longer range (about 13,000 kilometers) presumably earmarked it for use against American targets. By this time the PRC also had tested SLBMs and may have launched one operational SLBM-carrying submarine.

But the early 1980s was also a time when Washington regarded the PRC as something approaching a friend, when Beijing allowed American intelligence-gathering stations to be put on Chinese soil, and when discussions were held about possible sales of American (non-nuclear) weapons to China. The slow increase in PRC nuclear capabilities against the United States received very little attention, either from the American public or in the unclassified literature of specialists.

SUMMARY

The steady and continuing military buildup that the Soviet Union began in the mid-1960s, after the Cuban Missile Crisis, had very visible consequences in the 1970s. The USSR advanced toward rough equality with the United States across the whole spectrum of military power. In some technologies the Soviets continued to lag; on the other hand, they surged ahead of America in production rates of tactical aircraft, tanks, and some other weapons.

Their strategic buildup included developing the Backfire bomber, acquiring MIRVs sooner than the West had expected, deploying three new ICBMs, and first one and then another new SLBM. The ICBMs were very large and gave the Soviets a great superiority in throw weight, mainly because they were technically incapable of matching American miniaturization technology. By the end of the 1970s yet another generation of strategic missiles and a new strategic bomber were on the way, and Soviet ICBM targeting accuracy was improving almost to American levels.

Virtually all analysts in the West grew concerned about this buildup but they differed in their degree of alarm. Some attributed it partially or wholly to intentions other than aggressive; others emphasized the aggressive capability it gave the Soviet Union. The CIA "Team B" report argued that the Kremlin was driving toward general military superiority over the West. The Committee on the Present Danger and others pressed for a matching American buildup. Other specialists who doubted the need for "force matching" also became concerned as Soviet military power mounted.

The Soviet missile that was to become so well known in the West, the SS-20, was first deployed in 1976. Largely a replacement for earlier, more primitive Soviet LRTNF (long-range theater nuclear forces) missiles, the SS-20 did not initially excite American specialists, nor the Europeans at whom it was aimed. But there was internal disagreement in NATO military and diplomatic circles about deterrence and the role of nuclear weapons. In contrast to most American professionals, most Europeans traditionally accepted a doctrine of the early use of many nuclear weapons. According to this idea, the USSR would be best deterred if the Soviets were convinced that NATO would surely escalate to long-range nuclear warfare. It could be argued that this, in turn, suggested that NATO must demonstrate that it could not be intimidated by deployment of the Soviet SS-20.

European professionals had always sought, too, to "couple" any kind of nuclear warfare in Europe to all-out strategic war. American Pershing IIs and GLCMs, due in 1983, would reinforce this coupling, and without them NATO had nothing comparable to the SS-20. At the same time, some of the allies preferred to limit all Eurostrategic missiles. At the end of 1979, the alliance agreed that the U.S. missiles would be deployed if no arms control agreement could be reached by the time the Pershing IIs and GLCMs were ready.

Meanwhile the Soviet military buildup continued at its constant rate of increase. Even in categories of power in which the USSR had well passed the United States, the drive continued relentlessly. Long before the end of the decade, the United States had begun to react to the Soviet military buildup by deciding upon new weapons of its own and in other ways. To that story we now turn.

FOR FURTHER READING

International Institute of Strategic Studies, *The Military Balance*; and International Institute of Strategic Studies, *Strategic Survey*. 18 Adam Street, London: I.I.S.S. (annuals). These two reference sources, published each year, provide accurate, up-to-date and comprehensive information about developments in Soviet as well as American, and other nations', armed forces; and about major international events of strategic significance in the previous twelve months.

Kaplan, Fred M. *Dubious Specter: A Skeptical Look at the Soviet Nuclear Threat*. Washington, D.C.: Institute for Policy Studies, 1980. One of the best critical assessments of the Soviet buildup, written from the viewpoint that minimizes its significance.

Olive, Marsha M. and Jeffrey D. Parro. *Nuclear Weapons in Europe: Modernization and Limitation*. Lexington, Mass.: Lexington Books, 1983. A useful collection of essays, written from various points of view, on the issues surrounding Eurostrategic weapons in the 1980s.

Pipes, Richard. "Why the Soviet Union thinks it could fight and win a nuclear war." In *Commentary*, Vol. 64, No. 1 (July 1977). One of the "classic" statements of the community of analysts that became most concerned about the Soviet military buildup and advocated a strong American response. The author subsequently became, for a period, a high-ranking adviser to the Reagan administration.

SIPRI (Stockholm International Peace Research Institute), *World Armaments and Disarmament: SIPRI Yearbook: 1982* Cambridge, Mass.: Oelgeschlager, Gunn and Hain, Inc. (1982). Part One of this volume contains a good introduction to the issues of Eurostrategic weapons.

U.S. Department of Defense. *Annual Report to the Congress.* Washington, D.C.: United States Government Printing Office, annual. A yearly summary of the U.S. defense budget and plan, and a five-year projection of defense programs. This document used to be known as the annual Posture Statement. It presents the official Defense Department viewpoint on the Soviet threat, European defense issues, and other major questions in U.S. national security policy.

11

The American Buildup

The Soviet strategic buildup of the 1970s, impressive as it was, never raised the number of Soviet missile warheads to a total larger than the American force. The deployment of Minuteman III and Poseidon always kept the number of American MIRVs larger.

But when the Soviets deployed a new generation of large strategic missiles they did encourage the development of qualitative improvements, and eventually new weapons, in the American aresenal. At least equally important in shaping the evolving American program were doctrinal and weapons changes created by advancing technology. And at the beginning of the 1980s, the Soviet buildup as a whole, conventional as well as strategic, became the justification for a huge expansion in U.S. programs. This chapter sketches the weapons developments, and some of the evolution of doctrine, in the United States to early 1983.

FLEXIBLE TARGETING

The "sufficiency" doctrine of the Nixon administration meant that the United States would give primary emphasis to maintaining sufficient forces to deter Soviet attack. But on entering office in 1969, that administration had inherited much larger forces than were needed for destroying Soviet cities. Planners had needed to hedge against the possibility that the Soviets might expand the small ABM systems built in the 1960s around Moscow and Leningrad. Many more missiles would be needed to penetrate an expanded and improved system than to destroy undefended cities. And only recently had the Defense Department abandoned the goal of damage limiting by way of counterforce strikes.

But the Soviet ABM was still small and more missiles were available than were needed for assured destruction. Even when targets in Eastern Europe and China were included, and redundant targeting built in to compensate for malfunctions, there was still a surplus. The surplus remained targeted, as it had been, on Soviet military targets—i.e., on counterforce targets. An earlier chapter mentioned that counterforce targeting was never entirely removed from the SIOP even when significant damage limiting became impossible.

The MIRVed missiles Poseidon and Minuteman III began to enter the U.S. arsenal about a year later, whereupon the total number of warheads began to rise rapidly. Before the end of Nixon's first term the SALT ABM treaty removed any prospect of a large, effective Soviet ABM. Penetrating such a system had been a primary rationale for developing and deploying Poseidon and Minuteman III; that rationale had now been lost. Meanwhile the Soviets were not yet deploying MIRVs, although clearly they would before long.

In numbers of warheads the United States was moving ahead of the USSR. A situation was developing reminiscent, in some ways, of the one ten years earlier. Now as then, the United States was finding itself with many more warheads than needed to destroy Soviet society, and many more than the USSR had. In the early 1960s planners had moved toward damage limiting through counterforce. But in the early 1970s The USSR had SLBMs and its ICBMs in hardened silos. So what should the surplus in the U.S. warheads be used for?

In January 1974 the secretary of defense, James Schlesinger, announced that the United States would modify its nuclear war strategy to make possible strikes *only* on Soviet military targets. One motive was to find a purpose for the multiplying American warheads, although this was not stated. The announced purpose was to give the president additional options beyond those provided by Mutual Assured Destruction. Should the Soviets strike American military targets (but not cities) the United States should be able to strike back in kind. Schlesinger emphasized that the United States should never have to strike cities for sheer lack of alternatives.

Schlesinger's strategy was given the name Flexible Targeting, but an ambiguity remained whether it meant an ability to strike Soviet military targets in general, or Soviet ICBM silos in particular. If it meant only the former, most national security analysts had little objection to adding Flexible Targeting to the SIOP, and many favored it. However, if it meant targeting Soviet ICBM silos, this represented a great change in American strategy. It would amount to something like a revival of the counterforce strategy of the 1960s, in which the United States had threatened to destroy Soviet missiles on the ground.

That strategy had been abandoned when the Soviets had put their ICBMs *under*ground in hardened silos (as the United States had done also). The missiles of the 1960s and 1970s could not be aimed accurately enough for either side to strike the other's underground silos. However, technology was evolving to the point that by the mid-1970s scientists believed that highly accurate warheads would be possible. Should such warheads be developed, and eventually deployed on missiles, each superpower might come to believe that it could attack the other's missile silos. Counterforce targeting could be resurrected.

Accuracy in targeting was the critical issue behind Flexible Targeting, therefore. The interpretation of what Secretary Schlesinger meant turned on whether or not he requested funds from Congress for research and development of accurate warheads. He did so in the same month that he announced the Flexible Targeting strategy. Money was requested for the Mark 12A, destined to become the first of America's highly accurate warheads, and for other R and D on targeting.

The secretary did not, at least publicly, draw attention to the implications of this request, but he did publicly invite a "national debate" about American strategy. However, the succeeding months witnessed the climax of the Watergate drama that drove President Nixon from office. This drew the public's attention and there was little real debate in public before the funds for accurate warheads were approved. In this way, the United States began to move in 1974 toward developing what is called in the jargon a "hard target kill capability" — or simply, "silo busting."*

Many arms control specialists regretted this decision, and wished that an agreement had been worked out with the Soviet Union to ban all testing of accurate warheads. The logic of arms control in this area was the same as it had been with MIRVs. Testing of the new technology could have been monitored by each superpower's own "national means." Had it been pursued promptly and vigorously, a verifiable arms control agreement to ban these warheads might have been attainable. But once tested, the deployment of these warheads could not be monitored. Each side would simply assume that the other had put accurate warheads on all possible missiles.

Not only did the superpowers not reach such an agreement, they did not even seriously try for one. Once testing was complete, therefore, they entered an era in which each side had to fear for the vulnerability of its missile silos, or any fixed installation, however hardened. This development set the stage for some of the most serious problems of the late 1970s, early 1980s, and almost certainly the years to follow.

One of the ironies of this state of affairs is that in fact it does not offer a true resurrection of the counterforce strategy. What made counterforce genuinely attractive in the early 1960s was its promise of damage limiting. When Soviet ICBMs were few and above ground, and the USSR did not yet have SLBMs, it was at least arguable that a counterforce strategy might reduce sharply the damage that could be done to the United States. More recently the promise of damage limiting had been lost. Even if nearly all the Soviet ICBM silos could be destroyed in a U.S. counterforce strike (as we shall see, they probably cannot), Soviet SLBMs could devastate America several times over.

THE "WINDOW OF VULNERABILITY"

In many aspects of advanced strategic technology the USSR typically lags some five years behind the United States. The high accuracy that the United States developed in the late 1970s with the Mark 12A warhead is being reached by the Soviet Union only in the 1980s.

---

*Flexible Targeting was also sometimes called the strategy of "selective options," something discussed further on pp. 220–23.

Long before then concern mounted in the United States over the potential danger of *Soviet* counterforce strikes against *American* hard targets, especially the Minuteman silos. This concern resulted from the growth in sheer numbers of Soviet warheads, and the fact that the whole American ICBM force numbered only 1,054.

As pointed out in the previous chapter, the most dangerous aspect of MIRVs is the potential leverage they give to the side that takes the offensive first. In the era when ICBMs had only single warheads there was a one-to-one exchange ratio between missiles used and enemy silos destroyed, even if one assumed 100 percent reliability and accuracy. But with MIRVs each side can contemplate attacking the other's ICBM silos without having to use up an equal number of missiles.

As the decade of the 1970s proceeded, the arithmetic of the situation worked against the United States. The Soviets put the bulk of their strategic striking power on land; by 1982 some three-quarters of their total warheads were on ICBMs (almost, but not quite, entirely MIRVed). The Americans put the bulk of their power at sea; by 1982 about two-thirds of their total warheads were on SLBMs. On both sides the SLBMs were much less accurate than ICBMs, and were not usually considered weapons with which one could target the other's silos. This meant that the Americans had more silos to shoot at with fewer ICBMs, and the Soviets had fewer silos to shoot at with more ICBMs. By 1982 the Soviets could, in principle, allocate about six warheads for each U.S. missile silo. With this many attackers per target, the odds on destroying the silo may be respectable, even with only moderately accurate warheads, depending upon assumptions about the reliability of attacking missiles, the silo hardness, etc.

The Committee on the Present Danger gave much emphasis to this. Indeed, a period during which Minuteman would be vulnerable was the core of the present danger that so concerned the committee and its allies. Eventually the United States would be able to replace its Minutemen and Titans with other systems, but that would take time. Meanwhile there would be a "window of vulnerability" to Soviet strikes. (Later the "window of vulnerability" theme was picked up and used extensively in the 1980 Reagan presidential campaign.)

In the hypothetical scenario to which the committee often drew attention, the USSR could attack American ICBM silos at some point in the early or mid-1980s when its exchange ratio is greatest, and its accuracy had improved considerably. Calculations by the committee credited the USSR with the ability to destroy at least 90 percent of the Minutemen and Titans while retaining some ICBMs in reserve. Several million Americans would be killed in such a strike, primarily from fallout. In the committee's scenarios the president would be unable to retaliate because at this point the strategic disadvantage would be too great. Soviet cities could be destroyed by American SLBMs and bombers, of course, but such a counterstrike would be pointless. The ICBMs the Soviet Union still had in reserve could destroy the United States in return, and the USSR would still have its own SLBMs and bombers with which to dominate the world afterwards.

Other national security analysts rejected, and still reject this scenario. They argue that it presumes a rarefied kind of "strategic rationality" that fortunately is impossible for real political leaders in the Kremlin or anywhere. Soviet leaders would never feel confident that the scenario would actually work out this way, even if they believed that 90 percent of American ICBMs could be destroyed. Perhaps the president would strike back anyway, even if it seemed "irrational." Perhaps he would use the 10 percent remaining ICBMs to destroy the Soviet air defense system, and then order SAC bombing raids on the USSR while retaining American SLBMs in reserve. Perhaps other things might occur. The uncertainties in this kind of hypothetical, "unthinkable" realm are too great, these specialists argue, for decision makers in Moscow to gamble with the terrible hazards involved.

Analysts of the "present danger" viewpoint reply that the Soviet at tack need never actually come. The knowledge of both sides that the USSR could achieve a tremendous advantage by destroying most of the American ICBMs could make Moscow aggressive and Washington meek. The world balance, they say, would be tipped dangerously. The opposing analysts argue that there is no reason why this should occur, and that in fact neither Moscow nor Washington is actually behaving that way. Since this debate turns partly on psychological factors and on the general plausibility of the scenario, it cannot be entirely resolved.

Skepticism was not limited to this scenario. During the 1970s and early 1980s many analysts criticized the claim of Minuteman vulnerability from another viewpoint as well. They doubted that the *theoretical* accuracy that the advanced warhead technology was attaining could be translated into *actual* accuracy under wartime conditions. The United States, and later the Soviet Union, might be able to achieve very accurate targeting over their test ranges, under carefully planned and controlled conditions, for a single MIRV package at a time. Obtaining similar accuracies for most or all their MIRVs, under chaotic war conditions, flying completely different flight paths, and on the first try, would be quite a different matter. No ICBM has ever been flown on a north-south trajectory over the pole.

Wartime versus test-condition accuracies became the subject of a lively debate among analysts. The argument was and is too highly technical to be fully developed here, but two important ideas should be mentioned.

For some time military scientists had been aware that when either side's MIRVs arrived at their targets they would not hit simultaneously. Where the targets were fairly close together, as in ICBM fields, the explosions of the first warheads would be likely to damage or deflect those arriving some moments later. This is called "fratricide." It might be alleviated by slowing down the rate of attack, so that the effects of the first blasts would have dissipated by the time the next warheads arrived. But doing this would allow the opponent much more time to fire his own missiles.

Another problem is "bias," which may be defined loosely as a tendency for warheads to drift to one side of their targets due to anomalies in the earth's shape and gravitational field, and other causes. Some military scientists believed that advanced technology could overcome bias and related problems. But others became convinced, on examining all the factors that would reduce accuracy in missile exchanges between the superpowers, that the accuracies possible under ideal test conditions could never be reproduced in wartime with any foreseeable technology.

The effect of this debate was to cast a cloud of uncertainty over a whole set of strategic questions that the United States and USSR faced in the 1970s and thereafter. If targeting under real war conditions cannot be totally accurate, then the superpowers' fixed ICBM silos are not very vulnerable after all. In that case, nearly all the concern and debate around the "window of vulnerability" has been unnecessary. The similar concern that Soviet leaders have doubtless felt as U.S. test accuracies improved would also be rendered unnecessary. On the other hand, many military scientists and national security analysts in America (and no doubt in the Soviet Union) do not accept this premise, and believe that advanced warhead technology does permit accurate targeting even under wartime conditions. Many of the factors over which analysts argue cannot be tested except under these very conditions, so this debate, too, cannot be entirely resolved.

THE AMERICAN STRATEGIC SYSTEMS OF
THE 1980s

It is characteristic of the very complex, technically sophisticated weapons of our day that they take a long time to design and build. Between the decision to develop and construct a weapon system and its actual deployment in any significant number, ten years may pass. This does not count time for research on the various technologies that eventually will go into that system, and perhaps others. The Soviet Union experiences a similar "lead time" between decision and implementation. Therefore plans must be made on the basis, not of current realities, but of expectations for the future. U.S. national security specialists must meet future U.S. defense needs and develop arms control measures on the basis of predictions—necessarily uncertain—about what the strategic balance may look like a decade or more ahead.

Minuteman III and Poseidon were the mainstay American strategic systems of the 1970s, and both are expected to remain important through the 1980s and perhaps longer. But even as these missiles were being deployed, analysts were turning to the question of what newer weapons, if any, the United States might need later in the 1980s and into the 1990s. One system almost was decided upon, was canceled, and then revived later. Three other major systems were approved for deployment.

The canceled system was a new bomber, the B-1. Throughout the 1960s and early 1970s the air force, which naturally wants to have a modern bomber at all times, had advocated that the United States develop a follow-on aircraft to the B-52. After one design for a high-altitude bomber, the B-70, was rejected because Soviet high-altitude air defense was becoming too effective, the air force produced a new design for a low-flying bomber. First called AMSA (for Advanced Manned Strategic Aircraft), later modified and called the B-1, the new bomber would be able to fly below most Soviet radar, hugging the contours of the earth.

For some years the air force's plan was rebuffed by successive secretaries of defense, but the mood changed somewhat as Soviet military expansion continued and as Soviet air defense improved. In 1976 the Ford administration approved the B-1. But after the Carter administration assumed office the next year, it canceled production. The dollar cost of the B-1 promised to be very high. And the Carter administration concluded that the B-52s and FB-111s, periodically fitted with new electronics and other improvements, were still able to get close enough to their targets to fire their SRAMs. A new system was being developed that promised to extend further the life of these aircraft and give the United States other strategic options as well. (Research and development on the B-1 were carried on, and in 1981 the Reagan administration revived the airplane.)

The new system was the cruise missile. Cruise missiles fly a relatively level trajectory, like an airplane, while ballistic missiles ascend steeply to a very high altitude, and then plunge down at very high speed. Cruise missiles are hardly new. Nazi Germany used a primitive version, called the V-1 or "buzz bomb," against targets in England toward the end of World War II. In the 1950s the United States deployed several cruise missiles for a while, and later the Soviet Navy put cruise missiles on both surface ships and submarines. But all of these were and are relatively short-range missiles—a couple of hundred miles at most—and they are relatively slow and easy to shoot down.

Cruise missiles as a modern *strategic* weapon are another matter altogether. The long-range cruise missile on which development began in the United States in the 1970s can deliver a nuclear warhead with great accuracy over ranges into the thousands of miles. The exact range depends on the route and other details. The "cruise," as this kind of missile is called in the jargon, is as fast as a jet aircraft and, unlike its earlier cousins, highly maneuverable. It has the same ability to fly close to the ground, hugging the terrain, that was planned for the B-1 and that is already being used in some American tactical aircraft. For these reasons and because it is not very large, the cruise is hard to catch on radar and hard to shoot down. Cruises are also less expensive than most aircraft or ballistic missiles.

Cruise missile technology is another area in which the United States enjoys a technological lead over the Soviet Union—probably the usual five years or so. In the longer run the USSR will doubtless catch up, as it did with ballistic missiles, but there is and will be a period in the early and mid-1980s when America has cruises deployed and the Soviets will not. Creating such a period was one of the reasons why Washington decided to move ahead rapidly with cruise missile technology, and it represented one major American response to the expansion in Soviet military power.

In the United States all three military services are deploying cruises. The air force's missile will be carried on bombers or other aircraft. This ALCM—for Air-Launched Cruise Missile, pronounced "ALkem"—can extend the useful life of the B-52s and FB-111 considerably, since its long range will allow them to "stand off" around the Soviet periphery and not have to penetrate most of the Soviet air defense system. The ALCM was being deployed at the end of 1982.

A cruise launched from on or under the sea is called a SLCM, pronounced "SLIKem," for Ship (or Submarine)-Launched Cruise Missile. The U.S. Navy's SLCM is called the Tomahawk and is due for deployment in 1984.

A missile derived from the Tomahawk, adapted for use on land, will be deployed by the army starting late in 1983. A Ground-Launched Cruise Missile is called a GLCM, pronounced "GLIKem." The small size of cruises permits tremendous variety in possible launching platforms, including all sorts of aircraft (ALCMs), ships and submarines of all kinds (SLCMs), and almost any kind of truck (GLCMs).

Because of their extraordinary capabilities and because they are different in kind from bombers, ICBMs, or SLBMs, cruise missiles are sometimes regarded as a developing "fourth leg" on the American strategic triad. As cruises become available in quantity in the 1980s, they will give the United States what will be, in many respects, a new form of strategic power. For this reason some analysts look to them as a solution to the problem of Minuteman vulnerability: as one leg of the traditional triad becomes doubtful, it is replaced with a new leg. On the other hand, cruises are far slower than ballistic missiles.

While the cruise may be a solution to one possible problem, it also raises a severe problem of its own. It is an arms control nightmare. Because the missile is small and can be launched from so many different platforms, it may be impossible to control it. Until now the superpowers' "national means of verification" have been able to determine the size of each other's forces with what most (though not all) analysts have considered to be reasonable reliability. Missile silos and bombers on airfields can be counted by satellites, and submarines can be counted in port and in other ways. It was only this ability of each side to verify the size of the other's forces by its *own* means that enabled the SALT negotiators to get around the perennial Soviet refusal to permit inspection within the USSR, and achieve some strategic arms limitation agreements. But cruises can be deployed in so many ways that most analysts fear it will be impossible to count them. Without this verification it is likely that no agreement limiting them will be attainable.

Arms control specialists had hoped in the mid- and late 1970s that cruise testing could be halted before the technology was perfected, just as they hoped in the late 1960s that MIRV testing could be halted before that technology was perfected. As with MIRVs, each superpower *would* have been able to monitor and verify whether the other was *testing* cruises. If a joint agreement with the Soviets could have been reached, cruise missiles would never have been developed adequately, and the impossible problem of counting them once deployed would not have arisen. But again, all efforts failed to have American testing of cruises temporarily halted while an agreement was sought, and development proceeded. Naturally the Soviets cannot be expected to forego an entire weapons technology, once the Americans have produced and deployed it.

Cruise missiles were not deployed until well into the 1980s, but another new American system was decided on earlier and began to arrive earlier. This is a new submarine, the Trident, with new long-range SLBM missiles. It was produced partly because existing submarines were aging. Specialists had known that by about 1980 the first Polaris submarines would be twenty years old, a period widely (though not universally) thought to be nearly the maximum useful life of a submarine. Putting Poseidon missiles in them after a few years did not, of course, extend the lifetimes of the submarines themselves. Unlike the missiles, the subs are actually in use much of the time. They must spend time cruising "on station" and traveling back and forth between their stations and their home ports. They wear out.

In its first term the Nixon administration approved a plan for phasing in a new class of submarines, the Trident, as the older Polaris submarines reached their maximum lifetimes. The first ten Polaris submarines built were expected to wear out sooner than the thirty-one that followed, and partly for this reason the administration decided to build and deploy ten Tridents. The thirty-one later Polaris submarines are expected to remain useful well into the 1980s and possibly longer.

Since the MIRVed Poseidon missiles made each Polaris sub far more potent, it was not obvious that a new submarine was needed at all. The decision to proceed with the Trident program was made before the SALT I agreements were completed, and was justified as a conservative hedge against two possibilities. In the absence of any SALT agreement about antiballistic missile systems, the USSR might have gone ahead to build a "heavy" ABM designed to stop many American warheads. Secondly, the rapid expansion of the Soviet Navy included a considerable buildup in its antisubmarine warfare (ASW) effort. It seemed prudent for the United States to hedge against the possibility of Soviet ASW eventually becoming much more effective.

To have a larger part of the world's oceans to hide in, and therefore evade the Soviet Navy, American submarines would have to carry longer-range missiles. Achieving longer range requires a physically larger missile. But the Poseidon was already just about the biggest missile the Polaris submarine could carry; a substantially bigger missile would require a new submarine. A bigger missile would also be necessary to carry the heavy package of warheads and decoys that might be needed to penetrate a heavy Soviet ABM system. Hence an entire new system, of new submarines carrying new and bigger missiles, seemed indicated.

Some specialists suggested that the United States could better use the same money to build a considerable number of small submarines, each of which would carry only a few of the big new missiles. A candidate design was called the Narwhal. Small subs like the Narwhal would be quieter than large ones, and hence safer from Soviet ASW; and having many of them would make the loss of a few in wartime relatively less important. But the administration opted for the system that the navy submarine officers themselves preferred—just ten large submarines. The Trident, as finally designed, is as long as two football fields, and each carries twenty-four missiles. (The Polaris submarines carry sixteen each.) The first Trident was launched in November 1979; the rest are following in the early to mid-1980s.

As happened earlier with the Polaris submarine and Polaris missile, the terminology was confused somewhat because the same name was given to both the submarine and the missile. The Trident subs are carrying, in their early years, the Trident I missile. Though it has a considerably longer range (4,600 miles), this SLBM is only slightly larger than the Poseidon. Eight of the Polaris submarines built last were modified to carry it also. This is the one new strategic missile the United States deployed during the 1970s.*

It will be followed by the Trident II, the missile for which the new submarine was really designed. The Trident II will have a range of over 6,000 miles. With this SLBM the Trident submarines can strike targets in the USSR from virtually any point in the world's oceans. And the missile will carry a highly accurate new warhead, the D-5.

When the SALT I ABM Treaty was signed, a major justification for the Trident program was removed. Under the treaty no Soviet ABM system is permitted that might require advanced American missiles to penetrate. Even so the Trident program was continued, partly as a hedge against the better ASW capability the Soviet Navy may develop,

---

*The launch of a Trident I missile from a submerged Trident submarine is shown in the photograph on the front cover of this book.

partly as a general response to the Soviet strategic buildup. Expansion of the program beyond ten submarines, which was discussed for a time as a possible option, was dropped from serious consideration.

Cruise missiles and the Trident submarine and missiles were two of the new weapon systems approved during the 1970s. The third was by far the most controversial.

THE MX DEBATE

As Soviet strategic striking power mounted during the 1970s, elements within the U.S Air Force were among those at the forefront of concern about Minuteman vulnerability. Mindful of the ten-year lead time for major new systems, the air force began pressing for a new system that could replace the Minuteman in the 1980s. The service proposed a *mobile* missile that would not be vulnerable to Soviet targeting however accurate it might become—the Soviets could not aim at something whose exact location they did not know. The new system was designated the MX for "missile experimental," and substantial study was made of various ways to put it in the field—its "basing mode," in the jargon of the trade.

At one point the air force favored moving the MX back and forth in shallow underground tunnels. At time of launch the moving launchers would stop and break through the earth covering the tunnels. Later this concept was replaced with a "racetrack" plan, in which the launchers would move at random among hardened shelters along a vast, specially built highway network in Nevada and Utah. Other basing modes, including deployment at sea, or even nonmobile locations at the bottoms of lakes, were also considered.

These studies and advanced R and D on the system itself were begun in 1973 and President Ford, had he been reelected, planned to approve the MX for major development in 1977. But the Carter administration deferred this for several years (while continuing R and D), partly for further study of the basing mode, and partly from a hope that if rapid progress were made with SALT the MX would be unnecessary. The administration wanted an understanding with the Soviets that would keep either superpower from deploying mobile ICBMs.

Nothing of this kind, however, could be included in SALT II, and President Carter realized as negotiations continued that the treaty would face heavy opposition in the U.S. Senate. The administration came under pressure to demonstrate its commitment to enhancing U.S. power in the face of the long and massive Soviet military buildup. In September 1979, at the height of the SALT debate in the Senate, Carter approved full development and deployment of the MX system. The administration hoped that this decision might win over enough senators concerned about the Soviet expansion to win passage of the treaty. This bid failed, but another major new U.S. strategic system was now under way.

Public opposition to the MX began developing when citizens' groups in Utah and Nevada woke up to the fact that the racetrack basing mode would cover enormous areas of their states, would have serious environmental consequences, and would make their region a prime target in the event of war. Critics of MX also claimed that this basing mode would prove extremely expensive. When the Reagan administration entered office it reaffirmed the MX missile but scrapped racetrack basing.

Instead, it proposed a new mode formally called "closely spaced basing," or more informally, "dense pack." One hundred MX missiles would be put in very hard silos spaced only about 500 yards apart. The array would be located in Wyoming, where the public approved the deployment.

The dense pack concept depended on fratricide to protect the MXs against Soviet attack. Placing the silos so close together would mean that attacking warheads would have to come in almost on top of each other. The first few MXs might be destroyed, but thereafter fratricide would destroy most of the attackers. Most MXs would survive.

A new debate raged through 1982 over this scheme. Critics argued that the Soviets could pin down the whole MX force for hours by exploding one warhead over the dense pack every few minutes. The plan also seemed rather hypothetical, since no one has ever exploded many nuclear devices, one after another, over the same spot. The full extent of the fratricide effect, or the effect on the MX silos, could not be known exactly. Congress voted to continue money for the missile, but not for dense pack.

President Reagan than appointed a high-level commission to review the problem, named the Scowcroft Commission after its chairman. In April 1983, the Scowcroft Commission proposed deploying 100 MX missiles in existing Minuteman silos. The combined panoply of American ICBMs, SLBMs, and bombers was a sufficient deterrent, the commission concluded, that the "window of vulnerability" should be of little concern for some time to come. The commission also proposed that the United States develop, and deploy in the 1990s, a new, small ICBM with a single warhead, popularly dubbed "Midgetman." This missile might be mobile. Congress proved receptive to the Scowcroft Commission's report, and in July voted production funds for the MX.

THE AMERICAN MILITARY BUILDUP

American strategic systems of the 1980s consist of a mixture of new and modernized weapons: Trident submarines and the later-model Polaris submarines, carrying Trident I and Poseidon missiles; Minuteman III

TABLE 7.   American and Soviet strategic forces as of mid-1981

	Soviet Union		United States	
ICBMs	1,398	(includes about 770 SS-17, SS-18 and SS-19 missiles)	1,052	(includes 550 Minuteman III missiles)
SLBMs	989	in 84 submarines	576	in 36 submarines (includes 64 Trident I missiles)
Long-range bombers	150	Bears and Bisons	366	B-52s and FB-111s
Strategic cruise missiles	0			none yet deployed, but significant numbers due to enter the force within the next two years

Notes: The discrepancy between the 150 Bears and Bisons estimated at this time, and the 135 estimated in 1975, probably results from estimating uncertainties, rather than the actual addition of any bombers. The data do not include about sixty-five Backfire bombers deployed as of this time.

The FB-111 is technically a medium-range bomber, but acquires long range with aerial refueling, a technique long practiced and perfected with FB-111s.

The time difference in the entry of significant numbers of strategic cruise missiles into the two sides' forces is often estimated at around five years.

Source: International Institute for Strategic Studies, London: *The Military Balance, 1981–82*

with the Mark 12A warheads, plus some older Minuteman II missiles; and B-52 and FB-111 bombers carrying ALCMs and advanced electronics. The table gives numerical totals for mid-1981. By the middle of the decade there will be SLCMs and GLCMs and by the end, the advanced Trident II missile and probably the MX.

Ironically, the MX, the one new system that was developed most directly in response to a specific Soviet threat, was the one system that proved highly controversial. Cruise missiles and Trident submarines and missiles were systems less directly connected to any new Soviet challenge, yet they evoked little public or congressional controversy.

The fiscal 1975 defense budget of the United States was the last to show the decline in military expenditures that had accompanied the gradual winding down of the Vietnam War. In that year, total U.S. forces were smaller than they had been before Vietnam and so (corrected for inflation) was the defense budget.

With the 1976 budget the Ford administration began a slow increase that was accelerated under the Carter administration, to an average of about 5 percent per year (not counting inflation). The chart on the next page shows the trend in U.S. defense expenditures over the thirty-three year period 1949–82.*

The bulk of the new spending went to improve U.S. conventional forces: increasing the number of army divisions, navy ships, and air force tactical wings, and providing all the conventional forces with more supplies and better equipment. These increases were justified almost entirely in terms of the mounting Soviet conventional threat. A portion of the total went to fund the development of the cruise, Trident, and MX missiles, and the manufacture of Trident I missiles and Trident submarines—all expenses that had not appeared in the budget, or had been minor, before 1975.

Ronald Reagan's 1980 campaign for the presidency gave heavy emphasis to the continuing Soviet military buildup, and to what he asserted was American inferiority. At that time the American public, having heard about the Soviet buildup for years, and having recently witnessed the USSR's invasion of Afghanistan, supported further U.S. increases by a substantial majority. Congress gave ready support

---

*Note: expenditures are not the same, in any given year, as amounts budgeted, because not all the dollars budgeted can be spent that year. Table 8 shows expenditures, which took a small dip in fiscal 1976 although the amount budgeted rose.

The surges for the Korean and Vietnam wars are obvious. Otherwise American defense spending since Korea was remarkably constant until the late 1970s.

TABLE 8.   Budget Expenditures for Defense, in constant (Jan. 1982) dollars

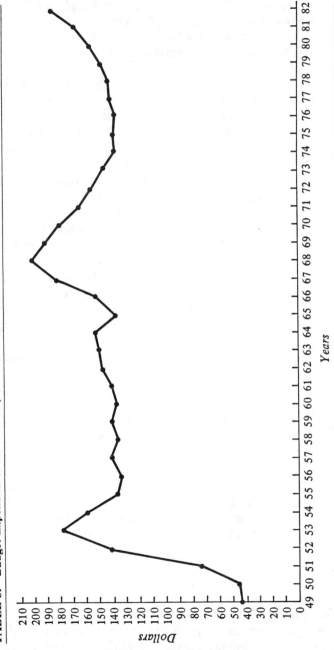

Units are in billions of dollars. Includes retirement pay; excludes veterans' benefits and services.

Sources: Statistical Abstract of the United States (Federal Budget Outlays for National Defense) and Survey of Current Business (Implicit Price Deflator for GNP).

when, about two months after entering office, the Reagan administration requested about $32 billion beyond Carter's budget. The new administration had not yet had time to develop an alternative defense plan; the extra money was intended mainly to accelerate existing programs.

In January 1982 the administration unveiled the first federal budget it had prepared, and a new five-year defense plan. Over five years the administration planned to spend about $1.6 trillion on defense. (The Carter administration had projected about $1.3 trillion for the same period.) The defense budget's rate of growth would be raised from Carter's 5 percent to about 8.1 percent annually. Again the bulk of the increase would go to the conventional forces. But strategic expenditures were increased also.

Several months earlier, in October 1981, the administration had unveiled its strategic weapons programs. These included the Trident submarines and the cruise, MX, and two Trident missiles, all begun earlier, and in some cases now given more funding. They also included a program for a new advanced bomber called Stealth. This had previously been an R and D program, begun under Carter. It was expected to produce, by about 1990, an aircraft that would be difficult to spot on radar. Once highly secret, the idea of an "invisible" airplane caught the public's fancy for a while. (Subsequently it was revealed that the Stealth technology would also be applied to later, more advanced cruise missiles.)

The Reagan administration's plans also included four other new elements. The nationwide civil defense program, which for many years had continued at a low level of funding and visibility, would be much expanded. Transferred to the Federal Emergency Management Agency (FEMA), a civilian agency not part of the Defense Department, civil defense would now include a program for evacuating the residents of American cities to the countryside in the event nuclear war seemed imminent. Subsequently this aspect of the new strategic program sparked public controversy, and a number of cities and towns voted not to participate. Many citizens found the evacuation plans unworkable and offensive.

A second aspect of the new program was a great improvement in the U.S. air defense system. Previous administrations back to Lyndon Johnson had chosen to deemphasize air defense, since the Soviets' bombers were few and their missiles (about which air defense can do nothing) were very numerous. President Reagan promised to modernize air defense with technology advanced enough to deal with the new long-range bomber the Soviets had under development, the Blackjack.

The new plans also called for upgrading the command-control-communications system (called c³ or "c-cubed" in the jargon) for connecting the nation's top leadership with the strategic forces. For some time analysts had pointed out that America's c³ was at least as vulnerable as the ICBMs to Soviet attack. While there were limits to how much could be done about this, some improvements could be made, including better communications with submerged submarines.

Finally, the Reagan administration revived the B-1 bomber. A more advanced version called the B-1B would be put into production as soon as possible, and 100 aircraft produced. Other than MX and the city evacuation scheme, this proved the most controversial element in the administration's strategic plan. Even the first B-1Bs would not be available until about 1985, and the Stealth was due to arrive only about five years later. With the B-52s soon to be mounting ALCMs, many thought it questionable whether the B-1Bs were worth the $35 billion they would cost.

In spite of these departures the Reagan administration's plans did not imply any radical change in the American strategic posture. The decisions shaping the main outlines of that posture through the 1980s and into the 1990s—Trident, cruise, and the design of the MX—had been made by previous administrations. The Reagan administration estimated the total cost of all strategic programs over the six years 1982–87, including its new ones, at $180 billion. Neither expenditures at this level nor the new programs, other than MX, the B-1B, and the city evacuation scheme, proved controversial.

SUMMARY

Throughout the 1970s and early 1980s the United States constantly had more nuclear warheads targeted on the Soviet Union than the USSR had targeted on America. There was never a time when the Soviets had more. It was true that the Soviets could deliver much more megatonnage. But this was because American weapons scientists, many years before, had decided there was no good reason for large-yield weapons and had deliberately designed U.S. weapons to be smaller. It was also true that the Soviets had somewhat more missiles, but the U.S. bomber force, equipped with SRAM attack missiles, could deliver far more weapons than the small force of Soviet bombers.

American missiles were, on the whole, more accurate than Soviet missiles throughout this time, and could be launched more quickly and with less preparation. Soviet missile-carrying submarines were somewhat noisy, and in a war some might be destroyed by superior American antisubmarine warfare; American submarines were quieter and Soviet ASW less effective. On balance there could scarcely be much doubt that overall, the effective strategic power of the United States was never less than the Soviets' and was probably marginally greater.

The bulk of the mounting U.S. defense expenditures after 1975 was devoted to countering the Soviet buildup in conventional forces, worrisome to almost all Western specialists. U.S. nuclear forces received more funding as well. For many analysts the rationale for new American strategic weapons was the perceived need to maintain the rough parity in the future. Because of the long lead-time in developing and deploying these complex systems, decisions had to be made on the basis of estimates about technical possibilities a decade or more ahead.

In this sense the real basis of the American strategic buildup was not current Soviet behavior, but the future of the technology itself. Thus Trident was intended to give the United States almost all the world's ocean space to hide submarines in, against the day that ASW technology improved to the point that more limited submarines might be locatable. The Stealth bomber and more important, the cruise missile, were developed substantially as expressions of technology itself: research was opening up new possibilities that offered exotic new capabilities.

Ironically, the one new system that most directly responded to a specific Soviet threat, the MX ICBM, was the only weapon (other than the revived B-1) that proved controversial. Soviet ICBMs were newer and larger than Minuteman. Some believed that a new US ICBM, also larger, seemed indicated, the more so if Soviet MIRVs were threatening the Minuteman silos. But the very "window of vulnerability" that arguably meant Minuteman had to be replaced also made it hard to find an acceptable basing mode for MX on land. Whether Soviet leaders had any real confidence that Minuteman was vulnerable was another question, since wartime accuracy was not the same thing as test-range accuracies.

Meanwhile, work on targeting accuracy was having its effect, not only on decisions about deploying weapon systems, but also on American thinking about the use and purposes of nuclear weapons. To this we now turn.

FOR FURTHER READING

Betts, Richard K., ed. *Cruise Missiles: Technology, Strategy, Politics.* Washington, D.C.: The Brookings Institution, 1981. This lengthy volume presents an important collection of papers on many aspects of cruise missiles.

Brookings Institution, The. *Setting National Priorities.* Washington: the Brookings Institution (annual). Each year the Brookings Institution, a major "think tank," publishes this book of assessments of U.S. policy issues, including one or two chapters on current U.S. national security questions.

Cockburn, Andrew and Alexander Cockburn, "The Myth of Missile Accuracy." In *The New York Review of Books* Vol XXVII, No. 18 (November 20, 1980). A good presentation of the many factors that make wartime missile targeting somewhat inaccurate, however great the accuracies that may be obtained over test ranges.

Fallows, James. *National Defense.* New York: Random House, 1981. One of the best-known assessments of the policies and problems of United States national security at the outset of the 1980s. This well-written book attempts to address the most significant general issues rather than particular policy decisions.

SIPRI (Stockholm International Peace Research Institute), *World Armaments and Disarmament: SIPRI Yearbook.* Cambridge, Mass.: Oelgeschlager, Gunn and Hain, Inc. (annual). This annual publication contains a wealth of information about world arms production, expenditure, and trade, and about a wide variety of security and military issues.

Utgoff, Victor. "In Defense of Counterforce." In *International Security* Vol. VI, No. 4 (Spring 1982). One of the most thoughtful published statements advocating some form of counterforce strategy for the United States in the 1980s and beyond. The journal in which this article appears is the leading American journal of security studies.

12

Strategy and Arms Control in the Early 1980s

The strategic program announced by the Reagan administration in October 1981 was a program for the procurement of various systems, and included little about policy for their use. Well before this the administration had made public its strategic thinking. The significant change that it decided upon was sometimes misunderstood to be a drastic new departure. In fact, just as the new administration had accelerated a buildup already well under way, not launched a new one, so it carried further and made more explicit a policy trend that also had been already under way.

"LIMITED NUCLEAR WAR"

In 1974 the Schlesinger Doctrine of Flexible Targeting had substantially increased the role of counterforce targeting in the SIOP, and major funding had begun for the Mark 12A warhead. In the following years little news was released about the technology of targeting, but progress was steady both in the development and production of the Mark 12A, and in research on still more advanced technology. Engineers looked forward to perfecting a new type of warhead called the MARV, for MAneuvering Reentry Vehicle. This warhead could not only change its course in flight, but would be extremely accurate because it could home in on its target.

Through these years R and D was also pursued to improve the quantity and quality of information that reconnaissance satellites could provide, including shortening the time between satellite observation and the delivery of information to decision makers. "Real time" satellite information became a prospect, which meant that decision makers would be able to select new targets, or restrike old ones, in the course of an ongoing war. A development in policy seemed a logical next step.

In July 1980 President Carter signed Presidential Directive 59, an order redirecting American strategy further along the line laid down by Schlesinger. Although P.D. 59, as it is familiarly known, remains classified, some of its contents have been discussed publicly.

The directive assigned *priority* to counterforce targeting, although naturally the assured destruction mission remained as well. Particular priority was assigned to targeting the hardened underground shelters that Soviet leaders planned to use in the event of war. (This kind of strike, designed to destroy a country's leadership, is called a "decapitating attack" in the strategic jargon.)

P.D. 59 also envisioned the possibility of a prolonged nuclear engagement lasting days, weeks, or even longer, and directed that emerging technology be exploited to locate fresh strategic targets and to evaluate the damage to targets already struck. The United States would acquire a "shoot-look-shoot" capability for nuclear war. In the same directive, Carter also set aside a portion of American nuclear forces as a strategic reserve, to be held back early in a war for possible use later.

Finally, it appears that P.D. 59 increased further the flexibility in U.S. targeting by ordering an increase in the number of targeting options. Some of the new options involved circumstances that the SIOP had not previously addressed, such as wars involving nuclear weapons that might be fought on or near Soviet borders, but that did not include strikes on cities. "Preprogrammed options," "selective options," or "limited nuclear options" are the jargon terms for developing plans, computer programs, and other prerequisites for serving up to decision makers targeting options for specific hypothetical situations.

After the Reagan administration came to office it superseded P.D. 59 with a new defense guidance plan and a National Security Decision Document that carried this strategy further. Though these documents remain classified, published reports indicate that they gave additional emphasis to the decapitation mission. They contemplated nuclear wars lasting weeks or even months, and they defined a new U.S. objective in such conflicts. Resurrecting an old term from the 1950s, they said the United States should plan to "prevail" in protracted nuclear wars.

Meanwhile the administration was saying publicly that, in the event fighting broke out with Soviet forces in one part of the globe, the United States might resort to "horizontal escalation." This meant that the United States might attack Soviet forces or interests elsewhere in the world. If the original conflict were conventional, these wider attacks might be too, but if the fighting had begun to include the use of nuclear weapons, the American attacks elsewhere presumably would also be nuclear. Horizontal escalation therefore could also bring limited nuclear options into play.

The whole period following Schlesinger's Flexible Targeting doctrine, and continuing into the 1980s, witnessed an ongoing debate among specialists about flexible targeting, limited nuclear options, and related issues. Steady advances were being made in the technology both for targeting and for command-control-communications-and-information (c^3i or "c-cubed eye," a variation on the older "c-cubed"). Throughout this time one wing of opinion among specialists argued that this technology would make possible "limited nuclear wars."

Although these phrases were sometimes used as if they had been freshly minted, they dated back to the lush period of strategic theorizing of the early 1960s, during the second era of American superiority. At that time some specialists had theorized about ways that nuclear weapons could be used for "war-fighting," not just deterrence. These theorists had suggested that if a nuclear war did begin, the United States should not confine itself to damage limiting and trying to end the war as quickly as possible. They had argued the United States might deliberately carry the war on in some controlled way for military and political objectives.

For a while an argument had gone on between those analysts who believed in war-fighting and those who believed that deterrence was the only feasible and legitimate role for nuclear weapons under all or nearly all circumstances. The latter group, of which Bernard Brodie was one of the prominent early spokesmen, was probably in the majority throughout the 1960s, and certainly as that decade advanced. This school emphasized the enormous destructiveness of nuclear weapons and the tremendous uncertainty that surrounded their use. Although a controlled use of nuclear weapons could be hypothesized, no one could be confident such a conflict would remain limited. History provided plenty of examples of wars escalating beyond the bounds that governments had originally intended and expected for them. In reply the advocates of war-fighting argued that knowledge of the devastation an all-out war would cause would prevent decision makers from escalating even—or perhaps especially—after a few nuclear weapons had gone off.

After being almost forgotten for some years while Mutual Assured Destruction and sufficiency were the guiding American doctrines, this idea was resurrected in the mid-1970s. The old argument was played out again. Effective damage limiting was no longer possible, but the prospect of accurate targeting and real-time c^3i encouraged some theorists to reconsider the possibility of "limited" or "controlled" nuclear war. (They were also encouraged by the need to find a rational purpose for the huge number of warheads being deployed.) Fighting such wars would require "limited nuclear options."

Theorists supporting the development of these options argued that the superpowers might employ only a fraction of their forces to carry out one or more of these options, then pause to negotiate. Or perhaps they might trade small blows in some kind of extended nuclear engagement. Having "limited nuclear options" available would allow various political and military objectives to be pursued by nuclear means, while avoiding an all-out holocaust.

Critics responded that this was a risky line of thought. Creating plans and hardware for "limited nuclear options" might make it all too easy for those options to be used in some intense crisis. If high officials became accustomed to thinking in terms of war-fighting and had a sophisticated array of supposedly "limited" options available, they would be more likely to begin nuclear warfare. The notion that such warfare *could* remain "limited" and "controlled" was purely hypothetical, and very questionable. Wouldn't such a war quickly escalate to larger and larger blows, and soon to all-out strategic war? Soviet military doctrine did not include the concept of selective options; it said that any nuclear strikes on the USSR would be answered by a full-scale attack on the enemy.

Some advocates of "limited nuclear options" agreed that it was too risky to plan on war-fighting, but that such options could strengthen deterrence. They made an argument similar to one of the original arguments for Flexible Response: Soviet decision makers must know the United States has options other than "nothing" or launching an all-out holocaust, or they may think the United States will back down in a crisis. Deterrence may fail. In turn, critics of "limited nuclear options" replied that this might be a good reason to have a small number of options that did not threaten the Soviets severely; but many of the "limited nuclear options" being programmed into the SIOP were too likely to trigger rapid escalation, and hence were dangerous.

Thus one of the sophisticated arguments in the 1970s over "limited nuclear options" was not whether to have them at all, but whether to have a few, carefully restricted, that posed minimal risk of escalation, or to have many diverse options that posed more risk. Critics feared that Presidential Directive 59, when it came at the end of the decade, meant that the United States was choosing the latter.

The directive apparently did order an expansion in the number of nuclear options. But just how seriously the Carter administration meant to move the United States toward the war-fighting doctrine was uncertain, even well after P.D. 59 was promulgated. Different administration officials seemed to hold somewhat different interpretations of the significance of the directive.

There was no question about the next administration's intentions. According to published reports, the Reagan administration's National Security Decision Document on this topic clearly instructs the Defense Department to prepare to win protracted nuclear wars, and the 1982 Defense Guidance Plan contains a strategy for fighting and supposedly winning such wars. Secretary of Defense Caspar Weinberger testified to Congress that "top priority" was assigned to acquiring "nuclear force parity across the full range of plausible nuclear war-fighting scenarios"; Deputy Secretary of Defense Frank Carlucci testified at the time of the Senate's confirmation of his appointment that his goal was a "war-fighting capability."

THE PEACE MOVEMENT

In simplified form, something of the Reagan administration's commitment to a war-fighting doctrine entered public awareness, both in

America and in Europe. As much as any one thing it became the trigger for immense popular movements against nuclear war on both continents. This is not to say that the public absorbed the intricacies of the debate over war-fighting versus deterrence, or that the administration's choice of war-fighting was the sole cause of the new "peace movement." Other causes included the great increase in the U.S. defense budget, and public awareness that the Soviet and American nuclear arsenals had grown enormously. But the policy shift in Washington was no less significant. What registered on the public mind, and frightened many people, was a simplified perception—now Washington was not just thinking about how to *prevent* nuclear war, but was planning how to *conduct* one.

This public perception was increased by some unfortunate public remarks by high-ranking officials during the administration's first year. Especially widely reported was a comment by President Reagan himself. When asked by a group of newspaper editors about the feasibility of limited nuclear war in Europe, he replied that he "could see where you could have the exchange of tactical weapons . . . without it bringing either one of the major powers to pushing the button." Not long afterward the *Los Angeles Times* published an interview with T.K. Jones, deputy undersecretary of defense for strategic and theater nuclear forces. Jones, whose responsibilities included aspects of the new civil defense plan, seemed to believe enthusiastically that a properly prepared United States could readily survive a nuclear war. He suggested that people "dig a hole, cover it with a couple of doors and then throw three feet of dirt on the top . . . It's the dirt that does it . . . If there are enough shovels to go around, everybody's going to make it."

Before long the administration realized that these and similar remarks were generating opposition to its defense plans. In its public declarations it backed off from the appearance of being casual about nuclear war. Defense Secretary Weinberger publicly denied, for instance, "that we mean to imply that nuclear war is winnable." But the public had already been frightened and the new peace movement was growing rapidly.*

It reached the dimensions of a mass movement earlier in Europe than in America. There had been much less consensus in Europe in

---

*Subsequent official documents did not suggest that the administration had reversed its preference for a war-fighting doctrine or its commitment to "prevail" in a protracted nuclear war.

favor of a Western buildup in the first place, and some imminent policy decisions had a more immediate meaning there. The December 1979 "two-track" decision by NATO had called for arms control negotiations with the Soviets about long-range theater nuclear forces (LRTNF) in Europe. Many Europeans hoped that success in the first track, negotiations, would make unnecessary any implementation of the second track, the deployment of new American Pershing II and cruise missiles. Some negotiations began in Geneva in October 1980, but languished, first while waiting for the American presidential elections, then for the new administration to decide its policy. As late as the early autumn of 1981 the United States had done nothing to press these talks forward with any vigor.

By then many Europeans concluded that the United States had decided not to take the negotiation track seriously and was interested only in missile deployment. Some thought the two-track policy had merely been a dodge all along, to hide a real decision to drop arms control in favor of a missile buildup. President Reagan's remark, widely publicized in Europe, that he could see how a limited nuclear war might be fought there, played straight into the Europeans' longstanding fear that the United States would somehow "decouple" itself from Europe, allowing the superpowers to survive a new war that would leave Europe a radioactive rubble.

In October 1981 the Reagan administration announced that it was reversing a Carter administration decision and would produce and deploy the neutron bomb. In the minds of most Western Europeans this was a weapon intended specifically for a European nuclear war. Demonstrations erupted. A protest march in Bonn drew a quarter million people, and was followed quickly by huge marches in London, Paris, Brussels, and Rome. In November, 400,000 marched in Amsterdam; the previous all-time record for a political demonstration in the Netherlands had been 80,000. Protest spread even to parts of Eastern Europe: three hundred thousand marched in Bucharest, the capital of Rumania. The demonstrations ceased only after Washington announced that the United States would immediately reopen arms control negotiations at a higher level and with a new policy (discussed below).

Meanwhile the new popular movement against nuclear weapons was spreading to America, where the issues were not so directly tied to NATO policy. Well before the European demonstrations, an American group called Physicians for Social Responsibility was trying to increase public awareness in the United States of the meaning of nuclear warfare. Headed by a Boston pediatrician, Helen Caldicott, the organization had a simple message: doctors would not be able to save people if a nuclear war came. Americans had grown used to being surrounded by a vast, sophisticated medical establishment that could cope quickly with most emergencies. And most Americans had only a dim notion of what nuclear weapons would do if used in quantity. PSR pointed out that the destruction would be so enormous that the medical establishment would vanish too. Not only would millions die at once; hardly anyone would be left to help the millions more of wounded and radiation-sickened.

A campaign had also begun for a public demand that the United States and Soviet Union freeze all their nuclear weapons programs at exactly their present point. Conceived originally by Randall Forsberg, an arms control specialist, the Freeze idea was an effort to cut through the endless complications of SALT and other arms control with a concept so simple that everyone could understand and back it. In November 1981, teach-ins were held on 151 American campuses, where the Freeze, NATO policy, the MX missile, and other nuclear questions were debated.

Early in 1982 Jonathan Schell published, first in *New Yorker* magazine and then as a book, a moving essay entitled *The Fate of the Earth*. Schell described in vivid and horrifying detail what wholesale nuclear war would mean, developed a philosophical argument that preventing the end of humanity is a moral value superseding all others, and argued for a radical change in direction. *The Fate of the Earth* was probably read and quoted more widely than any book about nuclear war ever written.

The antinuclear movement in America now gathered steam. In April, a new organization called Ground Zero sponsored a week of public-awareness activities nationally. On June 12 in New York City, 750,000 people marched to Central Park in the largest political demonstration in American history. All sorts of civic groups turned their attention to the nuclear issue, conferences and meetings were held everywhere, and for a while the danger of nuclear war seemed to be Americans' number one preoccupation.

A Freeze resolution in the House of Representatives was defeated 204 to 202, but the Freeze was put on the ballot in eleven states for the November elections. The basic issue for most people involved in the movement was the danger posed by the mere *existence* of vast numbers of nuclear weapons; accomplishing a bilateral Freeze of *current* arsenals became the movement's concrete symbol. Most attention narrowed to the Freeze as the immediate goal. In November it passed in ten of the eleven states, in most of them by sizable majorities. With more Freeze supporters elected to Congress as well, the campaign leaders looked forward optimistically to passing a freeze resolution in 1983, at least in the House.

THE INF TALKS

As the Freeze became the focus of the antinuclear war movement in America, the "two-track" decision and impending deployment of Pershing IIs and GLCMs became the focus of the movement in Western Europe. In November 1981 President Reagan made a speech proposing that high-ranking representatives of the two superpowers reopen negotiations in Geneva at once, on what he now termed "inter-mediate-range nuclear forces," or INF. The Soviets agreed.

The U.S.-NATO position, developed after consultation among the allies and announced in the president's speech, was soon called the "zero option" or "zero-zero solution." The president proposed simply that the Soviets remove all the SS-20s they were in the process of de-ploying, targeted on Europe; in return NATO would forego deploying any Pershing II or cruise missiles. Zero Soviet LRTNF missiles would be balanced by zero NATO LRTNF missiles. President Reagan named Paul Nitze to head the U.S. negotiating team.

Substantial parts of European opinion were satisfied by Reagan's offer, and shortly the mass protests ceased. At INF the Soviets rejected the offer. They argued, as they had in earlier arms control talks, that the Western view failed to count the British and French forces targeted on the USSR, or the American and allied "forward-based systems" of aircraft in Europe and on aircraft carriers on the Mediterranean. The Soviets alleged that these amounted to a greater capability than the USSR and Warsaw Pact had in their air forces (something NATO dis-puted) and that the SS-20s only righted the balance. The Soviets also thought it unfair that they were asked to give up a system already de-ployed, in return for the West not deploying systems that were yet to be perfected.

Even so the Soviets seemed genuinely concerned about those Western systems. The GLCMs were being developed with technology the USSR did not have yet, and would not have until later in the 1980s. Of even greater concern were the Pershing IIs, because these missiles would be very accurate and would have a short flight time.

From launch to impact would be only six to ten minutes, depending on trajectory details. Some of the USSR's command and control centers for Soviet *strategic* forces (targeted on the United States), as well as Eurostrategic forces, were within the Pershings' range. A counterforce Pershing strike against those centers could arrive far faster than could American ICBMs.

Such a strike might not have seemed very plausible at some other time. But this was just the time when the Reagan administration was announcing that war-fighting was its general policy and that the United States could and should prevail in a controlled nuclear war. Pershings and other systems were being developed or deployed that seemed to offer capabilities going beyond deterrence to a potential for highly accurate counterforce targeting. MX would be very accurate, and so too would the D-5 warhead for the Trident II SLBM. Some people wondered whether Washington was beginning to think about a first strike.

In the late 1970s and early 1980s the terminology of "first strike" had become somewhat smudged, in comparison to its earlier precise meaning. We recall that originally a "first-strike capability" had meant the ability to make a *disarming* first strike—one that removed all or nearly all of the opponent's ability to strike back. (Careful analysts still use the term in this strict sense.) In the era of submarine-launched missiles this had become impossible: no available means can find and destroy the submarine. But later the Committee on the Present Danger and others had drawn attention to a scenario in which one side saw nearly all its silos and bomber bases lost in a sudden attack, and would then be faced (it was argued) with such overwhelming superiority that it would not dare to employ its SLBMs and other forces.

To many analysts, this scenario was an example of what some called "nuclear theology"—hypothetical analyses too abstract to bear on the real decisions of real government leaders. But the frequent reiteration of this scenario generated a kind of modified idea first-strike capability: an attacker could gain some of the benefits of a true, disarming first strike by attacking only land-based missiles, bomber bases, and command centers.

The Pershing II appeared to the Soviets, and to some independent observers, as a logical component in just such a strategy.* When President Reagan produced an INF proposal that the Soviets felt was unacceptable, they announced a new counter to what they saw as the danger. They threatened to adopt a policy of "launch on warning."

---

*It must be remembered that many Soviet targets, including command centers, are outside the Pershing range.

Launch on warning means that a nation plans to launch its counterstrike when its radars and computers indicate that an enemy attack is on its way. In a sense this is the ultimate answer to fears that one's own missiles or control centers may be vulnerable. One does not wait for the enemy strike to wreak its damage; one fires while one's forces are still intact. A slight variation, called "launch under attack," calls for waiting until the last moment and then launching just before the enemy strike arrives.

The United States has never had a launch on warning policy, and the overwhelming majority of national security specialists have always opposed it. So far as known the Soviets have never adopted this policy either, although some Western analysts suspect that they may have moved close to it. It is so widely opposed because it is extremely dangerous. If a false alarm in the radar and computer systems indicates that an attack is coming when it is not, the nation with that policy would launch its forces. Then the other side, faced with a real attack, would presumably have to respond. The holocaust of all-out nuclear war would happen by accident.

This is no negligible danger. False alarms of one kind or another are frequent in the American warning system. From 1977 to 1982 there were no fewer than 159 incidents in which some kind of alarm was triggered, and on five occasions the strategic offensive forces were put on alert — bombers rolled down the runways, missiles were brought to readiness. Every time it was a false alarm. Presumably similar events have occurred in the Soviet Union. False alarms are so prevalent that many analysts fear a launch on warning policy adopted by either superpower would make a wholesale nuclear war likely within the foreseeable future.

When the Soviets threatened in 1982 to answer the upcoming Pershing deployment by shifting to launch on warning, Western officials denounced such statements as irresponsible, and as obviously designed to frighten Western Europeans and Americans. In this period U.S. and allied leaders worried about Soviet manipulation of the European peace movement. If the democratic governments of the West found themselves under public pressure to call off the Pershing and GLCM deployments — while the public in the Communist countries could not, of course, exert similar pressure against the SS-20s — the Soviets would have won cheaply a major political victory. Further intimidation would unquestionably follow.

This "political" interpretation of Soviet behavior received increasing credence as time passed and the Soviet play for Western public opinion became more overt. Especially critical were the West German elections of March 1983, because West Germany was the NATO ally on whose soil Pershings would be based. Only one of the two major parties, the Christian Democrats, really supported deployment. As the elections approached the Soviets expanded their campaign to influence the German public, culminating in a virtual barrage of declarations that a Pershing deployment would expose West Germany to nuclear destruction, and similar intimidating statements. (The elections were won by the Christian Democrats, substantially on the basis of domestic issues.)

But even if the Soviet threats of moving to launch on warning were only propaganda, they bore some relationship to a real issue, one that applies in fact to both the Pershings and the SS-20s. Accurate missile targeting tends to undercut what specialists call "crisis stability."

This strategic concept, the last to be introduced in this book, is especially important. Most analysts agree that "crisis stability" is one of the foremost goals to be sought for U.S., and for that matter other nations', nuclear forces—perhaps *the* foremost since it inherently includes deterrence. It means this: In a crisis that might escalate to nuclear warfare, government leaders should find that the configuration of forces on both sides encourages moderation and unhurried, careful decision making. The force configurations should *not* encourage rapid or major escalations or quick decisions. Let us pause for a moment on this.

It is well understood by now that both the content of the decisions that leaders make in a crisis, and the rationality of the process by which they formulate and make their decisions, are heavily influenced by the characteristics of the forces on both sides. For example, one or both sides may have important forces that are vulnerable to attack—by accurate missiles, by strike aircraft, or perhaps by ground assault in the case of systems based near the borders. Once fighting has begun, leaders may feel strong pressure to employ those forces quickly, to "use them or lose them." But often using them would mean escalating the crisis and perhaps triggering a much bigger war. The goal of crisis stability means creating, ahead of time, forces that will not generate this or similar kinds of escalation pressures.

This logic applies to LRTNF or indeed to any nuclear forces. The goal of crisis stability requires that each side's forces be as secure as possible for as long as possible, so that leaders will not feel they must "use them or lose them," and can make unhurried decisions. Accurate targeting, which is possible with both the SS-20 and Pershing II, tends to undercut that goal.

The same will be true with ground-, sea-, and air-launched cruise missiles, which, first on the American and later on the Soviet side, are and will be very accurate too. However, the flight time of cruises used strategically is measured in hours rather than minutes, so many analysts do not regard cruises as first-strike weapons. Even so their deployment will undercut crisis stability to some extent. Far more than two or three hours is needed for careful decision making. Most analysts believe, for instance, that one of the reasons why the Cuban Missile Crisis of 1962 did not escalate into a nuclear war is that leaders in Washington and Moscow had many *days* in which to think through their actions. If arms control agreements do not succeed in reducing accurate LRTNF to very low or zero levels, crisis stability in the future may not be as great as it has been in the past.

An agreement that would set SS-20s, Pershings, and GLCMs at some low, but not zero, level remains a possibility as of this writing. In the summer of 1982, Nitze and his opposite number at the INF talks, Yuli Kvitsinsky, privately discussed a compromise plan by which the SS-20s would be reduced to about seventy-five, and an equal number of American missiles would be deployed. At the time both Washington and Moscow quickly repudiated any such plan. In the spring of 1983 President Reagan made a similar offer in a public address. Moscow rejected it again, but many analysts remained hopeful that some such compromise might eventually be reached. Such an agreement might allow NATO and the Soviets to retain some of the weapons that strong military and civilian elements on both sides want, yet allow both to control their arms in a limited but useful way that would not undercut crisis stability too severely.

CONTROLLING STRATEGIC ARMS

Although Ronald Reagan had said repeatedly during his 1980 campaign for the presidency that the SALT II agreement was not in America's interests, on entering office his administration decided to continue the informal observance of its terms that Carter had begun. The United States would act in accordance with the SALT II terms even though the Senate had not ratified the agreement, so long as the USSR did the same. But the Reagan administration did not resubmit the agreement for Senate consideration, and did not advance any new plans for strategic arms control for well over a year after entering office. For these and other reasons, many arms control advocates concluded that the administration was not seriously interested in limiting strategic arms, at least anytime soon.

In May 1982 President Reagan offered a new departure. Calling for fresh talks with the Soviets, the president argued that previous negotiations had been flawed by concentration on setting ceilings rather than seeking reductions. He proposed replacing "Strategic Arms Limitation Talks" (SALT) with "STrategic Arms Reduction Talks" (START).

He also offered a specific reduction proposal. Each side would cut back its total number of ballistic missile warheads—ICBM and SLBM both—to 5,000. At the time this represented about a one-third reduction. Of this total, neither side would be allowed more than half, or 2,500 warheads, on land-based missiles. Finally, neither side would be allowed more than 850 ballistic missiles, ICBMs and SLBMs together. The president also suggested a later, "second stage" agreement that would put a ceiling on total missile throw weight, to be set below the current U.S. total.

Two features of this proposal were innovative. One was the size of the reductions. On some earlier occasions reductions *had* been discussed, notably the sudden American suggestion, early in the Carter administration, of a ten percent cut. But never had either side officially proposed cuts of this magnitude. The other innovation was the president's proposal to make numbers of warheads a central criterion. SALT had always counted launch vehicles—missiles—primarily and counted warheads only secondarily. President Reagan suggested reversing this.

The Soviet premier, Leonid Brezhnev, responded in ten days, accepting the proposal to resume strategic arms control negotiations, but rejecting the president's specific plan. As Western arms control specialists had anticipated, he argued that the U.S. plan was grossly unfair to the Soviet Union. The requirement that no more than half the total warheads be on ICBMs would pose no difficulty at all for the United States, which had well over half its missile warheads on SLBMs already. But as Washington well knew, some three-quarters of the total Soviet warheads were on ICBMs. If the USSR had to cut back to only 2,500 ICBM warheads, adding its relatively few SLBM warheads would leave it with a total much lower than that of the United States. The Reagan administration justified its proposal on the grounds that land-based missiles were becoming vulnerable on both sides, whereas SLBMs were still secure. But the American advantage in SLBMs was undeniable.

The Reagan administration proposal seemed to favor the United States in two other respects also. The limit of 850 missiles happened to be almost exactly half the total the United States then had deployed. The Soviets, who had a total of about 2,300 missiles deployed, would have to give up more. Their relative sacrifice would be even greater under the proposed terms of the "second stage" to come later. Their total throw weight came to over eleven million pounds; the United States had about four million pounds of throw weight deployed. Setting a ceiling below four million would require only a minor American reduction but a huge Soviet one.

In fact it would be an even greater sacrifice than these numbers suggested. The United States had its throw weight "fractionated" across a larger total number of warheads than the USSR had. The huge Soviet throw weight represented fewer warheads because individual Soviet warheads, lacking Western miniaturization, were much bulkier and heavier. Unless and until the USSR mastered the necessary miniaturization technology, agreeing to equal throw weight would mean agreeing to considerably *fewer* warheads in fact (no matter that legally the Soviets would be allowed an equal number).

Secretary Brezhnev denounced the Reagan administration proposal as favoring the United States so much as to be "unilateral in nature." The secretary also claimed that the U.S. proposal had left unmentioned, and thus entirely uncontrolled, those weapons in which America had the greatest technological lead: cruise missiles and strategic bombers. But in fact the president had said, a few days after making his proposal, that no systems would be excluded from negotiation. In a speech televised throughout the USSR, Brezhnev agreed to open START talks and countered the Reagan plan by proposing the freeze.

This in turn was unacceptable to an administration convinced that the Soviets were ahead. Even so the START talks got underway in Geneva shortly thereafter. The two sides began so far apart that Western arms control specialists expected, at best, a long and difficult negotiation. (Some of them believe, in fact, that the Reagan administration position was designed to give the public appearance of being a serious effort to halt the arms race and reduce arms, while actually being so one-sided as to ensure that no agreement would be reached.) In any case little significant progress had been made in START a year later, when this book was completed.

SUMMARY

There were no strategic arms control negotiations between the superpowers from mid-1979, when the finishing touches were put on the SALT II agreement, to mid-1982, when START began. During those three years U.S. cruise missiles advanced from a technology still under development, almost to the point of deployment in the ALCM version. In retrospect it seems probable that those years were the last in which strategic cruise missiles might have been controlled. Any final chance that might have still been possible at the opening of START soon vanished. The two sides began far apart, cruises were only one item on a complicated agenda, and no rapid progress was made in the talks. ALCM deployments began within months, with GLCMs scheduled to follow a year later and SLCMs soon thereafter.

Negotiations about Eurostrategic systems did begin in October 1980, but little could be accomplished, first until the presidential election in the United States, and then until the new administration developed its position. President Reagan and his advisers entered office believing that the United States and the West were inferior in central strategic systems and in Eurostrategic systems both, and also believing that past administrations had been too eager to reach arms control agreements. It is not surprising that the Reagan administration did not regard opening negotiations as an urgent priority.

The "peace" or antinuclear war movements, first in Europe and then in America, stimulated the administration quickly to bring forth its arms control proposals. Mass protests in Europe in the fall of 1981 were followed by President Reagan's November proposal of INF talks and a "zero-zero solution" to the problem of SS-20s, Pershing IIs, and GLCMs. The expanding Freeze campaign the next spring in America was followed by his May 1982 proposal of START talks and a one-third reduction in warheads. The Soviets agreed to participate in both negotiations, but regarded both specific proposals as one-sided. By mid-1983 little had been accomplished in either forum.

The USSR tried to sway European public opinion with a propaganda campaign. The goal was to prevent any Pershing or GLCM deployment, without having to give up any SS-20s in a negotiated agreement. Among other things, the Soviets threatened to shift to a policy of launch on warning, claiming the Pershings could strike Soviet military command centers. In fact the majority of these centers were not within Pershing range. But it did appear that to some extent both these missiles and the SS-20s threatened the vital goal of crisis stability.

The antinuclear war movements had arisen, in part, as a reaction to public perception that the United States had suddenly decided to plan on fighting "limited nuclear wars." The perception was a much simplified version of the truth. Debate whether the purpose of nuclear weapons was "deterrence only," or deterrence plus "war-fighting" under some circumstances, had begun in the early 1960s. Debate subsided when the Soviets achieved parity a few years later, and revived in the 1970s when the flexible targeting doctrine and the many available MIRVs had made "limited nuclear options" attractive to some analysts. Improved missile accuracy and c^3i had led President Carter to expand counterforce targeting and the number of preprogrammed options in Presidential Directive 59. To this the Reagan administration added the goal of "prevailing" in a "protracted" nuclear war, and a clear choice of the war-fighting doctrine.

FOR FURTHER READING

Ball, Desmond. "Can Nuclear War Be Controlled?" *Adelphi Paper No. 169.* London: International Institute of Strategic Studies, 1981. The classic analysis, in the open literature, of why planning for controlled, limited nuclear warfare is not feasible.

Freedman, Lawrence. *The Evolution of Nuclear Strategy.* New York: St. Martin's Press, 1981. An extensive history and assessment of the development of U.S. nuclear thinking. In scope, approach, and subject matter it somewhat resembles the present volume, but is pitched at a more advanced level and incorporates more detail.

Harvard Nuclear Study Group. *Living with Nuclear Weapons.* New York: Bantam Books, 1983. A widely noted, widely read introduction to questions of nuclear weapons and strategy. Intended in part as basic education, in part as a reply to Jonathan Schell and the Freeze movement.

Knorr, Klaus, and Thornton Read. *Limited Strategic War.* New York: Praeger, 1962. The first, and probably still the best, general introduction to its topic, from the viewpoint of comprehensive strategic analysis.

Schell, Jonathan. *The Fate of the Earth.* Boston: Houghton Mifflin, 1982. Extremely widely read, this polemic became the "bible" of the American anti-nuclear war movement.

Smoke, Richard. *War: Controlling Escalation.* Cambridge, Mass.: Harvard University Press, 1977. An exploration of how difficult it can be to control escalation processes, and of how those processes work.

13
Conclusion: U.S. Security and the Nuclear Dilemma in the Late Twentieth Century

This survey of the American experience of security in the nuclear era ends in 1983. This short concluding chapter offers several observations about that experience as a whole, and closes with a brief glance at the prospects before the American people in the years to come. Let us begin by summarizing the experience of the decades since World War II.

For a brief time just after that war, Americans enjoyed a world position that has never been equaled by any people in history. It was a position drastically different both from the isolation that had gone before, and from the relative insecurity that came after, which by now is all that most Americans can remember. The atomic bombs that ended the war made the United States temporarily supreme on the planet. In that unique position Americans were able to give full rein to the idealism, tinged with innocence, that at that time was a natural part of their culture. They were sincere in wanting to turn the "collective security" of the whole world over to the United Nations Security Council, in desiring only small U.S. military forces, and in supporting a plan that gave up control of atomic energy to a powerful international agency.

At the same time, the American concept of collective security and the Baruch Plan would have tended to further a world economic order favorable to American interests, and would certainly have maintained the U.S. monopoly on knowledge of how to construct an atomic bomb. When the Soviet Union rejected that plan, and used its Security Council veto to protect its own policies from UN "interference," the American people began to reorient their attitudes. Now (and only now) the phrase "national security" became part of their language, and institutions for a large, standing military establishment were created.

The Soviet determination to maintain an Eastern European empire acquired by force, the completion of that empire by an engineered coup in Czechoslovakia, and above all, the Berlin Blockade, convinced most Americans that the USSR was a political enemy whose ambitions were creating a state of "cold war." Only the American monopoly of the atomic bomb, it seemed, prevented the USSR from becoming an immediate military enemy as well. For a while this monopoly was a reliable source of security in spite of the cold war. The deterrence that the bomb seemed to provide automatically was expected to keep the Red Army at bay; the containment policy and practical expressions of it like the Marshall Plan and NATO were expected to rebuild and protect Western Europe.

The surprisingly early Soviet explosion of a test atomic bomb, together with the fall of China to Mao Zedong's Communists, shocked the Truman administration into a thorough reassessment of U.S. national security, NSC-68, and a decision to proceed with the hydrogen bomb. The Korean War intervened before the full implications of NSC-68's main conclusion could be weighed—that deterrence was becoming complicated and problematical, and would have to be sought at conventional as well as nuclear levels. In the face of a potential Soviet atomic threat, the U.S. strategic posture was greatly upgraded. Interest in disarmament waned, new jet bombers were given to SAC, and air defense and nuclear bomb production were expanded.

The Eisenhower administration entered office to find that the real Soviet strategic threat was still relatively small. The nation had passed through a cycle from supremacy, through a marked sense of danger, and was now coming back again to superiority and optimism. But after Korea, Americans wanted no more frustrating small wars. Eisenhower decided to enhance the American technological advantage over the Soviets in his "New Look," and to exploit that advantage to extend deterrence further. Even as specialists of a new kind — "national security analysts" — became interested in the questions of limited war that Korea had posed, Secretary of State John Foster Dulles announced a policy of Massive Retaliation should the Sino-Soviet bloc launch a new war.

Soviet strategic striking power grew during the 1950s, and between Moscow's increased confidence and Washington's realization that the U.S. superiority would not last indefinitely, serious disarmament negotiations were begun. But the arrival of long-range missiles, symbolized for the public by Sputnik, complicated the negotiations and raised what seemed to be a grave threat of a "missile gap" in the Soviets' favor. Specialists worried that a dangerously delicate balance of terror might result from the Soviets — or either side — being tempted to preempt in a crisis, striking the other's vulnerable, above-ground ICBMs before its own were destroyed. They urged that the United States deploy "secure, second-strike forces," especially SLBMs.

The Kennedy administration accelerated the already vigorous American ICBM and SLBM programs and, though it discovered that the missile gap had not materialized, decided to deploy over 1,700 missiles in anticipation of imminent Soviet deployments. But the Soviet missiles did not appear for years. In the meantime Americans found that the cycle through a sense of threat, vigorous effort, and back to marked superiority had repeated itself a second time.

The new era of advantage, spent exploring damage limiting options (especially by way of counterforce targeting) passed when the long-awaited Soviet missile buildup materialized in the second half of the 1960s. Secretary of Defense Robert McNamara and his successors concluded that stable, Mutual Assured Destruction had arrived, and that a new bid for superiority was infeasible. The Nixon administration settled on a policy of "sufficiency," though later the development of highly accurate warheads would lead it to reemphasize counterforce targeting, even without the prospect of accomplishing much damage limiting.

Meanwhile the 1960s saw the development of a new approach to security—arms control. As advancing technology seemed to render complete disarmament infeasible, analysts became interested in constraining and slowing the arms race, with the ultimate aim of halting it. The Limited Test Ban Treaty, the Nonproliferation Treaty, and several other agreements brought some progress along these lines, while SALT I put a ceiling an offenseive missiles and stopped the deployment of ABM systems. But MIRVs, cruise missiles, and accurate warheads were not forestalled, as they might have been by agreements to ban their testing. The Vladivostok accords set offensive force ceilings quite high. The promise of an early SALT II agreement evaporated in delays, and when it was finally signed at the end of the 1970s it was not ratified by the U.S. Senate.

The decade of the seventies also witnessed a continuing Soviet military buildup, to the point where the USSR came to surpass America in some categories of power, and one body of opinion in the West feared the dawn of a new and unprecedented era of overall Soviet supremacy. In Europe, the deployment of the SS-20 late in the decade led to a NATO "two-track" decision to seek an arms control agreement limiting long-range theater nuclear forces, and failing that, to deploy its own missiles. But serious negotiations opened only after the United States, in the wake of public pressure from Western Europe, proposed high-level U.S.-Soviet talks. After similar pressure at home the United States also opened fresh negotiations on controlling strategic arms. But in INF and START both, the Soviet and American positions were so far apart that no early arms control success could be expected.

The Ford and Carter administrations did increase spending on defense in response to the Soviet buildup, and the Reagan administration increased it much more. Some believed that American ICBM silos were becoming vulnerable to increasingly numerous and accurate Soviet MIRVs, but no domestic consensus could be reached on basing a new ICBM, the MX. In the 1980s new Trident submarines and missiles entered the American forces, along with air-, sea-, and ground-launched cruise missiles. As the technology of accurate targeting improved, Washington moved toward planning for "limited," protracted nuclear war. The Reagan administration announced that this kind of "war-fighting," not just simple deterrence, was now American doctrine.

THE POST-WORLD WAR II ERA

What observations emerge from viewing this era as a whole? One involves the cycle of American superiority. So noticeable during the first twenty-five years following World War II, the cyclical character of the U.S. arms advantage in the world has *not* continued, at least not at all in the same way. Twice in earlier years an unexpected surge in the Soviet threat seemed to nullify a previously advantageous American position, whereupon a powerful new American effort restored a superior posture — in fact a better one than anticipated. Since about 1970 the stalemate of Mutual Assured Destruction has dampened down this cycle.

Furthermore, at each turn of the wheel the *relative* position of the United States was less advantageous than before. When the era of superiority represented by Massive Retaliation arrived and the Eisenhower administration said the United States would "prevail" in a general war against the USSR (which had only a few atomic weapons and limited ability to deliver them), this was a less desirable situation than the absolute supremacy that had accompanied the American atomic monopoly earlier. When the second (and briefer) era of superiority arrived, the Kennedy administration only explored, with some doubt, the possibility that a counterforce strategy might accomplish some damage limiting in the event of war. This was quite different, and less advantageous, than the Eisenhower administration's belief that damage to the United States would be so slight that America could credibly threaten to *begin* a nuclear war. When these cycles ended, the superpowers found themselves roughly equal in their capacity for Mutual Assured Destruction, an ultimate kind of equivalence that has continued to the present in spite of each side's continual jockeying for minor advantages.

It might be thought that the great Soviet buildup of the 1970s, followed by the American buildup of the 1980s, represents a third cycle in the series. Didn't President Reagan enter office saying the United States was falling behind, and launch a fresh American effort, just as President Kennedy had in 1961?

A minor difference is that the two previous cycles each lasted less than one decade rather than extending over two. A much greater difference is that the previous American efforts had resulted, not very deliberately, in tremendous and very real superiority. Massive Retaliation and counterforce for damage limiting had both put the United States in a position, for a while, that would have been decisive had an all-out war occurred. Nothing remotely like this was in prospect for the American buildup that began in the late 1970s and accelerated in the 1980s. The capacity of the USSR to destroy the United States completely could not be challenged. The new American effort was motivated merely by a judgment that the prior and continuing Soviet effort must be matched. A rough balance in forces must be maintained, or in the Reagan administration's perception, restored.

Another observation to be made of the post-World War II era is of a gradual, but more or less steady erosion of what was once the United States' overwhelmingly commanding technological position. America emerged from World War II technologically supreme by a wide margin, not merely by virtue of its atomic monopoly but in many other ways as well. In aircraft design and technology, in electronics, in the size and power of its navy, and in many other respects the United States was far ahead of all other military powers. In the 1950s the Soviets also came to possess nuclear weapons, and were even ahead briefly in building long-range rockets; but the United States retained a commanding lead in other categories. During the 1960s that lead narrowed, and in the 1970s the Soviets caught up in many areas.

Even by the 1980s the *total* breadth and depth of Soviet technological capability had not yet begun to equal that of the United States. The Soviet economy as a whole is technically backward compared to the Western European, Japanese, or American economies. But by concentrating a high fraction of its total technological capabilities into *military* technology, the Soviet Union has succeeded in becoming highly competitive with the United States in weapons.

This dribbling way of the American technological superiority has been the result of two factors, both inevitable. First, it is politically impossible in the United States to spend taxpayers' dollars (particularly as more and more of them would be needed) to remain four or six steps ahead of the nearest competitor. The taxpayer will not pay for more than a moderate advantage. (The United States does remain up to five years ahead of the USSR in some military technologies, primarily those related to electronics.)

Second, the technological progression itself has been relatively homogenous. The invention of nuclear weapons represented a sharp discontinuity in the evolution of military technology. The nation that possessed them was in a completely different military category from the nation that did not. But it is an accident of nature that no similar discontinuity has appeared since, nor so far as known is any in prospect. Since 1945 the evolution of technology has been homogenous, each single step ahead in research being marginal. The Soviet leaders were determined to sink all the resources needed into catching up with the United States, and as the USSR is a country of roughly comparable population size, and greater natural resources, in time they were able to do so. Unable to find some new corner to turn into a wholly new technology, and unable to keep many steps ahead in the known technologies, the United States inevitably found itself being overtaken. Henceforward the competition presumably will proceed on a roughly equal basis.

Americans are used to thinking of their country as the strongest military power on earth and have been slow to accept that it is no longer. The breadth and depth of the Soviet technical and industrial base for military programs is now at least equal to America's. The size of the forces the two sides *actually* create will be the result of policy decisions, but broadly speaking, the military *potentials* of the two superpowers are now roughly equal. They will remain so in spite of any effort Americans can make or are likely to try to make. That the USSR no longer *can* be surpassed by any reasonable U.S. effort — as it could be, and twice was — has probably not yet been realized by many Americans.

THE PROSPECTS AHEAD

The simplest observation to be made about the last few decades is that the American people now find themselves less secure than they ever have been (except briefly during the most intense cold war crises). The total destructive power the USSR can visit upon the United States, which by the late 1960s was already ample to wipe out every sizable American city, has grown hugely since then and continues to increase. So does the equivalent American power against the Soviet Union. Nothing in the history recounted in this book gives much hope that the mutual piling up of destructive force, or the continuing threat to American security, is likely to be reduced anytime soon.

The "nuclear dilemma" mentioned in this book's title refers to the fact that the United States dare not, by itself, halt this piling up of weaponry, even though the net effect of both the United States and USSR continuing it is that both are left even less secure. As Americans experience it, the nuclear dilemma is fundamentally this: efforts to increase U.S. nuclear power are matched by Soviet efforts, and both sides end up even more threatened than before; yet for the United States *not* to continue its efforts while the USSR still did obviously would leave America even more vulnerable and insecure.

The prospect is not bright for effective, verifiable agreements between the superpowers to halt the competition together. Unless entirely new social or political forces come into play, or unforeseen events change the world considerably, the long-term trend toward continuing and even increasing insecurity will go on. This book closes with a brief look at the prospect Americans face in the coming years.*

Ever since the commanding superiority of the United States was replaced by the basic stalemate of Mutual Assured Destruction, the best hope for improving Americans' real security—or at least halting the slide toward increasing insecurity—has lain in arms control efforts. As noted earlier, arms control is not an alternative to national security; it is one avenue toward achieving it. The Joint Chiefs of Staff have agreed. They have repeatedly supported the various SALT agreements explicitly on the grounds that limiting Soviet arms would limit the threat to the United States. Arms control becomes a *principal* avenue toward achieving security, when unilateral action to remove the threat is impossible, as it has been between East and West for decades.

But the record of actual arms control achievements, at least to date, is not very satisfying. With the outstanding exception of the ABM treaty, efforts to limit strategic weapons have accomplished little. A decade and a half after SALT began, the Soviet and American arsenals are much larger than they were at the outset! While it is often argued, and may be true, that in the absence of SALT they would have grown even greater, one cannot believe that the arms race is being brought under any effective control when both sides have some five times the number of warheads they had when the effort started. They are also developing new categories of weapons (e.g., cruise missiles).

Note: a discussion of future prospects often involves value judgments to a degree greater than a description of past events and conditions. The reader should be aware that in the rest of this chapter the author's values are expressed openly.

Other efforts to limit arms, conventional as well as nuclear, are also languishing. In the 1980s a mood of pessimism grips many of those who specialize in arms control.

There is reason for pessimism other than the meager results achieved so far. Events of recent years have gone a long way toward undercutting one of the main bases for hope, namely a belief that parity between the superpowers would drain away much of the competitiveness of the arms race. We recall from chapter 8 that when national security specialists turned in the early 1960s from grand disarmament schemes to arms control, they did so not only because the grand schemes seemed pointless, but also because they had, or thought they had, positive reason to think that a strategy of slowing and halting the arms race would work. At that time the balance of terror seemed "delicate." Each side's vulnerable forces of bombers and primitive missiles might be wiped out by the other's first strike. Also, the two arsenals were badly "out of synch" in terms of time. First the USSR seemed to be profiting from a "missile gap," then a real missile gap in reverse gave the United States superiority for awhile. Throughout those years many analysts believed that the intensity of the arms race was a product of these imbalances and fears. When the forces facing each other became roughly equivalent in size and were deployed in relatively secure silos and submarines, they thought, the two sides would be able to relax and the competition could be slowed and halted by degrees.

To some small extent this expectation was realized. The SALT process got underway when, and only when, these conditions began to be fulfilled. But events since have suggested that these conditions are *not* enough for the competition to be significantly slowed. Parity, reasonably secure forces, and the more relaxed atmosphere these things helped bring have not led Moscow and Washington to brake the arms race. Instead the competition has continued at a rapid pace. Evidently more conditions, perhaps unknown ones, must also be met before it can be slowed and halted. The hope of the 1960s, a force that launched the whole arms control movement, has been largely dashed.

It is hard to avoid the conclusion, too, that the technology simply moves faster than can efforts to control it. It is true that neither side, and certainly not the United States, pushes weapons technology ahead as rapidly as it *possibly* could, and in that sense the two sides are not "racing" and there is no arms "race." But they push it noticeably faster than they pursue arms control. After SALT I, the rapid deployment of MIRVs forced negotiators to accept much higher force ceilings at Vladivostok. While they were still trying to codify those in a SALT II treaty, the technology was already moving on to cruise missiles and accurate warheads. Before a strong effort could be mounted to control those at the testing stage, they had been tested. The result is that the strategic environment of the 1980s has been greatly complicated. If it was difficult to negotiate meaningful ceilings before, it is doubly hard now.

The onrush of the arms race is all the more troubling because in recent years its underlying character has changed in a way that gives it less and less reasonable relationship to security. Of course any arms race poses dangers. But an element of irrationality has appeared in the Soviet-American competition that it did not used to have. As recently as the mid-1960s much of what was occurring in that arms competition made a considerable amount of sense and, despite the claims of some critics at the time, the forces the two sides were deploying were not wildly excessive. Today that cannot be said. Not everyone understands that in the 1970s, an element of absurdity entered the arms race that had not been present previously.

When the United States built over six hundred B-52 bombers in the 1950s, it was on the assumption that a Soviet sneak attack would destroy some on the ground and others would be shot down by Soviet air defenses. Since destroying the USSR as a modern military and economic power meant destroying several hundred targets inside the Soviet Union, having this many bombers was not extreme.

Even when the United States deployed more than 1,700 missiles in the 1960s, this was originally decided on the basis of a calculation that a Soviet first strike might destroy most of the bombers on the ground, half of the Polaris submarines in port, and a few of the ICBM silos. The missiles of that day were less accurate, and not too reliable; some would fail to put their one warhead near the target, and many would malfunction. The Soviets were beginning an ABM system that might shoot some warheads down. Though all these factors together still left a margin of safety, again the deployment of 1,700 missiles was not too extreme.

Today things are very different. Just two Trident submarines can wreak as much destruction as the entire U.S. missile force of October 1962, when the Cuban Missile Crisis occurred. One Trident submarine carries twenty-four missiles, each of which has eight warheads for a total of 192 warheads. Three hundred eighty-four warheads on two Trident submarines is approximately the size of the entire American missile force in October 1962. There are only 218 cities of 100,000 or more population in the whole Soviet Union.

It is true that if one adds significant Soviet military bases and installations (other than missile silos) the number of possible targets increases by several hundred. It increases still further if one adds military targets in Eastern Europe. It is also true that in a war one or more Trident submarines might be sunk before they could fire their missiles.

Even so American striking power is outlandishly excessive, and so is Soviet striking power. Ten Trident submarines are being deployed. In addition, the United States will retain for an indefinite period thirty-one Polaris submarines, each of which carries either 128 or 160 MIRV warheads. There are also 1,000 land-based missiles, more than half of which carry three warheads each. In addition there are over 300 bombers that also carry multiple bombs and warheads. And on top of that the United States will be deploying hundreds, probably thousands, of strategic cruise missiles. Obviously the total destructive power the United States can rain on the Soviet Union is mounting far in excess of the number of feasible targets. The same thing is true of the destructive power the USSR can rain on America. The popular term for this is "overkill."*

A full-scale nuclear war between the superpowers would destroy them utterly and would have the gravest consequences far beyond their borders. This had not been the case in the earlier years of the Soviet-American competition, even though some people were inclined to think so. The general public discovered in the late 1950s that the USSR could launch hundreds of bombers carrying nuclear bombs toward the United States, more than a few of which would get through. Suddenly there was a tendency for Americans' previous feeling of considerable security (which had not been justified) to be replaced by the equally simple, opposite feeling that nuclear war meant the end of the world (which was also not justified). At that time and for a while thereafter, a nuclear war would have been an unprecedented catastrophe but would not have been the equivalent of doomsday.

But more recently the popular fantasy has become essentially true. The armories on both sides have reached a point where a general

---

*This discussion presumes correct the many scientists who say that actual wartime accuracy would differ considerably from accuracy on test ranges, and hence that neither side could attack the other's ICBM silos with any confidence of destroying most of them. Even on the opposite assumption, the great majority of U.S. missile warheads in the early 1980s are not highly accurate even on test ranges. In any case, both sides' plentiful and secure SLBMs mean that no disarming first strike is possible under any conditions, which leaves little point or purpose even to attempt "silo busting."

war — in which nuclear weapons are targeted on cities as well as on military targets — would all but obliterate the United States and the USSR.

In spite of the absurd and dangerous quantity of nuclear weapons, there is hardly any promise of a real braking of the arms race. Rather, the prospect is for its more or less steady continuation in the coming years. The planned cruise missiles probably will be deployed in great numbers, first by the United States and a little later by the USSR. Either or both may deploy mobile ICBMs in quantity, and both are working on weapons for use against targets in space, such as the other side's satellites. Advanced bombers and advanced SLBMs will be deployed, along with other new systems supporting nuclear and other warfare on the ground, on and under the seas, in the air, and quite possibly in outer space.

Some of these systems, certainly the cruises, will be impossible to keep track of by reconnaissance satellites or any other means available. Once they are produced in quantity, no verifiable limit or freeze on their deployment will be possible. Neither side would permit the very extensive and intrusive inspection practices that would be needed to count and track them manually. The first American cruises were deployed in late 1982. These major components of strategic power, and later their Soviet counterparts, can multiply uncontrollably.

Putting a ceiling on the overall total of each side's strategic nuclear forces, then reducing them, was and is the fundamental goal of strategic arms control. At some date in the early to mid-1980s, when the cruises have been deployed in enough numbers to make a difference, that goal will be rendered impossible. It will remain impossible for as far into the future as one can see. Some other nuclear forces may continue to be limited, and certain other measures, such as a comprehensive ban on atomic testing, will still be feasible. But the basic goal of capping and then reducing the two sides' total nuclear striking power will have been lost, perhaps permanently.

Technology itself evidently offers no natural stopping place for the arms competition. There is no reason for it not to go on and on, barring some unpredictable change in underlying Soviet-American hostility, or other unforeseeable event. The prospect before the American people is continuation of the arms race, with all its costs, absurdity, and danger, almost without hope of any end.

Epilogue

The nuclear threat has been the preeminent challenge to American national security since shortly after World War II, and will continue to be for as far ahead as anyone can see. Generations of nuclear weapons and delivery systems have come and gone; more will follow. The nuclear threat dominates all thought about security. Unlike earlier eras, when Americans were secure on their own continent far from enemies, when the lines between civilian and military were sharp, and when most of life fell on the civilian side, insecurity now pervades the background of American life. The future seems likely to bring only more of the same, at best.

But the threat is much greater now than it was in the days when the superpowers could destroy each other as modern nations, but not much more. The huge forces deployed on both sides recently have changed the character of the threat qualitatively, not just quantitatively. They jeopardize not the two nations alone, but civilization itself.

A general war between the United States and USSR — no targets barred — would inflict drastic, although not precisely predictable, damage over the whole globe. The impact on the increasingly fragile world ecology would be far more devastating than any of the other things environmentalists warn about. Fallout around the globe would create wholesale radiation sickness, cancer, and long-term genetic damage. There would be total economic breakdown and epidemics of disease. The psychological and social shock would be incalculable. There is real doubt whether civilization would survive.

For a country to put at risk its own national existence is one thing. History gives precedents for this. But for one country, or two, to put at risk the whole of human civilization is another thing altogether. The "nuclear threat" is not just a Soviet threat or an American threat. It is a threat to everyone, a threat created by the weapons themselves.

This qualitative change in the nuclear threat does not mean that all earlier thinking about a Soviet threat to the United States, and the deterrence of it, is invalidated immediately and completely. But it does mean that serious new thinking and completely new approaches are needed. The danger to civilization has introduced an extraordinary new element into human history. Some kind of equivalent change is needed in the whole concept of security and the nuclear threat.

Just this thought has arisen lately from opposite ends of the American political spectrum. The antinuclear war movement seeks not only for both sides to freeze the arms race but also for them to turn away from their basic reliance on nuclear weapons as instruments of national policy. Whatever its other successes or failures, the antinuclear war movement has convinced many people that some fundamentally different way of approaching security must be found.

President Reagan voiced the same idea in a televised address to the nation on March 23, 1983. Before announcing that he would order research on a defensive security system, intended to shoot down missiles before they could reach the United States, he said that what is needed is "a new vision of the future that offers hope." Deterrence has worked for decades, he said, but the Joint Chiefs and other advisers had "underscored the bleakness of the future before us" if no fresh approach is taken. At a news conference the following day he said it is "inconceivable" that the superpowers would continue indefinitely "like people facing [each other] across a table each with a cocked gun, and no one knowing whether someone might tighten the finger on the trigger."

The specific proposals of the antinuclear war movement and of President Reagan — respectively, for abandoning reliance on nuclear weapons and for a new defense against them — are different, but the basic idea behind both is the same. New thinking is needed. Humanity cannot continue down the current road indefinitely.

For decades the foundation of American national security has been deterrence. But more and fancier weapons will not resolve the nuclear threat, only add to it, and deterrence cannot be counted on to be a reliable foundation of security forever. To continue indefinitely the thinking and the practice of recent decades will only bring into reality "the bleakness of the future" of which the president has warned.

Appendix
National Security
as a Field of Study

"National security affairs" refers both to a class of policy problems for the United States (and for every other nation) and also to a field of study. This book has addressed itself to the evolution in the post-World War II period of major American policy problems involving nuclear weapons, and to the parallel evolution of important concepts associated with these policy problems. A few passages have also commented in passing about national security as a field of study. This appendix offers some additional observations, in a more academic vein, about national security as a field of study.

No formal definition of national security as a field has been generally accepted; none may be possible. In general, it is the study of the security *problems* faced by nations, of the *policies and programs* by which these problems are addressed, and also of the governmental *processes* through which the policies and programs are decided upon and carried out. As practiced in American research institutes, governmental agencies and universities, it naturally focuses on the problems, policies, and processes of the United States government.

National security differs from traditional "military science"; that field involves strategy and tactics in a narrower sense. Military science does not concern itself with decision-making processes at the pinnacle of governments, nor with the ways in which one government's decisions interact in broad and long-term ways with another government's decisions. Conversely, national security affairs does not concern itself, as military science does, with such questions as air tactics, deployment of naval fleets for battle, or the proper use of armor on the battlefield.

National security affairs partially overlaps the traditional fields of "international politics," "foreign affairs," and "diplomacy," but also differs from them to some extent. Specialists do not completely agree on just where the dividing lines should be drawn. In general, national security focuses more than these fields on the role of force in relations among nations, and on the implications of advancing military technology. It focuses more than "international politics" and similar academic subjects on policy: what should a country (the United States, say) do about an existing or foreseeable threat, and how should it go about deciding?

In the 1970s, national security affairs was renamed "international security affairs" at some research centers that wanted to accent a world perspective rather than an American, and there is a journal entitled *International Security*. Generally speaking, the substance of the problems addressed did not change markedly from what national security specialists had been working on earlier.

Quantitatively speaking, the field is overwhelmingly dominated by literature concerned with the practical security problems of particular nations. And of this, the literature in English is overwhelmingly dominated by analyses of the security problems of the United States and NATO. Distributed through this "policy analysis" literature is a conceptual dimension of the field, made up of analytical ideas that have emerged over the years. An example is the distinction between "counterforce" and "countervalue" strategic strikes. Many of these ideas have an abstract validity independent of their application to any particular circumstances. In other words they would apply, in principle, to all times and places, or at least to all that involved something resembling modern technology. We will return below to this quantitatively minor, but important, body of "theory."

The national security field as a whole possesses some distinctive qualities. One is that national security questions are greatly affected by changes in the many relevant technologies, and also by changes in the international environment. To be sure, the more abstract theorization, and also a few perennial policy issues, such as how decision making for national security should be organized within the executive branch, evolve slowly or not at all. But most national security questions are *sensitive to changes* in the international or technological parameters almost to an extreme degree.

Indeed, there are few other fields within the political and social sciences in which so many of the issues can be drastically affected by so many changes in circumstances. Great questions may turn on changing technical details—for instance the targeting accuracy of MIRVs (discussed on pp. 199 and 202 above). They may also turn on international events that can be quite sudden—for instance, the Cuban Missile Crisis and its outcome. More slowly, but still quickly by the standards of most social sciences, changes in circumstances can alter even abstract theorization. Some of the theoretical dynamics of deterrence, for instance, may be different in a world of a few nuclear powers, a world of a dozen, or a world of thirty.

Major changes in power balances and blocs around the world are rather unpredictable, except for some of the broad trends, but many of the worst possibilities may never occur. The continual rapid evolution of military technology has just the opposite characteristics. It is considerably more predictable (out to a time horizon of ten to fifteen years, and with a certain irreducible chance of surprise) but it also seems to be inevitable. The alterations wrought by technical change in many aspects of national security (certainly including nuclear issues) are often more drastic over a few years than the alterations wrought by world events during those years. Military technology is advancing so rapidly, in fact, that many national security specialists find themselves devoting a significant amount of their time simply to keeping up with present and projected weapons and other technical systems, and to creating the ideas needed to understand and cope with their novelties. Indeed, the pace of technological change is so fast that it is often necessary to theorize about the implications of systems that have not been built yet.

Although the technical characteristics that are intended and desired for future systems can be specified, there remains some *technological uncertainty* that can be important. For instance, during the debate that raged in 1969 among national security specialists and others concerning the Nixon administration's proposed Safeguard ABM system, part of the debate turned on whether one imputed relatively high or relatively low technical effectiveness to the system. Respectable opinions were offered on both sides of this question, but since at the time most of the critical system components had not been built, even in prototype, it was impossible actually to know.

Technological uncertainty becomes a constraint on the role and usefulness of national security theorizing, yet the theorizing is, if anything, needed all the more where the possibilities are so open. In such situations the theorist can and should specify his conclusions in contingent terms—"if we assign value *a* to factor *x*, then thus-and-such, but if we assign value *b* to it, then so-and-so." Even so, final judgments will have to be made by decision makers on a partially subjective and political basis.

This uncertainty, and the sensitivity to rapidly changing circumstantial detail, gives national security affairs a somewhat different flavor from many other fields involving the analysis of contemporary social and political issues. National security is a field dominated by policy analysis and relatively lacking in general theories. Most of the national security literature does not concern itself with drawing general conclusions or developing theory. Rather, it explicitly or implicitly assumes a technical and situational context similar to the one actually existing at the time of writing, and goes on to examine policy problems and associated intellectual problems that exist within that context and derive their meaning and force from it.

This *problem-oriented* quality of the national security field also derives from the fact that one's basic goal or purpose is largely predetermined. In the field of overlapping foreign policy studies it is possible—in fact mandatory—to ask: "What goals do we want a foreign policy to accomplish?" But in national security there is no parallel question. It is "given" that the goal is to enhance security. An entire dimension of potential theorizing—everything that concerns questions of multiple purposes—is simply absent. This applies equally whether one prefers to emphasize security through arms control or through unilateral measures such as deploying a new weapon system.

A related aspect of the national security field is its transient quality. Even more than most kinds of policy analysis, concepts and policies tend to be conceived, live briefly, and die. The premium on trying to keep up with the onrushing pace of world events and of technology creates a tendency toward *ahistoricism*. The few small islands of stable abstract theory are awash in the shifting tides of the ideas of the moment, and the relevance of past situations and problems to the present is often ignored. Debate over counterforce targeting in the 1970s and 1980s was often conducted without reference to what was similar or different from the time when counterforce as a general doctrine flourished in the early 1960s. And few remembered that that doctrine had been foreshadowed by a similar theory within the Strategic Air Command, called Bravo-Romeo-Delta, of a decade earlier. Wheels not recalled are reinvented—perhaps better, but often not.

The ahistoricism also helps narrow the range of forward vision down to the immediate future. If the literature rarely asks how 1985 resembles 1965 or 1955, it also rarely asks how it may resemble, or differ from, 1995 or 2005. Even less often does it ask whether, or how, the overall trends of the last several decades can continue; and if not, what might take their place.

The great majority of studies that focus on the policy analysis of current issues is supplemented by a small but significant body of abstract theorization. Some of the literature on strategic deterrence, for instance, concerns itself with the pure theory of deterrence between two nations that possess nuclear weapons and long-range means of delivering them, not just the particulars of the Soviet-American relationship. Some of the limited war literature also inquires into the general attributes and dynamics of limited war and escalation.* Certain other topics such as governmental processes and decision making for national security, and alliance politics, have also been approached partly from a theoretical perspective.

Beyond this there is an additional domain that not all national security specialists would regard as part of their field: basic research in conflict resolution and security. We know very little about the whole range of social, political, and psychological processes through which security may be reduced or increased, or the full menu of means for reducing, managing, mitigating, and resolving human conflict. Providing more understanding into these subjects is among the most important contributions the security field, broadly defined, could make.

But it is also the area where least progress has been made, partly because these are among the most difficult problems to be found in the

---

*An example of the former is Glenn Synder's *Deterrence and Defense*; of the latter, Thomas Schelling's *The Strategy of Conflict*. Citations are given on pp. 102 and 82, respectively.

social sciences, and partly because they have received grossly inadequate effort. It is a great irony that the United States alone has spent trillions of dollars on military forces since World War II, yet basic research on security has received less than, say, a single B-1B bomber. Much more attention needs to be given to the social roots of war, psychological and anthropological research on human aggressiveness and related questions, and to alternative approaches to security such as new negotiation systems, "civilian defense," and imaginative kinds of nonviolent techniques.

The importance of this basic research is not limited to the results it might provide, which might be disappointingly meager or excitingly great. Such research would also have a more indirect, but important benefit. Pursuing such work, or even reading about it, tends to enlarge one's awareness of the manifold possibilities inherent in "security" and "conflict resolution."

There is a tendency, born of a basic continuity in human thought and experience, for our perception of these problems and our imagination about possible solutions to remain bound within the frameworks that seemed fairly satisfactory in the past. In the national security literature, as well as in national security policy, this tendency shows itself in a continuing drift toward interpreting challenges to security almost exclusively in terms of deterrence strategies, usually implying military threats. Options that would cope with a possible challenge by, for instance, a carefully limited act of conciliation, are rarely thought through. Neither is there much analysis of limited acts to *initiate* changes in the international system that could enhance long-term security.

Basic research on human conflict and on alternative approaches to its resolution tends to make possibilities other than the usual ones for strategy, for managing conflict, and for enhancing security, more "visible," more recognizable, and more plausible. Enlarging the bounds of what specialists and policy makers thought possible and reasonable would in itself be a valuable payoff for developing this side of the security field.

Glossary

ABM	Antiballistic Missile. A missile intended to destroy an incoming ballistic missile reentry vehicle.
ACDA	Arms Control and Disarmament Agency. The principal agency of the U.S. government for arms control affairs.
AEC	Atomic Energy Commission. For about three decades following World War II, the federal agency responsible for the design and manufacture of atomic weapons. Subsequently absorbed into the Federal Energy Agency, which was absorbed into the Department of Energy.
ALCM	Air-launched cruise missile. Any cruise missile designed to be carried by, and launched from, an airplane.
APC	Armored personnel carrier. A heavily armored vehicle that carries a small number of troops.
assured destruction	The American name for the policy, pursued by both the U.S. and USSR, of deterring the opponent from striking one's homeland by threatening to devastate his own in retaliation.

ASW	Antisubmarine warfare. All measures intended to identify, track and destroy enemy submarines.
ballistic missle	A missile that rises on a steep trajectory to a high altitude and then plunges back very fast, also at a steep angle.
bias	The tendency for a ballistic missile RVs to drift to the side of its intended target because of anomalies in the earth's shape and gravitational field, and other factors.
catalysis	A process by which a small-scale conflict, such as one among Third World nations, ignites a much larger conflict, usually one between the superpowers.
CBW	Chemical and biological warfare. (Weapons of these kinds, if grouped together with nuclear weapons, are also called ABC weapons, for atomic-biological-chemical.)
CIA	Central Intelligence Agency. The best-known of many U.S. intelligence agencies, charged, among other things, with synthesizing the information gathered by the others together with its own.
COIN	Counter-insurgency warfare. Warfare against guerrilla forces.
counterforce	The targeting of one's missiles and other forces against enemy strategic forces, especially missile silos. Also, an American strategic doctrine of the early to mid-1960s, revived less formally in the late 1970s and since, the goal of which was and is to destroy the bulk of Soviet ICBM forces.
countervalue	The targeting of one's missiles and other forces against what the enemy values most: usually cities.
crisis stability	A condition in which the superpowers are not much tempted, in a crisis, to escalate to nuclear warfare, in part because most or all of their strategic forces are relatively secure.
cruise missile	A missile which flies a roughly horizontal trajectory, like an airplane.
damage limiting	An American strategy during the 1960s, intended to reduce the damage suffered by the United States in the event of nuclear war, by both offensive and defensive means.
decapitation	A strategy of destroying an enemy country's leading governmental officials, on the premise that this will make it impossible thereafter for the country to carry on the war coherently.

DIA	Defense Intelligence Agency. The principal intelligence service of the Defense Department. It includes the separate intelligence agencies of the military services.
DOD	Department of Defense.
DOE	Department of Energy. Branches of this department, not DOD or the military services, design and manufacture U.S. atomic weapons.
first-strike capability	Not the capability to strike first, but to largely or entirely disarm one's opponent in a first strike.
Flexible Response	A loose doctrine that emphasizes the creation and maintenance of "multiple options" and the flexible decision making and communications that go with them, for managing crises and conflicts. Flexible Response holds that strategic nuclear, theater nuclear, and conventional forces will all be maintained to deter the opponent's use of equivalent forces.
Flexible Targeting	An American strategic doctrine since the mid-1970s, emphasizing the ability to strike either Soviet cities and/or Soviet military targets, including missile silos.
forward-based systems (FBS)	A term, originally introduced by the Soviets, for the American systems located in Europe, Asia, and on ships around the Soviet periphery, capable of delivering nuclear weapons into the USSR.
fratricide	Destruction or deflection of incoming warheads by the nuclear explosion of other warheads that have just preceded them.
general purpose forces	A generic term for all combat forces other than those armed with nuclear weapons. Synonymous with "conventional forces."
Graduated Deterrence	An American strategic doctrine of the late 1950s, which sought to supplement the threat of Massive Retaliation with the additional threat that relatively large conventional attacks on U.S. allies might be met with nuclear strikes in the local theater.
horizontal escalation	Enlarging a conflict by bringing in nations previously uninvolved, or by attacking the opponent's forces or interests elsewhere in the world. (See, by contrast, "vertical escalation.")
IAEA	International Atomic Energy Agency. A United Nations-related agency that monitors compliance with prescribed safeguards against the misuse of nuclear materials; and also promotes peaceful applications of atomic technology.

ICBM	Intercontinental ballistic missile. A ballistic missile with a range sufficient to travel from the United States to the USSR or vice versa.
IRBM	Intermediate-range ballistic missile. A missile with a range from 1,500 up to five thousand kilometers.
JCS	Joint Chiefs of Staff. The four senior officers of the four American military services, plus an elected chairman drawn on a rotating basis from the services.
kiloton	Equivalent to a thousand tons of TNT. Used as a measure of the yield of nuclear weapons. The Hiroshima bomb, for instance, was about 15 kilotons, or the equivalent of 15,000 tons of TNT.
LRTNF	Long-range theater nuclear forces. Weapons with ranges from 1,000 to 5,500 kilometers.
MAD	See Mutual Assured Destruction.
Massive Retaliation	An American strategic doctrine of the 1950s, which threatened the USSR and China with large-scale atomic strikes on their homelands in the event they sponsored a military attack on U.S. allies, of not-precisely-defined magnitude.
megaton	Equivalent to a million tons of TNT. Used as a measure of the yield of thermonuclear weapons.
Minuteman	The backbone of U.S. ICBM forces since the mid-1960s. The Minuteman I was phased out in favor of the more modern Minuteman II (deployed starting in 1966) and the MIRVed Minuteman III (deployed starting in 1970).
MIRV	Multiple independently targetable reentry vehicle. Multiple warheads for missiles, in which each warhead can be aimed at a separate target.
MRTNF	Medium-range theater nuclear forces. Weapons with ranges from 200 to 1,000 kilometers.
MRBM	Medium-range ballistic missile. In some usage, a missile roughly synonymous with MRTNF. In other usage, a missile with range up to about 1,500 kilometers.
Mutual Assured Destruction	The principle that the United States and Soviet Union, each possessing an assured destruction capability against the other, mutually deter each other from launching a nuclear war.
NIE	National Intelligence Estimate. A formal, systematic assessment of a foreign nation's capabilities and intentions, or of other questions, prepared on the basis of all available data.

NPT	Nonproliferation Treaty. Completed in 1968 and signed by over a hundred countries, this treaty obliges nuclear powers not to transfer, and non-nuclear powers not to receive or manufacture, nuclear weapons or the immediate components thereof.
NSC	National Security Council. A legally instituted group of senior advisors to the president on national security issues, including the secretaries of state and defense.
OSD	Office of the Secretary of Defense. The analysts and other staff serving the secretary.
PNEs	Peaceful nuclear explosives. Atomic explosive devices intended for civilian purposes such as digging canals.
preemption	To strike an adversary quickly, before he strikes and in the expectation that he is about to.
RV	Reentry vehicle. The warhead, and some associated parts, of a ballistic missile.
ride out	To absorb an enemy's strike before responding.
SAC	Strategic Air Command. The branch of the USAF that includes ICBMs, strategic bombers, and their command and control.
SAM	Surface-to-air missile.
saturating	In the context of ABMs, the process of sending so many warheads against the defensive system that its interceptor missiles are exhausted.
second-strike capability	The ability to ride out an enemy attack and then retaliate effectively.
SIOP	Single Integrated Operations Plan. The basic American war plan for general nuclear war.
SLBM	Submarine-launched ballistic missile. A ballistic missile, of intermediate or intercontinental range, launchable from a submerged submarine.
SLCM	Ship- or submarine-launched cruise missile. A cruise missile launchable from a ship or a submerged submarine; usually "strategic," that is, intended for use against the enemy's homeland.
SRAM	Short-range attack missile. A U.S. missile carried by B-52 and FB-111 bombers, enabling them to avoid flying over the most densely defended targets.
thermonuclear	Pertaining to hydrogen (fusion) rather than uranium or plutonium (fission) weapons or processes.

throw weight	The total weight that can be carried by a missile to the target.
TNF	Theater nuclear forces.
triad	The long-standing American strategic doctrine that the United States must maintain three kinds of strategic forces: ICBMs, SLBMs, and long-range bombers.
USAF	United States Air Force.
USN	United States Navy.
vertical escalation	Intensifying a conflict by bringing new forces to bear, employing new types of weapons, or in the extreme case by attacking the enemy's homeland.
yield	The explosive force of a nuclear blast, measured in kilotons or megatons.

Index

ABMs. *See* Antiballistic Missiles
ABM Treaty. *See* SALT I Agreements
Accidents Agreement, 143
Acheson-Lilienthal Report, 129–30
Afghanistan, 1979 invasion of, 171, 212
Air alert (SAC), 98
Air defense of U.S., 60, 69, 71, 118, 153, 214
Air defense of USSR, 68–69, 153
Air-Launched Cruise Missile (ALCM), 205, 206, 211, 215, 230

ALCM. *See* Air-launched cruise missile
American University speech (John F. Kennedy), 139
AMSA (Advanced Manned Strategic Aircraft), 204
Ann Arbor speech (Robert McNamara), 114
Antarctica Treaty (1959), 143
Antiballistic Missiles (ABMs), 118–21, 153, 155, 157, 198, 240; ABM Treaty. *See* SALT I Agreements
Antinuclear war movement, 224–26, 250

Antisubmarine warfare (ASW), 157, 207, 208
Antitank guided missiles (ATGMs), 188
ANZUS Treaty, 67n, 68
Area defense, 212
Argentina, nuclear options of, 142, 146
Armored personnel carriers (APCs), 180
Arms Control and Disarmament Agency (ACDA), 137
Arnold, Gen. H. H., 83
Aron, Raymond, 15
Assured destruction mission and capability, 112, 114, 122, 123, 136, 151, 157
ASW. *See* Antisubmarine warfare
Athens speech (Robert McNamara), 114
Atlas missile, 97, 107, 109
Atomic Energy Act (of 1947), 47
Atomic Energy Commission (AEC), 47, 54
Atoms for Peace proposal, 131
Automated battlefield, 18

B-1 (bomber), 204–5, 215
B-36 (bomber), 53, 68
B-47 (bomber), 19, 53, 68, 70, 92, 109
B-52 (bomber), 68, 70, 71, 92, 96, 111–12, 154, 162, 176, 178, 204–5, 211, 246
B-70 (bomber), 204
Backfire (bomber), 167–68, 170–71, 178, 211
Baghdad Pact, 67
Baruch, Bernard, 36–37, 129–30
Baruch Plan, 129–30, 133, 238
Basing mode, 209
Battlefield nuclear weapons (short-range theater nuclear forces), 190
Bear (bomber), 109, 122, 178, 211

Berlin Blockade (1948–49), 39–41, 55, 238
Berlin Crisis of 1958–59, 74, 100
Berlin Crisis of 1961, 100, 116
Bias, 203
Biological weapons convention (1972), 143
Bison (bomber), 109, 122, 178, 211
Blackjack (bomber), 179, 214
Black shoe navy, 48
Blue-water navy, 181
BMEWS (Ballistic Missile Early Warning System), 98
Bolt from the blue, 115
Bomber gap, 70
Bravo-Romeo-Delta, 255
Brazil, nuclear options of, 142, 146
Brezhnev, Leonid, 122, 154, 165–66, 182, 232, 233
Britain. *See* Great Britain
Brodie, Bernard, 77, 222
Brown shoe navy, 48
Bush, George, 183
Buzz bomb, 205

Caldicott, Helen, 225
Capitalism, 8, 11
Carlucci, Frank, 223
Carr, E. H., 13
Carter administration, 168–69, 171–72, 183, 204–5, 209–10, 212, 214, 220, 240
Carter, Jimmy, 168, 169, 171, 189, 209–10, 214, 220
Castro, Fidel, 115, 142, 168
CBW (chemical and biological warfare), 142–43
CENTO (Central Treaty Organization), 67–68
Central Intelligence Agency (CIA), 46, 183–84
Checkpoint Charlie, 100
Chiang Kai-shek, 57

China, People's Republic of: U.S. threats against, 74–75; nuclear weapons of, 120, 140, 145, 192–93

Chinese civil war, 56–57, 238

Christian Democrat Party (CDU, West Germany), 229

Churchill, Winston, 29, 31, 33, 36

City avoidance, 114

Civil defense (U.S.), 179, 214

Civil War (U.S.), 24, 26

Closely spaced basing, 210

Cold war, 31–43, 51–52, 238

Cold War As History, The (book), 33

Collective security: universal sense, 28–31, 38, 42, 67, 129–31, 238; alliance sense, 42, 67

Command-control-communications (c-cubed), 214–15

Command-control-communications and-intelligence (c-cubed eye), 221, 222

Committee on the Present Danger, 183, 184, 201–2, 228

Comprehensive test ban (CTB), 140–41

Concert of Europe, 10

Condottieri, 6

Congress of Vienna (1815), 10

Containment doctrine, 49–52, 56, 238

Controlled strategic war. *See* Limited nuclear war

Counterforce: targets and targeting, 113, 114, 198, 199, 220, 227, 239; doctrine or strategy, 113, 114–15, 118, 123, 136, 176, 199, 200, 227, 241–42, 255

Counterinsurgency, 16

Countervalue, targets and targeting, 112, 113

Coupling, 187, 225

Credibility, and deterrence, 86–88, 91

Crisis stability, 230–31

Cruise missiles, 167, 170, 191, 205–7, 211, 212, 215, 225, 227, 233, 240–41, 247, 248

Cuban Missile Crisis, 91, 96, 115–18, 122, 230–31; aftermath of, 138, 139, 141, 142, 182

Czechoslovakia: 1948 coup, 39, 55, 238; 1968 invasion, 152

D-5 warhead, 208, 228

Damage limiting: by offensive means, 113, 114, 115, 122, 176, 198, 200, 222, 239, 241–42; by defensive means, 118–20

Dayan, Moshe, 18

Decapitation, 220, 221

Defense budget (U.S.): late 1940s, 54; early 1950s, 62; Eisenhower administration, 69; Kennedy administration, 103–4; during and after Vietnam War, 187; under Ford and Carter, 212; under Reagan, 212–14; 1949–82, 213

Defense expenditures (USSR), 177, 184

Defense Guidance Plan (of 1982), 223

Defense Intelligence Agency (DIA), 47

DeGaulle, Charles, 87

"Delicate Balance of Terror, The" (article), 96, 98

Delta submarine, 178

Dense pack, 210

Department of Energy (DOE), 47

Deterrence, 74, 249; in immediate postwar era, 52–56; in NSC-68, 60–62, 89–90; under Eisenhower administration, 73–75; and credibility, 86–88, 91; in Flexible Response, 89–90, 186–87; long-term feasibility, 134–35; finite deterrence, 135

Directorate of Defense Research and Engineering (DDR&E), 49
Disarming first strike, 93, 228
Dove (terminology), 182
Dulles, John Foster, 67, 239

Eisenhower administration, 66–75, 79–80, 85–87, 88, 90, 92, 94, 100, 104, 107, 108, 239, 241
Eisenhower Doctrine, 51
Eisenhower, Dwight D., 66, 68, 105, 131, 132
Enhanced radiation weapon. *See* Neutron bomb
Essential equivalence, 155–56, 165, 172
Eurostrategic weapons, 164–65, 189–92
Exchange ratio, 158

False alarms, 229
Fate of the Earth, The (book), 226
FB-111 (bomber), 111, 162, 176, 178, 204–5, 211
Federal Emergency Management Agency (FEMA), 214
Federal Energy Agency (FEA), 47
Finite deterrence, 135
Finland, 34–35
First-strike capability, 93, 228
Fission weapons, 58–59, 63n
Flexible Response, 88–92, 223; implemented, 103, 110
Flexible Targeting strategy, 199, 200n, 220, 221
Force structure, 137
Ford administration, 168, 204, 212
Ford, Gerald, 165–66, 167, 209
Foreign Affairs (journal), 50
Forsberg, Randall, 226
Forward-based systems, 70, 154, 164–65, 227

France: nuclear weapons of, 132, 140, 145, 164, 191; and NATO, 187, 188, 191
Fratricide, 203, 210
Freeze campaign, 226–27
Fusion (hydrogen) weapons, 58–59, 63n, 239

Gagarin, Yuri, 97
Gaither Report, 92
General and complete disarmament, 134
General purpose forces, 110, 186, 187–88; Soviet, 179–82
Geneva: negotiations on long-range theater nuclear forces, 225; INF negotiations, 227–31; START negotiations, 233
Geneva Protocol, 142, 143
Germany: in pre-WWII Europe, 13, 129; joins NATO, 41; 1983 elections, 229
Glassboro summit meeting, 151–52
GLCM. *See* Ground-launched cruise missiles
Graduated Deterrence doctrine, 80, 88
Gravity bombs, 162
Great Britain, nuclear options of, 132, 164, 191
Greek Civil War, 36, 55
Grotius, Hugo, 7
Ground alert (SAC), 96, 98, 107
Ground-Launched Cruise Missiles (GLCMs), 191–92, 206, 211, 227, 229, 230
Ground Zero (organization), 226

Halle, Louis, 33
Hard target kill capability, 200
Hawk (terminology), 182
Hiroshima and Nagasaki, 1, 27, 54, 55
Horizontal escalation, 221

Hotline, 138
Hydrogen bomb, 58–59, 63 n, 239

Ideology, 7, 15
Incidents at Sea Agreement, 143
India, nuclear test by, 146
Indian Ocean, Soviet naval deployments in, 181
Industrialization, 8, 11–12
INF (intermediate-range nuclear forces), talks on, 227–31, 240
International Atomic Energy Agency (IAEA), 131
Iran, at end of WWII, 35
Iron curtain (speech), 36
Israel, nuclear weapons of, 147

Jackson, Henry, 155–56
Johnson administration, 119–20, 214
Johnson, Lyndon, 119, 151, 152, 214
Joint Chiefs of Staff (JCS), 46, 75, 119, 244, 250
Jones, T. K., 244
June 12, 1982 rally. *See* New York Central Park rally
Jupiter missile, 185–86, 190

Kahn, Herman, 114, 124
Kaufman, William, 79
Kennan, George, 49–52
Kennedy administration, 91, 103–4, 106, 108–11, 117–18, 186, 239, 241
Kennedy, John F., 91, 100, 104, 106, 108, 117, 134, 137, 139, 145, 147, 242
Khe Sanh, battle of, 75
Khrushchev, Nikita, 99, 105, 116, 117, 118, 134, 139, 182
Kissinger, Henry, 78, 80, 166
Korean War, 51, 62, 65–66, 74–75, 239; consequences of, 72–73, 76–80, 81; constraint on, 76–77

Kosygin, Alexsei, 151, 152
Kvitsinsky, Yuli, 231

Labour Party (Great Britain), 189
Laser weapons, 121, 163
Lawrence, T. E. (Lawrence of Arabia), 18
Launch on warning, 228–29
Launch under attack, 228
Lead time, 204
League of Nations, 13–14, 28, 29, 137, 142
Lebanon Crisis of 1958, 74, 75
Lebanon War of 1982, 180
Leningrad ABM system, 153, 157, 198, 246
Limited nuclear options, 221–23
Limited nuclear war, 220–23
Limited Test Ban Treaty (1963), 138, 240
Limited war: in Europe (seventeenth to nineteenth centuries), 8–9, 24–25, 76; in the nuclear era, 55, 75–80, 239
Lincoln, Abraham, 24–25
Lippman, Walter, 37
Lisbon force goals, 185
Long haul competition, 51, 66, 69
Long-range theater nuclear forces (LRTNF), 190, 225, 227–31

MacArthur, Gen. Douglas, 18, 78
McNamara, Robert, 106, 108, 112, 114, 119–20, 123, 151, 186, 240
Manhattan Project, 47
Mansfield resolutions, 187
Mao Zedong (Tse-tung), 56–57, 238
Mark 12A warhead, 199, 200, 211, 220
Marshall Plan, 37–38, 39, 51, 238
MARV (maneuvering reentry vehicle), 220
Massive Retaliation doctrine, 72–76, 99, 123, 186, 239, 241, 242; critique of, 85–88, 92–94

MBFR, 188
Mediterranean Sea, balance of forces in, 177, 181
Medium-range theater nuclear forces, 190
Middle Ages, war in, 6, 33
Mideast War of 1973, 138, 188
Midgetman missile, 210
Minimum deterrence, 135
Minuteman missile: Minuteman I, 107, 109, 154, 158; Minuteman II, 158, 176, 211; Minuteman III, 158, 160, 161–62, 177, 197, 198, 201, 204, 211
MIRV (Multiple independently targetable reentry vehicle), 156–60, 162, 176, 183, 201, 240, 245
Missile gap (1957–61), 98, 99–101, 104–6, 133, 239, 245
Mobile ICBMs, 209, 248
Moscow ABM system, 153, 157, 198, 246
Moscow summit meeting (May 1972), 154
Mr. X article, 50
Multilateral force, 145
Multiple options, 91, 111
Mutual and balanced force reductions. *See* MBFR
Mutual Assured Destruction (MAD), 123, 176, 199, 222, 241, 244. *See also* Assured destruction
MX missile, 209–11, 214, 215, 226, 228; basing mode debate, 209–10, 240

Napoleonic Wars, 9–10, 11, 25, 34
Narwhal, 208
National Intelligence Estimates (NIEs), 183
National Security Act of 1947, 46–47
National security affairs, as a field of study, 85, 86, 128, 136, 251–55
National Security Agency (NSA), 49

National Security Council (NSC), 47, 92
National Security Decision Document, regarding Reagan administration nuclear strategy, 221, 223
NATO (North Atlantic Treaty Organization): formation, 41, 238; early years, 53–55, 60–61, 90, 185; and U.S. troop deployment in Europe, 87–88, 185; and Flexible Response, 91, 186; and European balance, 90, 110, 180, 186; Multilateral Force, 145; and Eurostrategic weapons, 186–92; differing concepts of deterrence, 186; "two-track" decision, 192, 225, 227; INF negotiations
Naval infantry (Soviet term), 181
Neutron bomb, 189, 225
Never Again Club, 66
New Look, 68–72, 81, 239
New York Central Park rally, 226
New Yorker (magazine), 226
Nike series of missiles, 68, 69–70, 71, 118–19
Nitze, Paul, 183, 227
Nixon administration, 120–21, 123, 161, 187–88, 198–200, 240, 254
Nixon, Richard, 154, 165, 199
No cities policy, 114
No first use, 75, 132
Nonproliferation Treaty (1968), 144–47, 240
NSC-68, 59–62, 68, 69, 89–90, 92, 123, 183, 239
Nuclear dilemma, 1, 244
Nuclear-free zone, 142
Nuclear Weapons and Foreign Policy (book), 78

Office of Strategic Services (OSS), 46
Office of the Secretary of Defense (OSD), 46, 48
Offset payments, 188

On Thermonuclear War (book), 114
Open Skies proposal, 132
Operation Skywatch, 57
Outer Space Treaty (1967), 141
Overkill, 247

Paasikivi, Juho, 34–35
Parity, 123
Partial Test Ban Treaty. *See* Limited
    Test Ban Treaty
Particle beam weapons, 121, 163
Peaceful nuclear explosives (PNEs),
    140, 146; Treaty regarding, 140
Peace movement, of the late 1950s,
    134–35; of the early 1980s, 224–
    26, 250
Penetration aids, 157
People's Republic of China. *See*
    China
Pershing I missile, 190
Pershing II missile, 191–92, 225,
    227–31
Persian Gulf, 75
Physicians for Social Responsibility
    (PSR), 225–26
Pin down, 210
Plate glass, 87–88, 185
Point defense, 121
Poland, in 1945, 32
Polaris missile, 107, 154, 162, 176
Polaris submarine, 108, 154, 162,
    208, 211, 246, 247
Poseidon missile, 108, 157, 158,
    160, 177, 190n, 197, 198, 204,
    208, 211
Powers, Francis Gary, 105
Precision-guided munitions (PGMs),
    188
Preemption, 95
Preprogrammed options. *See* Limited
    nuclear options
Presidential Directive 59, 220–21,
    223
Prevention of Nuclear War agree-
    ment, 143

Preventive war, 53
Proliferation, 144–45, 146–47
Prussian Army, 11–12, 17
Pugwash Conferences, 137

Quemoy-Matsu Crisis, 1954–55 and
    1958, 74, 75

RAND Corporation, 83–84, 96
Rapacki Plan, 133
Reagan administration, 172, 212,
    213–15, 219, 227, 231–32, 240–
    41, 242
Reagan, Ronald, 75, 168, 201, 212,
    213–15, 224, 225, 227, 228, 231–
    32, 241, 250
Reconnaissance satellites, 105
Reentry vehicle (RV), 119, 156
Revolutionary War (U.S.), 24
Ride-out, 93
Rio Pact, 67n
Romantic dimension of war, 17–18
Roosevelt, Franklin D., 29, 30, 31
Russell, Bertrand, 53

SAC. *See* Strategic Air Command
Safeguard ABM system, 10, 153, 254
SALT I agreements, 120, 153, 154–
    55, 155 (table), 160, 162, 164,
    176, 198, 207, 208, 240, 245;
    formal expiration of interim
    agreement, 169
SALT II agreements, 141, 166–72,
    231, 240, 246, 170 (table); debate
    over, 171–72
SALT negotiations, 121, 152–74,
    176, 226, 231, 232, 244, 245–46
Samos satellite, 105–6
Sanitized, 114
Scenario, 115
Schell, Jonathan, 226
Schelling, Thomas, 79, 124
Schlesinger, James, 199–200, 220,
    221
Scowcroft Commission, 210–11

Seabed Treaty (1971), 141
SEATO (Southeast Asia Treaty
    Organization), 67–68
Second-strike capability, 93–94, 96,
    123, 163, 239
Selective options, 200n, 220–23
Selective service, 54
Sentinal ABM system, 120, 192
Ship- or Submarine-Launched
    Cruise Missile (SLCM), 206, 211,
    230
Short-range theater nuclear forces
    (battlefield nuclear weapons), 190
Silo-busting, 200
SIOP (Single Integrated Operations
    Plan), 114, 198, 199, 220, 223
SLCM. See Ship- or submarine-
    launched cruise missile
Social Democratic Party (SPD,
    Germany), 189
Solid-fuel missile technology, 107
"Sources of Soviet Conduct, The"
    (article), 50
South Africa, possible nuclear test
    by, 147
Soviet Union: nuclear forces of, 1,
    60–61, 69, 72, 80, 86, 92, 98–99,
    105, 106, 109–10, 121–22, 154,
    167–68, 177–79, 201; military
    expenditures, 177, 184; civil de-
    fense, 179; general purpose forces
    of, 179–82; deployments vis-a-vis
    China, 180, 183, 184; economy
    and technology, 242
Spanish-American War, 24, 25
Spartan missile, 119
Sprint missile, 119
Sputnik, 97, 100, 239
Spy-in-the-sky satellites. See Recon-
    naissance satellites
SRAM (short-range attack missile),
    162–63, 205
SS-3 missile, 186
SS-4 missile, 186, 190
SS-5 missile, 186, 190

SS-17 missile, 177
SS-18 missile, 177
SS-19 missile, 177
SS-20 missile, 185, 189, 190, 191,
    227, 230–31, 240
Stalin, Joseph, 29, 33–35, 51, 75
Standing Consultative Commission
    (SCC), 154
START (Strategic Arms Reduction
    Talks), 231–33, 240
Stealth bomber, 214, 215
Strategic Air Command (SAC), 53,
    55, 56, 68, 70, 73, 92–96, 98,
    132, 239, 255
Strontium 90, 138–39
Submarine-launched ballistic missile
    (SLBM), 107–8
Sufficiency doctrine, 123, 175, 198,
    222, 240
Supercarriers, 48
Survivability, 94

Tactical nuclear weapons (mis-
    nomer), 70–71, 80
Taiwan, 57
Targeting accuracy debate, 201–3
Taylor, Gen. Maxwell, 79
Team B Report, 183–84
Technology, role in war, 11–12
Tehran Conference (1943), 29, 33
Thirty Years War (1618–48), 7, 11,
    15
Thor missile, 185–86, 190
Threshold Test Ban Treaty (1974),
    140
Throw weight, 107
Titan missile, 97, 107, 108, 109,
    122, 154, 201
Tlatelolco, Treaty of (1967), 142
Tomahawk cruise missile, 206
Triad doctrine, 111–12
Trident I missile, 208, 211, 212,
    214, 215, 240
Trident II missile, 208, 211, 212,
    214, 215, 228, 240

Trident submarine, 207–8, 211, 212, 215, 240, 246–47
Trip-wire, 87–88, 185
Truman administration, 36–37, 45–46, 48, 49–51, 53–54, 55, 57–58, 59, 62, 69, 129–30, 238–39
Truman Doctrine, 36, 51
Truman, Harry S., 36, 45, 48, 57 59, 62, 131
Turkey, 36
Two-track decision (NATO), 192, 227, 240
Typhoon submarine, 178

U-2 aircraft, 104–6, 116
United Nations, 29–30, 31, 36, 45, 129–30, 131, 137, 142, 151, 238
U.S. Air Force (USAF): origins as Army Air Corps, 27, 46; within DOD, 46
U.S. Army (USA), within DOD, 46
U.S. Navy (USN), within DOD, 46
Universal military training (UMT), 54
Use them or lose them, 230–31
USSR. *See* Soviet Union
Utah nerve gas incident, 142

V-1 missile, 205
Vance, Cyrus, 168

Vienna, SALT II signed, 170
Vietnam, U.S. war in, 12, 14, 16, 18, 51, 54, 75, 81, 121, 142, 187, 212
V-J Day (1945), 27
Vladivostok Accords, 165–66, 166 (table), 240, 246

War-fighting, 211–23, 224n, 227, 240
War of 1812, 24
War plans, late 1940s, 55; 1950s, 71; 1960s, 114–15
Watergate, 200
Weinberger, Caspar, 223, 224
Window of vulnerability, 200–203
Wohlstetter, Albert, 96, 98
World War I, 13, 14–15, 18, 19, 25; as example of unwanted escalation, 78
World War II, 13, 14, 19–20, 27–28

Yalu River, 65–66, 76, 79
Yield, 58
Ypres, Battle of, 14

Zero option (or zero-zero solution), 227